THESE HOLY SPARKS

These Holy Sparks

THE REBIRTH OF THE JEWISH PEOPLE

ARTHUR WASKOW

1817

Harper & Row, Publishers, San Francisco

Cambridge, Hagerstown, New York, Philadelphia
London, Mexico City, São Paulo, Sydney

For Shulamit D'vorah,
dark lady of the Song
that is all songs

THESE HOLY SPARKS. *The Rebirth of the Jewish People*. Copyright © 1983 by Arthur Waskow. All rights reserved. Printed in the United States of America. No part of this book may be used or reproduced in any manner whatsoever without written permission except in the case of brief quotations embodied in critical articles and reviews. For information address Harper & Row, Publishers, Inc., 10 East 53rd Street, New York, NY 10022. Published simultaneously in Canada by Fitzhenry & Whiteside, Limited, Toronto.

FIRST EDITION

Designer Jim Mennick

Library of Congress Cataloging in Publication Data

Waskow, Arthur I.
  THESE HOLY SPARKS.

  1. Judaism—Essence, genius, nature. 2. Judaism—United States.
3. Fellowship—Religious aspects—Judaism. 4. Israel and the Diaspora. I. Title.
BM565.W28 1983   305.8'924'009041   83-47737
ISBN 0-06-069263-4

83 84 85 86 87 10 9 8 7 6 5 4 3 2 1

In memory of
Emil Grinzweig and Issam Sartawi,
an Israeli and a Palestinian,
who learned from the thousands of war dead around them
to seek peace with each other—
and who died for daring to try.

May You Who make peace in Your high places
teach us to make peace among ourselves—
among all the children of Israel,
all the children of Ishmael,
and all who share the earth.

Oseh shalom bimromav hu yaaseh shalom alenu
v'al kol yisrael v'al kol yishmael v'al kol yoshvai teyvel.

Contents

Foreword: From 1492 to 1945

During the centuries between 1492 and 1945, the age-old life-paths of the human race and of the Jewish people were utterly remade—and the two processes marched in eerie parallel.

In August of 1492, the King and Queen of Spain sent Columbus on the voyage that stripped away the veils that had separated the Eastern and Western continents. The Americas were opened to European conquest and settlement. So there began the transformation in the knowledge, wealth, numbers, and technology of humankind that we call the Modern Age. That transformation shattered the old world, the world as human beings had known it for millennia.

On the very day before Columbus set sail, the same King and Queen expelled all the Jews from Spain.

These two events did not merely coincide in time and place. They were two sides of the same coin: the first experiment in shaping the "modern" nation-state. Internally, that state wanted uniformity—and the quickest way to get it was to expel the indigestible Jewish minority. Externally, that state wanted colonies to rule over—and found them by using the most advanced technology of the day to "dis-cover" America.

The triumph of the modern nation-state was built upon the shattering of traditional communities—Jews at home and Incas overseas. As modernism spread, the shattering also spread. The first victims—the shattered community of Spanish Jews—drew on their own experience to create a world view not of their shattered self alone, but of the whole wide shattered world—and of how to heal it. Some of these exiles regathered in the town of Safed in the Land of Israel. As they struggled to understand what had happened to them, they worked out a new version of Jewish mysticism—a version that was ready to explain the shattered world and teach how to repair it. It was almost as if a possible cure had entered the world at the same moment the "dis-ease" became manifest—a possible cure that would become useful centuries later, in our own days.

During the Modern Age that began in 1492, the human race became more and more convinced that it was master of the world. All its old habits of mind and action came unraveled. The traditional economies of farm and village and commercial town were transformed into giant industrial cities and wretched shantytowns. The great fossil fuel deposits of coal and petroleum replaced the daily sun and firewood as the key sources of energy. Continental states and global corporations shaped and controlled the intimate lives and thoughts of billions through mass media, and in some cases were themselves controlled by hundreds of millions of people scattered across whole continents who could debate and have some hand in choosing their future. The inner secrets of biology and physics became knowable and known. Biological species that had taken millions of years to emerge were exterminated in a few decades. A net of communication was flung across the globe by which any human being anywhere could talk with any other. Organizations and parties proclaimed—and proved—their ability to plan, shape, and transform the histories of nations, classes, the whole human race. Millions of humans who would in previous generations never have had the chance to explore their own individual thoughts and talents, began to do so. Even the nature of consciousness and thought itself became subject to conscious, thoughtful examination and control.

For countless ages, all human cultures had been respectful of the Mystery that shrouded the world. Now the many religious traditions that had in their various ways honored and celebrated Mystery became embarrassed and rueful in the face of the new ideologies that proclaimed human mastery—and proved it. It is the cluster of these new ideologies and the life-practices that accompanied them—nationalism, liberalism, socialism, science, industrialism—that I mean by modernism.

We may name 1945 as the date on which the triumph of modernism was fulfilled—so fully that it ended. In that year, a medium-sized nation, highly schooled in modern civilization, almost completed its chosen task of destroying the Jewish communities of Europe, by using an extraordinary combination of modernized bureaucracy and sadism. And in that same year a continental superstate perfected the techniques of modern physics and industrialism in order to destroy at one blow an entire city—by using an early, feeble prototype of nuclear weapons.

In 1945, the human race's self-confident sense of human mastery became a haunted nightmare: If the human race could do anything it wanted, it might in fact do anything it wanted. The very fact of total mastery might be used to "total" the world.

These dates, these milestones in the biographies of the human race and of the Jewish people—from 1492 to 1945, from the "discovery" of America to the invention of the atomic bomb; from 1492 to 1945, from the expulsion from Spain to the "invention" of the Holocaust—are profoundly intertwined. The career of modernism as it affected the human race and the Jewish people; the hypertrophy or elephantiasis of modernism as it is now affecting the human race and the Jewish people; finally, the possibilities of renewal and recovery in the lives of the human race and the Jewish people—these are, of all subjects of inquiry, most worthy of our study as we stand in the present moment. For now is when modernism—which shattered the ancient traditions and pathways—has itself been shattered by its own successes. We stand in the ruins of the old world-systems, barely covered by the more recent ruins of the new ones. We have not yet drawn the blueprints for some new living spaces in which we can live out a human span.

For the human race, those new ruins are as yet only intellectual and spiritual. In the Jewish people, the ruins are physical as well as intellectual and spiritual. The Holocaust may have again made the Jews into humanity's prophets, humanity's canary-people in the poisonous air of a poisoned mine-shaft, humanity's early warning system of the danger of a global holocaust.

In the same way, the efforts of the Jewish people to begin shaping a new version of Jewish peoplehood may be of use to other peoples and to the human race as a whole, as all of us try to move past modernism into a new shape of human society. How can we fuse those partial truths that are within modernism into a fuller truth that goes beyond modernism? How can we draw on the ancient wisdom without being trapped in the ancient ruins? Can glimmers of possibility emerge from the way some contemporary Jews have begun to deal with these questions?

Some contemporary Jews. For among Jews, as among all the peoples, there has been a broad spectrum of responses to the modernist triumph and disaster. Some Jews responded by trying to draw on the best of modernism to defend themselves against the worst of it—and these Jews struggled against great odds to create the state of Israel. Other Jews have tried to restore religious practice as it was before the Modern Age began—and they have helped create a wave of neo-Orthodoxy. We will try to understand how these sparks of the spectrum may become part of a new whole. But we will focus on those Jews, mainly in America, who are drawing on but looking beyond even the best of modern and even the best of premodern practice.

This book will examine the efforts of these "postmodern" Jews to draw on the truths in modernism as well as on the truth of its hypertrophy—and to wrestle with the ancient wisdom in order to make something new out of it. It is these Jews that we will be calling "the movement for Jewish renewal." Renewal rather than restoration only, or defense only, or survival only. And this book will also suggest some ways in which these Jewish efforts for Jewish renewal may illuminate the possibilities for all human beings to work for world renewal.

In order to do this, we will look first at how the unity that was the Jewish people before the Modern Age was shattered into the many scattered sparks of Jewish peoplehood that we now live with. And then we will look at some recent glimmering efforts to reunite these sparks, especially in the world of American Jews during the past two decades.

Then we will look more closely at the specific forms or aspects of separation, alienation—and at the efforts to cure these alienations. One way to imagine these specific forms of alienation and regathering is to see them in five concentric spheres of Jewishness—the inmost spheres of the individual and the family, the sphere of the face-to-face local congregation or community, the worldwide sphere of the whole Jewish people, and finally, outermost, the relationship between the Jewish people and the other nations.

But we will not be looking at these five spheres in the seemingly "logical" order that goes from inmost to outermost. In the actual growth of the movement for Jewish renewal, change did not begin with renewal of the individual and then flow into renewal of the world. The midlevel sphere, that of face-to-face community and congregation, was where most people began to create new forms. It was only as the existence of new communities strengthened individuals in their own willingness to change that two things happened: In one direction, inward, the individual Jew began to reconnect the alienated aspects of body, mind, and spirit into one whole person, and then women and men began to rework the meaning of *mishpacha*, family. In the other direction, outward, as the intimate communities grew stronger, more participants began to address the macro-issues of Jewish peoplehood and the fate of the earth.

So a road map of this book would show Chapters 1–4 like a highway moving straight ahead, focused on face-to-face communities and their efforts to deal with knowledge, money, and politics; Chapters 5 and 6, branching off in a fork to the individual and family; Chapters 7 and 8, as another fork to issues of Zionism, Israel, and Diaspora; and finally both these forks reconnecting in Chapters 9 and 10, on God and secularism, and on Israel among the nations.

There is another element of "road map" that may be of help to readers. This book does not stay in any of the usual genres of expository prose. Woven into it are strands of autobiography, analytical social and political history, and *midrash*—a peculiarly Jewish form of biblical interpretation that itself is woven of poetry, pun, and philosophy. I move back and forth among these strands and approaches, as each seems useful to illuminate a problem. I hope that you will find that this weaving bears an interest of its own. It has some resemblance to two odd literary forms: dreams and the Talmud. Perhaps this is because, like them, it tries to explain reality without reducing it to a formula and tries to tell real stories without reducing them to idiosyncracy.

A gateway is a gateway; find the *mezuzah* that welcomes you most warmly.

There was a great Menorah
whose lamps reached up toward Heaven
so high that it attracted
all of the firmament's
explosive lightning fire
In its twisted black-gray wreckage
among its black-gray ashes
there remained some scattered embers
a puff of flying sparks
Alone each cooled to gray and black
Until there came a breath of wind
that warmed the sparks to points of blazing light
and sent them flying toward each other
blazing in the air a glowing wholeness
 a fiery shape
a new Menorah
made of sparks and light
All light

1. *Shattered Worlds and New Departures*

We begin with the vision of those Jews who gathered from the Spanish exile of 1492, whose lives had been shattered by the very first moments of the explosion that created what we have come to call the "modern world." They gathered in the light-filled northern hills of the land of Israel, not far from the "Sea of Galilee"—the lake that is shaped like a harp, Kinneret. They came together about four hundred years ago, a whole but tiny townful of Jewish mystics, to sing, to pray, to study—and to *see*. From the dazzling light of the Spanish explosion, these mystics of the town of Safed drew the intensity and illumination to let them see and speak of the cosmic explosion that created the universe itself. Not just the physical universe, but the moral, ethical, and spiritual universe as well.

Their imagining of the Creation is one of the most illuminating insights of Jewish tradition:

Divine energy poured into the void, creating an utterly harmonious, seamless vessel of supernal light—a holy universe. But God-energy was so intense that its very holiness shattered the vessel it was shaping. The seamless vessel of supernal light exploded into infinities of sparks.

The sparks of holy light dispersed. Because they were no longer in touch with each other, because each now stood in isolation, in alienation, each holy spark of light became obscured by a husk or shell of darkness and unholiness. At the root of every soul, every act, every relationship in the universe we live in . . . is the darkened spark of holiness in exile.

It is, said the Kabbalists, our human task—though with God's help—to gather the sparks, to bring them back into a holy whole, and so to remove the husks of alienation that disguise them. How do we repair the holy vessel? Our every act of love and decency lifts up a spark; our every act of death and meanness lowers one.

This cosmic insight of the Kabbalists of Safed had its roots in their experience of their own society and history shattered. Perhaps because the vision was rooted in this experience, we can take their insight and reconnect it to the realm of our society and history; for their paradigm, their metaphor, can help us understand the whole transformation of the earth and the human race in the Modern Era. And it especially applies to the modern life of the Jewish people, which has embodied in itself a history-in-miniature of the general human experience of this great upheaval.

Four centuries ago, the Jewish people was something like a holy vessel. While not quite seamless, it was an organic community.

At the grass-roots level, there was a path of Jewish life—the *halakha*, literally "the walking." In it were encompassed celebration and prayer, work and money, sex and the family, food and politics. The individual, the community—even the whole people, far-flung in Diaspora around the world—walked this path together.

For the individual, the bodily acts of walking through a life—birth, puberty, marriage, work, childrearing, death—were deeply entwined with the emotional, intellectual, and spiritual acts of understanding the world.

For the face-to-face community, there was a similar intertwining. The communal functions of celebration and prayer were intimately connected with *tzedakah*, the collection of money to help those in urgent trouble. So was *gemilut hassadim*, the sharing of the tasks of kindness toward the poor, the sick, the desperate. And so was the task of "the redemption of captives" and related tasks of communal defense and "foreign policy"—working out relationships with the powerful and often hostile non-Jewish world. All these necessities of communal life were bound together by the process of Torah-study, so that what the community should do in practical matters was infused with holiness by reexamining and reinterpreting a holy tradition.

And also at the level of the far-flung people—at the level of theory and vision—the great Jewish ideas were intertwined. The visions of a universal God and of a single holy people, the dream of Zion and the dream of Messiah, the process of working out the everyday details of the *halakhic* path-of-life, and the long-range re-visioning and remaking of that path by midrash and *aggada* (reinterpretation and storytelling). All were intertwined.

Let us not be romantic. In that organic community there was much suffering—some of it because life was hard and short for almost everybody, some of it because the community's very uniformity smothered individual differences and desires. But there was a sense and a theory of organic unity.

Into that organic community, in the last five centuries, there came pouring the energy of modernism. It was the energy of science and industrialism, the corporation and the nation-state, the press and mass media, universal citizenship and elections, the pursuit of individuality, and the affirmation of free choice. Modernism was in many ways a good and useful energy. It made possible the solution of age-old problems of poverty, sickness, isolation. It put new tools—physical and organizational tools—into the hands of human beings. And so it lit the way to far more effective human action—both individual and social.

But the energy of modernism was so intense that it shattered the community as it transformed it.

The effectiveness of human action in reshaping the world seemed so enormous that the traditional sense of the world as independent and "other" faded away. The sense of natural rhythms, of natural limits, of reaping what we sow, faded away. As human beings began to imagine themselves omnipotent, the sense of an Omnipotent God faded away. As the new ideas of science and organization grew more powerful, students of Torah grew fewer and became more embarrassed about applying the tradition to the burning issues of modern life.

So the holy vessel of Jewish life-practice flew apart into many separate sparks.

Some Jews focused on the land of Israel, turning away from God and Torah. They built a secular Zionist movement, invented the kibbutz, rescued Jews from Europe and the Middle East, and ultimately they built the state of Israel.

Some Jews focused on the prophetic vision of the days of peace and justice—when all the nations would beat their swords into plowshares and rejoice in the One Universal God, and when each individual conscience would guide each individual human in a holy path. They built a liberal version of Judaism that was able to communicate with those who held other worldviews and was able to infuse modern individualism with a prophetic bent for social justice. But in doing so they turned away from the Land and halakha because they felt these were narrow and restrictive.

Some fastened on secular socialism as the modern, realistic version of Messiah—and turned away from God and Land and Torah all at once. They built the Jewish labor movement and many universalist socialist groupings, too.

Some focused on a static version of halakha as a code of law, to the exclusion of any outward universal vision and even of the stories, reinterpretations, mystical insights—all the different fountains of new energy from the tradition that had for ages watered the halakhic tree.

And so each subcommunity of Jews centered around one holy spark, one valid fragment of what had been an organic whole. But with their separation, the sparks took on the husks of alienation and unwholeness. Alone, halakha became rigid. Alone, universalism became assimilationist. Alone, Zionism became bureaucratic and superpatriotic.

The energy of modernism had its dark side, too. Modernism provided both the physical technology and social-organizational techniques that could be turned toward mass destruction. And by dissolving the traditional sense of limits and proportion, modernism permitted the expression of old hostilities toward Jews in a newly total, unlimited way. Thus old pogroms could now become something new—the Holocaust. So, especially in the last generation, the Jewish people had to respond to the physical destructions posed by the demonic side of modernism.

They responded by building strong national-political institutions:

the state of Israel and the American Jewish "polity." But they let the spark of politics and the spark of Jewish categories of thought get separated from each other. So the new secular Jewish institutions used modern secular ideas—rather than the unfolding Torah—as the basis of their action. The *Am Kadosh,* the Holy People, became *am* and *kadosh*—apart.

And it was not only these great themes of Jewish thought and practice that were scattered when the vessel shattered. The communal functions also split apart. Especially in America, where the shattering was most thorough because more organic communities were left behind not only in time but also in space—back in Europe. So in America, where the alternative would probably have been the total collapse of Jewish life, the Jews made brilliant adaptations of such modernist American institutions as professions and bureaucracies. There grew up professional organizations and specialists: one set in what had been the process of Torah-study, once broadly participatory but now focused on a professional rabbinate and synagogue denominations; a second in tzedakah, once the acting out of religious righteousness by giving money to the poor and suffering, now turned into professional fund-raising and philanthropy; a third in gemilut hassadim, once the religious act of loving-kindness through direct personal service to mourners and wanderers, now centered in professional Jewish social-service agencies; another in what had been *pidyon shevuim,* the communal effort to ransom Jews who were imprisoned, now transformed into professional "defense organizations" against anti-Semitism.

And at the level of the individual Jew, the path of holy life was shattered into—

Work.

And leisure.

And art.

And sex.

And family.

And sports.

And politics.

And health.

And prayer.

All separate categories, separate sparks. All dulled, by their separation, into unholiness.

Now, to our generation, there falls the task of regathering these sparks:

The task of recreating a life cycle in which there is a sense of rhythm and of wholeness, in which the physical acts of walking through a life are infused with meaning.

The task of recreating organic, grass-roots communities in which Torah, tzedakah, gemilut hassadim, and pidyon shevuim are all intertwined.

The task of reconnecting, revitalizing, and reaffirming both the far-flung Jewish communities of the Diaspora and the Jewish state of Israel.

The task of infusing the new, powerful, Jewish political institutions with the authentic Jewish process of wrestling with Jewish tradition as the way of working out what to do in the present.

The task of reconnecting the sense of special Jewish peoplehood and the special Land of Israel with joyful celebration of the universal God of universal justice.

The regathering of the holy sparks is taking many forms. In America, one of the most vigorous and creative efforts has been the *havurah* movement—the movement to create small, intimate, face-to-face congregations without hired functionaries—"fellowships" of fully participating Jews seeking to recreate a participatory Judaism. The *havurot* are the seedbeds in which many Jews have learned to renew their own individual Jewish lives, and some of their successful approaches might be used in other situations.

Three aspects of the havurot have made them both different from the recent past, and extraordinarily effective in reaching toward the future: They encourage amateur participation, drawing on but not deferring to professional expertise; they try to reconnect and intertwine the physical, emotional, intellectual, and spiritual; and they reject the notion of themselves becoming a new elite for the Jewish community and instead have tried to teach all *amcha*, all the Jews, "how to do it."

But the havurot are not *the* solution to the problem of the shattered vessel of Jewish peoplehood. They are but one step on an open-ended path toward an unknown destination—a path of Jewish venturing perhaps as risky as the one that Abraham walked down when he left the town of Ur, or Yokhanan ben Zakkhai when he left the burning Temple.

Neither the pioneers of modern Israel nor the mystics of Safed were the first generation of Jews to face this moment of shattering and renewal. The moment goes back to Jewish beginnings, and has been repeated in all the crucial generations of Jewish history— whenever the Jewish people and Judaism hovered at the edge of dissolution, and then renewed themselves with deeper life.

When the Jewish people departed from Egypt, they turned that physical exodus into the spiritual "new departure" of Sinai, the Ten Commandments, Torah. When the Jewish people departed from the Land of Israel into Babylonian Captivity and then back again, once more they turned those leavings into the new departure of the Prophets: the warning and the promise of destruction and redemption. When the Jewish people departed from the Second Temple— or it from them—the new departure they created was the Talmud, the discovery that within the ancient Torah had been concealed a new path of life, a path of prayer and study. And so from the Romans' destruction of the Temple and the Romans' defeat of Bar-Kokhba, there emerged as "normative Judaism" the practices and processes of the rabbis, which then for almost two millennia defined the Jewish way.

Just so, the mystics of that town near the Kinneret—the Kabbalists of Safed—four centuries ago drew from their physical departure from Spain the new spiritual departure that infused the Jewish people with Kabbalistic fervor.

These moments of departure have usually held deep pain, anger, collision. For when an old pattern is destroyed, and the sparks fly apart, before a new holy pattern forms, each scattered spark thinks itself the heart of holiness—and sees only in the others the alienation that makes each spark unholy.

When Moses stood in the wilderness—Sinai behind him and the golden calf before his eyes—he unleashed a bloody civil war, and thousands died before the new holy pattern that we call Torah was accepted.

Just before and after the destruction of the Second Temple, Jews fought—not just with words, but with swords and spears—over whether the Sadducees' adherence to the sacrificial system, or the Pharisees' devotion to Torah-study, or the Qumran commitment to ritual purity, or the Zealots' urgency to clean the land of Roman desecration, or the Christian insistence that Messiah had come— was truly Jewish. Only by looking backward do we know who won that struggle.

Only with hindsight do we even see Yokhanan ben Zakkhai—who after the Temple fell became the great hero, teacher, and refounder of the rabbinic process—as one who kept the commandments. For in his own day, *what the commandments were* was the deepest issue; those he chose became what the commandments were for almost two thousand years.

The lesson of all these periods is the same: a generation of exile, physical departure, loss, and alienation can create a new departure in Jewish creativity. This is what has begun to happen in the generation of American Jews who in the 1960s experienced an "expulsion," an alienation from their home society. For such expulsions do not need to be physical and geographical in order to create the sense of shattered vessels that can spur a new creation. They can come from a sense of home itself being turned inside out.

And this indeed is what it felt like: America being turned inside out. The America of social peace riven by riots, strikes, assassinations. The America of noble vision pouring rivers of fire on a peasant countryside. The America of universal human culture breaking up into Blacks, Hispanics, ethnics. The America they had grown up considering the protector of world Jewry, standing silent for a week of fear in 1967 while Israel seemed in danger of destruction.

In the late sixties out of their sense of alienation from America, these American Jews began to cluster together—not in one town like Safed, but in a dozen out-of-the-way houses and unused rooms scattered across the continent. In each place, to begin with, there were only twenty or thirty of these people; later, the number of groups began to multiply while the groups themselves stayed small and intimate. The number is still growing. For just as the mystics of Safed spoke to some deep hunger in the far-flung Jewish people of that day—just as the Jews of their century adopted songs and words and meditations out of Safed—so some of the new approaches of these "new Jews" rang true to many others. What is more, the sense of bafflement, of alienation from an America turned inside out did not end when the Vietnam War and the Black uprisings ended: so new waves of "new Jews" have kept emerging.

There were many paths that led to the new communities:

In Boston and New York, clusters of rabbinical students who felt suffocated by their seminaries decided to create a way of Jewish learning in which students and teachers could talk and laugh and argue and eat with each other—a path in which learning and loving would not seem mutually exclusive.

In Washington and Philadelphia, clusters of people who felt their passion for peace and social justice was rooted in prophetic Jewish anguish came together as Jewish activists, radicals who celebrated rather than fled their Jewish roots.

In Chicago and Los Angeles, women and men who had learned the beauties of Jewish prayer rebelled at being separated from each other, at being frozen into rigid rows of pews, at being told only the hired rabbi could lead the congregation, at being forced to use only the printed prayer book as a guide for their approach toward God.

In a New England summer camp for Conservative synagogue youth, teen-age girls demanded to learn how to put on *t'fillin*—and a Hassidically trained rabbi began to teach them not only how but why. In a Massachusetts town, a woman who had been bored into sullenness by rigid Jewish schools began to experiment with "open Jewish classrooms." At Brandeis University, a graduate student began to experiment with translating the Bible into English as Martin Buber and Franz Rosenzweig had translated it into German—with breathing patterns, puns, and a sense of oral poetry intact. At Rutgers, an undergraduate started writing Hebrew songs with echoes of Country-Western rhythms. In Washington, a young draft-resister lit the *Shabbos* candles with his burning draft card—"From death to life!" he said. In Berkeley, a Jew who had taken part in the Sufi mystical movement, rooted in Islam, returned to Jewish life and brought with her the Sufi dances, to dance the Jewish prayers.

And so on. From myriad outposts of diminished Yiddishkeit— from the scattered sparks of Jewish peoplehood—something began to happen. The scattering had been quite comfortable; the pleasures of America had been quite pleasant. But now the scattering, the shattering, brought discomfort. The pleasures of America had grown *too* pleasurable. For many Jews, sating themselves with pleasures, avoiding and forgetting pain, had become a kind of painfulness.

For me the moment came in April, 1968. I lived just off Eighteenth Street in midtown Washington, D.C. On every block of Eighteenth Street there stood a knot of soldiers, relaxed but watchful. Friends and couples walking in the April breezes hushed their conversations as they sidled past the Army.

Just ten days before, Martin Luther King, Jr. had been killed. After eighteen hours of intense tension, crowds from the Black community had burned three major streets to ruins. Food, doctors, lawyers—all these had disappeared. But a network I was part of had been trying to bring them back: getting food to hungry ghetto neighborhoods, getting doctors to the sick and injured, getting lawyers to the jails. We roamed the streets despite the curfew, since we were white and the police did not care. We had been feeling daring, feeling virtuous, feeling useful. And now I was feeling relaxed, happily tired. Happily exhausted.

Tonight, however, was a time for being home. Tonight would be the beginning of Passover. It was the time for my encounter with the sacred past—the sacred past of the Jewish people, the sacred past of my own family.

It was safely "past"—and therefore, *therefore*, sacred. A time to recite in high and solemn tones the archaic English of my old *Haggadah*. A time to look again at its old drawings, at the faded inscription that said it was a present for bar mitzvah, at the stains of ancient dribbled wine. A time to leave the turmoil of America, of 1968, of burning streets and napalmed villages, of a murdered saint and murderous presidents. A time for ceremonious pleasure.

But not this afternoon. As I walked up Eighteenth Street toward my house, my steps began to drum an eerie sentence:

This is Pharaoh's Army . . .
And I am on my way to do the Seder.

This is Pharaoh's Army . . .
And I am on my way to do the Seder.

Block after block, I remembered the words King spoke the night before he died . . . the words that echoed Moses: "I am standing on the mountain top, looking across into the Promised Land. I may not get there, but my people will."

And when I turned the corner at Wyoming Avenue, there it was still: a United States Army jeep, machine gun still pointing vaguely at my house. The rhythmic chant came back again, this time a question:

This is Pharaoh's chariot . . .
And I am on my way to do the Seder?

The Passover Haggadah had come alive to stalk the streets.

That night, for the first time, I broke open the form of the Haggadah to talk about the streets and what had been happening to us. For the first time I felt the Seder a moment not for high and solemn recitation, but for burning passion and hard thinking. For the first time, we paused to talk about its meaning.

Not even in my childhood home in Jewish Baltimore had we paused to talk about the Seder's meaning. Passover had been a thing apart, a solemn but not a lively holy day, an act of memory, not of hope and struggle. My neighborhood had been a microcosm of the shattered Jewish people—together out of habit, not vision.

The neighborhood was centered on an Orthodox *shul*—though a number of families, including mine, were nonobservant. Between the Jews who did and those who did not live by Orthodox practice, there was a sense of shared neighborhood, colored by a dull and muted discomfort, but no passionate conflict. There was no conflict because there was no passion about the Jewish future. So traditional practices became habit and custom:

- We bought chickens from the ritual slaughterer, not because my family kept kosher—but because that was where the chickens were.

- I carried the books I loved to the nearby branch library every Saturday afternoon—even though I had to bear the imprecations of the older men: I was a *goy* for violating Shabbos. They did not even try to teach me there were other books with a deeper meaning that I could read on Shabbos. They did not try to teach me some meaning to the Shabbos prohibitions against carrying burdens from a private to a public domain. Maybe they did not know. Maybe for them as well, it had all become mere habit.

- My father, to earn some extra money, taught an afternoon class in world history at the nearby Orthodox high school—and told us stories of how his students rebelled against learning about the Church, the Pope, the Reformation.

- My mother and my grandmother spoke Yiddish to each other—but never, never ever, to me.

- My father fasted on Yom Kippur—but he would not go to synagogue because he hated the system for buying tickets to rent 2 seats to pray in.

- And I was "bar-mitzvahed" (so we said it) in the neighborhood shul. Bar-mitzvahed by learning flawless chanting and no meaning. By learning to recite the Hebrew, not to read it. By becoming letter-perfect—perfect in each letter—with the words, the sentences, and the architecture of the prayer book utterly opaque.

But I wanted meaning. I was hungry for meaning, passionate for learning, romantic about justice. None of these seemed to be what being Jewish was about.

So I went off to a world in which meaning, learning, and justice were important—the world of the universities. It turned out to be a world of other Jews (almost a "Jewish neighborhood") where in a Jewish context I learned to think, learn, mean, share—"Jewishly" in fervor and in flavor, but with no Jewish words, no Jewish concepts, no Jewish texts or explications.

Whole departments of psychology, sociology, physics and whole seminars in history were full of Jews but empty of Jewishness. Here, in the most modern reaches of the modern world, there was no Inquisition burning Torah—and there was no Torah. There was no ban against Yiddish—and there was no Yiddish. There was no outlawry of Zionism—and there was no love of Zion.

From that world, once the 1960s dawned, it was easy to move into the struggle for peace and social justice. Again, this was a "neighborhood of Jews"—but Jews who had only the vaguest sense that "Justice, justice shall you pursue" and "Seek peace and pursue it" were commands of Torah.

I was not alone in moving through this line of Jewish neighborhoods, declining in their Jewishness from the 1940s to the 1960s. There were tens of thousands of Jews of many ages who followed precisely this pattern. It had been the classic pattern of American Jewry: in the absence of any burning sense of Jewish focus, generation after generation had preserved the ties of Jewish contact without the content of Jewish thought, music, culture. Even in reaction to the Holocaust, even in response to the rebirth of Israel, American Jewry expressed itself by boundary-building—not by "center"-building. We organized against pressure from outside rather than by redefining our identities within.

So the moment of the Seder in April, 1968—the moment when I reconnected the spark of "telling" and the spark of "acting," the spark of "Jewish" and the spark of "universal," the spark of memory and the spark of hope, the spark of ceremony and the spark of spontaneity, the spark of outer practice and the spark of inner meaning—this was the moment when, for me, the path of my life began to turn to a new direction, to new directedness.

And I was not alone. All over America, for many different reasons, out of very different biographies, Jews began in those moments of the sixties to regather some sparks. For some it was a moment in 1967 of stark fear for Israel's survival; for others, a moment of unutterable joy just a few weeks later, when Jews came to pray again at the Wailing Wall; for others, a moment of revulsion from the America that was lurching toward a genocide in Vietnam; for others, a moment of attraction to Black music or Eastern mysticism or some other life-path richer than that displayed in American mass media.

With all, it was a moment of bringing together a spark from the communal Jewish past with a spark from their own personal present-growing-toward-a-future. Some need of a growing life—a need for ecstasy or for community, for the grounding whereon to struggle or the breathing space wherein to rest—resonated with a remembered word, a melody, an image from their storehouse of Jewish experiences.

There was a chaos of experiments, and out of them by 1971 a new form had emerged: the havurah or fellowship. The heart of it is Shabbos, the holy Sabbath day of meditation and repose. Radiating out from Shabbos is a sense of community: the sharing of all the concerns of life, both Shabbos and workday, among a cluster of people who feel to each other like an extended family. And giving intellectual focus to it all is Torah: the process of wrestling with all of Jewish tradition, seriously and joyfully and playfully and angrily seeking to learn from that process how to live.

How did it look? In those early days, those days still flavored with the sixties, the tone was strongly countercultural. There have been changes since then; as the participants grew more comfortable with being different, they grew less strident in their difference and more relaxed in the face of a range of styles and approaches.

But this is how it was at the beginning:

A number of people, usually between twenty and forty, gather on a Friday night. Their clothes are loose, relaxed, colorful, pretty—the kind of clothing that encourages its wearers to move around, sing, hug each other, sit cross-legged on a cushion or the floor. They gather in a rough circle—some on cushions, some on chairs. A five-year-old walks around to greet his grown-up friends. Someone picks up a guitar; someone else passes out prayer books. The conversation hushes; the guitarist begins to chant a wordless tune. The others join in; the tune repeats, repeats again, and still again. Bodies start to sway; taut muscles start to loosen. The tune develops into a song, into a prayer. The guitar rests.

Someone begins to chant, not just read, a paragraph of prayer in English. The community joins in. There is a pause. Someone says, "It's hard for me to 'give away' what happened to me Tuesday. I had a fight. I still feel angry. I'd like to be rid of that for Shabbos." There are tears in her voice. Someone next to her takes her hand; she does cry a little, shakes her head, smiles. The guitarist begins again with a line from the Psalms: "From the tight spot I cry out to God: You answer me with open space."

A little later the community stands up, faces westward and sings a greeting to the Shabbos Queen who is arriving as the sun is setting. The singing soars, murmurs, falls away into a whisper: stops. There are a few moments of deep quiet. Someone says "Good Shabbos, *Shabbat shalom!*" and people start to gather wine, bread, cheese, fruit, egg salad, noodle kugel for a potluck meal.

So goes Friday night: a time to sing, to relearn body movements, loose and flowing to ease the mind.

And then on Shabbos morning, another clustering of people, some new, some the same as those the night before. They are perhaps a little older—psychologists, lawyers, computer pro-grammers, lobbyists, English teachers, a sprinkling of people trained as rabbis. Again they gather in a circle, but this time there is a sense of a little more formality, a little more structure. Using the traditional prayer book, a woman begins the service with the wake-up blessings of the morning: "Blessed is the One Who opens the eyes of the blind," and she touches her eyelids; "Who makes firm the earth above the waters," and she pats the floor; "Who engirds the People Israel with power," and she draws the *tallis* close around her for a moment. Some members of the community join her in phys-ically acting out the blessings in their own ways; some look still too sleepy and simply murmur "Amen." The service slowly rises in intensity, climbing from the individual "warm-up" of the Psalms to the warmth of communal presence and unity that is signaled by the responsive chanting of *Bar'chu* to the private, individual intensity of the standing *Amidah*.

As the leader repeats the Amidah aloud, a visitor blinks: he has heard for the first time what the community is used to, that God is celebrated not only as the God of our fathers Abraham, Isaac, and Jacob, but also as the God of our mothers Sarah, Rebekah, Rachel, and Leah.

Then comes a change in tone. The service is about to move from the reawakened body to the reawakened mind, from song to story, from chanting toward God to hearing God's word in the Torah. But first there is a transition. Singing tunes more regal in their melody, the havurah turns its attention to a portable hand-carved wooden Ark and to the Torah scroll within it. The Torah is taken out, handed from person to person around the room: each one holds it, cradles it almost like a baby, kisses the cover in a loving way, and the last puts it on a special table to be undressed, unrolled, and finally read. It is as if the ceremonial richness is a veil, and when the veil is gently laid aside, there in the Holy of Holies is something much plainer—a word. A Name.

Ceremonial baroqueness gives way to a businesslike demeanor. Several people come up to share in reading from the scroll. When they are finished, someone else takes out a copy of a new translation, and it moves from hand to hand as people read aloud, in English, the portion for the week.

What happens next can be, often is, the high point of the week for members of the havurah. For example:

A havurah in Washington reads the passage late in Exodus that everyone "knows" is pretty boring. The Torah describes the building of the *Mishkan*, that portable tent in which God's indwelling Presence moved through the wilderness of Sinai. In detail the text explains how board was joined to board and post to post. Then it turns to the sacred clothing of the high priest: What precious stones shall he wear on his chest? What fur shall hem his gown?

These details dry the mind. Who can remake a modern Jewish life by playing with these dusty facts of architectural design and garment fashioning?

And yet, and yet . . . The havurah finishes reading this passage, and turns to hear one of its members speak brief words of Torah, comment on this passage:

God tells the high priest how to make and wear some sacred clothing. What does this mean about *our* clothing? Is there a spiritual discipline in what we wear? Does clothing screen us from God's awesome, overwhelming presence—or does some clothing bring us closer, like the priest's? Did nakedness in Eden represent a closer spiritual contact with God? As Eden disappeared, was the first set of clothing that Eve and Adam made for themselves, a screen against God out of fear? Was the second set, the clothing God made for them, a tender mesh of reconnection? And do these stories teach us anything about how to treat our clothing?

Suddenly there is a burst of energy in the room: What is the connection between the spiritual and the physical? How do we get past words, or through words, to the body of our people, the body of each person in experiencing the wholeness of the world? Clothing, buildings, art, dance, sacrificial blood—how do we use these to offer our selves—and to withhold ourselves? Is a building a kind of suit of clothes for a body of people, a community, a physical boundary that says *we* are in here, *they* are out there? And after an hour of intense discussion, when the initiator asks the traditional question, "Does anyone who has not yet spoken at all want to say something?" there comes at first a hesitant and then a vigorous comment:

I spent four whole days last summer on a nudists' beach at Martha's Vineyard. It was amazing, it shook me and . . . Those days felt drenched with sexuality, and with spirituality too. We were open, utterly open—unable to conceal our bodies, our fears, our embarrassments, our attractions, our desires. . . . And we responded by caring about each other, caring for each other, worrying for each other's sakes about our skin, our sunburn. People came back to the same places every day. We became a community.

And again, a burst of energy in the room: This time it is silent but intense, a glowing network of erotic connection—sexual but more than sexual. The speaker had unified the message with the medium. In talking about her days naked on the beach, she had stripped her feelings naked, bared her self. And the havurah had responded to her spiritual nakedness as the bathers had responded to physical nakedness: by forming a community.

From below, the disparate group of Jews had become for a moment the mystical Community of Israel. From above, the Presence, the *Shekhinah,* the female aspect of God, had entered in the midst of the discussion. The distant, veiled, transcendent Deity had for a moment unveiled Herself, revealed Herself, come naked—as it were—into the congregation.

The letters of Torah, in all their plainness, had become so powerful an attraction, so much a center of gravity-pull, that they had created a small community of Israel.

The tradition recognized this Torah-power long ago: at Sinai, said the rabbis, God and Israel were wedded with the Torah as *ketubah*—the written covenant of marriage. The analogy has irony, for the ketubah seems a plain and boring legal document, a contract. It does not speak of love or passion, yet it binds together two people in what can be a passionate embrace.

The question today is whether Torah can bind together the large community of Israel as it does the havurah.

It used to. Until Sinai, the Israelites were a camp of allies, facing outward against the dangers of Egypt and the Wilderness. At Sinai they became a people, a community, facing inward toward a Center.

And in the *Ahavah* prayer of the daily service, the prayer that celebrates the Torah-giving God, Jews say to God, "With intense love you have loved us, Lord our God," and recognize that through the Torah their scattered selves are reunited from the four corners of the earth into harmony and community.

But in the modern era, the Jewish people has been scattered—not only geographically but far more deeply, into an inner disarray. Even the physical reunion of a sizable part of the Jewish people in the Land of Israel has simply reemphasized the deep divisions between different kinds of Jews: The division between those who live in the Land and those who live in Diaspora. The division between those who have shrugged and turned away from the tradition and those who have bowed down before it—both, in different ways, refusing to engage it, wrestle with it, make love to it. What can reunite our people, not as an armed camp facing outward against enemies, but as a community looking inward toward the Center?

The havurah experience teaches that there is a binding power in the Torah process. It comes not from bowing down to Torah, but from making love with Torah: not from blind obedience to a Torah wrapped heavily in expert guidance, but from open-eyed enjoyment of the naked Truth.

To draw on that power, however, it is necessary to unwrap the Teaching as the scroll itself is unwrapped: it is necessary for Jews to make close contact with the ancient stories and precepts, to make close contact through real urgency and caring about a real issue in our lives.

That is what the havurot have been doing. Questions about work and friendship, about the anger and love between brothers and sisters, about war, peace, and the military draft, about when to make more money and how to give money away, about the agonies of Israel and the Palestinians—all these concerns have found a place in havurah Torah discussions, and all of them have changed their shape when Torah has been brought to bear on them.

It will be necessary to search more deeply into the kind of Torah-study that has evolved in the havurot, in order to understand how that process might become more useful to the Jewish people as a whole. But to do this, it would be important to understand how this core of the havurah—the two-way communication with God through prayer and Torah-study—ripples out into the rest of havurah life. And we will need to look at how people who from one moment to another may feel they have a sense of God—and do not—and do again—can talk with God at all.

We will see more of this. But there is more than Torah to the havurot. What happens after Torah-study? The rest of Shabbos will be a tranquil drifting, usually more individual than communal. After the Torah discussion, the service comes quickly to an end. People talk together for awhile, then drift off in twos and threes to walk, nap, have lunch, chat.

And during the rest of the week?

• Saturday night there may be a party; or a gathering of friends within the havurah to go to a baseball game; or the showing of a Yiddish film.

• Sunday afternoon there may be a wedding; or a volleyball game; or a committee meeting to work out how to apply Jewish traditions and values to issues of energy policy; or another committee planning how to help the Ethiopian Jews, who are being harassed by all sides in the Ethiopian civil war and ignored by the official Jewish leadership in America and Israel.

• On any weekday night there may be a meeting of Jewish study groups. One may be learning elementary Hebrew, another studying the structure of the prayer book, still another reading and discussing a history of the Holocaust. One group may be studying Martin Buber, another a section of the Talmud, still another an esoteric mystical text of Kabbalah. All are sitting together around a table, talking, responding to a teacher and to each other, rather than quietly listening to a lecturer. And all include some people who are utterly new to the exploring of their Jewish selves, as well as some veteran members of the havurah.

• One night a month, about fifteen people will gather who have been pooling some percentage of their incomes to help people and projects for the poor, the sick, the desperate. They may be reporting on how a new project is operating, or voting how much money to give the different projects on the list, or arguing about what tzedakah really is.

• On another night, six or seven people may gather to create a "dance," a set of movements and gestures, that expresses through body language the meaning of a psalm or a prayer—a dance that they can teach others as part of a service. Others may gather around a kiln to finish a ceramic Passover Seder plate.

And so, out of the separated threads of an alienated life—out of the concerns of friendship and family, politics and money, body and intellect, artistry and hanging-out, there will be woven together a community. Not only because the people around the circumference of the communal circle like each other (indeed, sometimes they do not); but because all of them around the circle are facing toward a center: the Jewish struggle with God.

This is where the North American movement toward Jewish renewal began. It has not stopped there. Secularists as well as the religious, synagogues as well as havurot, dancers, calligraphers, and historians as well as rabbis and storytellers have contributed their skills and knowledges. And the renewal has not stopped within the walis of Jewishness. The very questions of what it means to be a Jew and Jewish, what and where the boundaries are with other peoples, are being explored.

And indeed the energies toward Jewish renewal are a special case of efforts among many peoples to renew many ancient traditions. The energies of modernism shattered many an ancient holy vessel, not just the Jewish one. Many peoples are struggling first to understand and then to regather their scattered sparks, though here we will examine and learn from a particular case, the Jewish one.

2. The Fusion of Learning and Loving

In traditional intimate Jewish communities and congregations before the coming of modernism, the process of studying Torah was at the very core of what it meant to have or to be a Jewish community. Two other processes—dealing with money and dealing with power by wrestling with Torah—were crucial to bringing Torah into the public world. In all three of these aspects, the shattering of the traditional Jewish pattern by modernism has turned the traditional process into something quite different.

In the study of Torah, objective understanding has been separated from passionate concern. And with Torah-study itself thus diminished, the relationships between Torah and the community's use of money, Torah and the community's use of power, have also been broken. Thus in its own inwardness of study and outwardness of action, the face-to-face local community found itself divided from itself: separated from its own process.

To see what it might mean to recreate a holistic Jewish community in any given place, we need to look at these three areas: study, money and politics. With each of them we need first to understand what it was in this particular aspect of community life, that got separated, alienated, estranged. Let us begin with Torah-study, and ask ourselves: What were the specific sparks of holiness that had been united in Torah-study as it was done in the traditional Jewish world, that were driven apart by the modernist explosion, and that most need to be reunited?

One way to understand is by closely examining the Hebrew word for knowing, *yoday-ah*. It is used in the Hebrew Bible in several senses: for "knowing" and understanding facts and ideas; for making love; and for achieving deep intimacy between God and humankind. When the Bible was translated into English as the King James Version, the translators had no trouble using "know" when they met yoday-ah in any of its senses: not only in relation to facts and ideas, but also in regard to ethical and emotional intimacy. Thus, "Adam *knew* Eve his wife, and she conceived," and "The earth will be full of the *knowledge* of the Lord as the waters fill the sea." But now we find this usage strange. Why?

When the King James Version was published, in 1611, it did not seem strange—inside or outside the Jewish world—to sense that "knowing" was what a scholar and a lover would both do. For scholarship was understood to be passionate—both utterly objective and utterly involved. It was understood that learning and teaching required a deep and loving intimacy with the facts and ideas being learned—a two-way intimacy like that of lovemaking, in which the facts and ideas could change the learner and the learner could change the facts and ideas.

But the world in which "knowing" was intimately interrelational and "loving" was objective was the world before modernism transformed and conquered it. Now, three hundred fifty years later, we have separated these ways of connecting ourselves to the world.

"Knowing" we have made utterly objective and wholly uninvolved. We have turned the facts into "foreigners," alien, distant from ourselves.

"Loving" we have made utterly involved and wholly romantic, unobjective. In love we make *ourselves* the foreigners, tourists enchanted by the Disneyland of some fantastic other.

And so both our knowing and our loving became emptied of wisdom, separated obscured sparks. For wise learning must be like loving—objective, yes, and also wholly involved, wholly open to the Other we are learning from. And wise loving must be like learning—intimately involved and open, yes, and also utterly objective, seeing the Other as the Other truly is. So in the modernist world where the sparks of "knowing" and "loving" got separated, the results were analytical universities and romantic, fragile families.

In the Jewish world, transformed as well by modernism, even the intimate knowledge from Hebrew that yoday-ah means "intimate knowledge" was not able to prevent the separation of the sparks of knowing and loving. Especially in the most modernized region of world Jewry, the Jewish community in America, this had disastrous effects on the process of Jewish learning—on the very communication of a Jewish culture to the succeeding generations of adults and children. By 1960, Jewish learning was so emptied of emotional connection to the world that it was almost emptied of intellectual interest as well. Indeed, Jewish learning was something that happened only to children—and rabbinical students. From age six to thirteen, boys and girls were pushed, begged, bribed, and screamed at to get them into Sunday schools and afternoon religious schools. They were bored, tired, angry, and either resigned or rebellious. Few indeed were excited, joyful, or curious about the next unfolding leaf of Jewish thought or history, Jewish dance or music, Jewish pottery or woodcuts. Few boys survived to go on to more schooling after bar mitzvah, and hardly any girls were able even to experience a *bat mitzvah*.

Those who did survive, who found themselves touched by an extraordinary teacher or a moment of spiritual insight, might persevere at being Jewish until (if they were men, of course) they made their way into a rabbinical seminary. If they had grown up in the Reform movement, they were taught how to give a bombastic sermon on a magazine article or on the social issues of the day. If they were Conservative, they were taught the apparatus of historical investigation into the development of Jewish tradition. If they were Orthodox, they were taught the minutiae of halakha and how to defend it against the creeping inroads of assimilation.

As for the women who survived this "educational" torment with a sense of exploration or joy in being Jewish—they became Sunday school and afternoon schoolteachers themselves, and learned how to live through hours of frustration and boredom teaching children who were bored and frustrated. Or they joined Hadassah and learned enough about Israel and about effective middle-class fundraising to raise money for Israeli hospitals with precision and élan. For only in the arena of restoring a Jewish presence in the Land of Israel did the analytic, the ethical, and the emotional—the cerebral and the physical—stay connected.

Such were (in something of a caricature) the possibilities of "Jewish learning." Few American Jews imagined that there was anything Jewish that might engage the mind or body of a Jewish grown-up, on a grown-up level.

By 1980 the situation had been transformed. By then, for example, thousands of energetic, excited Jews in their twenties, thirties, and forties had gathered at summer conferences of the Coalition for Alternatives in Jewish Education (CAJE) to learn—usually by doing, and always with passion, love and caring.

They read Bible passages like the binding of Isaac or the wedding of Jacob and Leah. They then improvised short dramas, acting out with their own bodies not the story they had just read but the unwritten stories that come just afterward—Abraham coming down the mountain with an Isaac broken inwardly, Jacob and Rachel and Leah and Laban confronting the fact of an unintended marriage.

They studied passages from the Talmud and from Martin Buber on war and peace—and struggled to connect these ideas with their own lives and the lives of their students in the thermonuclear age.

They learned how to put on t'fillin, the traditional leather straps and boxes worn on arm and head for morning prayer—and said out loud the feelings and thoughts the archaic instruments aroused in them.

They grilled Jewish "lay leaders"—that is, people of wealth—about how the organizational structures work, and they practiced on these leaders, trying to "raise money" till they began to understand how to get past the hardness of doing it.

They giggled and guffawed at a rabbi who, as a stand-up-comic, ran an auction to pay off the Conference's own deficit, and they learned new twists of Jewish humor.

They learned—and thereby learned to teach. They learned a Jewishness that was adult enough to excite and stretch them—and thereby learned a Jewishness that was adult enough to excite and stretch their children.

This new approach to Jewish learning was at the same moment experiential and textual; at the same moment it used the newest means of full emotional involvement and the oldest passages and problems of Jewish cognition. How had this happened, and what might it lead to next?

One of the roots of this new approach was the enrichment of Jewish summer camping. Jewish camps during the sixties had become places for hands-on Judaism, where learning Torah chant, calligraphy, and midrash making were intertwined with swimming and volleyball and campfire building.

Out of these camps came many of the people who formed the havurot in the late sixties and early seventies. There, as they shaped their own experiential-traditional Judaism, they also began to experiment with teaching children. Some early havurah members in Boston and New York, Chicago and Los Angeles, were graduate students who supported themselves in part by teaching in Jewish schools on afternoons or Sundays. They were influenced by their own experience in Jewish camps that they remembered as far more attractive and effective in teaching than their official schools had been. And they were also influenced by the new or revived use of radical, progressive, or experimental educational theories and techniques that were characteristic of American education in general in the late sixties and early seventies: the open classroom, learning by doing, child-centered education, attention to the process of learning as more important than any particular product, the confluence of emotional, ethical, and cognitive learning, voluntary and self-directed rather than compulsory education.

These ideas of what education was about fit in very well with havurah ideas of what Jewishness was about. In a society rooted in the First Amendment, being Jewish was no longer a compulsory caste or status, but a voluntary act with many definitions; in a society of physical and sexual openness and spiritual search, being Jewish was no longer simply a head trip but one that engaged the body and the soul. So for these young teachers, the integration of new ways of learning with new ways of being Jewish felt absolutely natural.

They began to use the new techniques in their own teaching.

Some of them even opened new schools, tied more or less loosely to havurot. Some of these schools were parent co-ops in which parents themselves did most or all of the teaching. In others the havurah members did the teaching, but parents were deeply involved in planning and began to study among themselves. In all of them, the atmosphere was that of the best summer camps in which learning happened organically as part of living, in which the learners and the teachers felt themselves part of a community rather than producers and consumers.

Many of these young Jewish teachers were also activists, change-makers. Some of them had been involved in Jewish student organizations, and had begun to create networks of people like themselves all across the country. They wanted to remake the Jewish world, not only their own lives. So through networks of active Jewish students and havurah people, they reached out to create the Coalition for Alternatives in Jewish Education.

For several years within CAJE there was a tension between what might be called "pressure-group" activism and "model-process" activism. Those who preferred the first approach saw CAJE as a pressure group to insist on such changes as wider use of nonsexist Jewish textbooks; on more respect and higher salaries for Jewish teachers; on larger allocations of money by the Jewish Federations to education (as against hospitals, Jewish Community Centers with low Jewish content, and other mammoth physical projects with high potentials for ethnic pride but low potentials for deepening Jewish culture). Some talked about the unionizing of Jewish teachers, to permit collective bargaining with schools and boards of Jewish education.

On the other hand, those who preferred the "model-process" approach thought CAJE's major usefulness would be changing the way teachers teach by engaging them in new ways of learning and teaching and by making alternative approaches visible. They assumed that questions of power, money, and content in the educational structures would be dealt with as the Jewish community became increasingly excited over the revival of Jewish education.

After a few years, CAJE clearly moved in the second direction.

Some boards of Jewish education and various local federations began to support the annual CAJE conferences by paying teachers' travel expenses to the meetings and subsidizing the organizations' staff and office costs in preparing for the conferences. Confrontations between CAJE and these funding sources became less and less frequent.

Unless CAJE builds its own financial base as a teachers' (or teachers, parents, and rank-and-file lay) organization, its activism will continue to take the model-making form. Perhaps this approach will continue to appeal to increasing numbers of people and so will transform the existing educational structures from within. On the other hand, it may turn out that the liberating effect of the new approaches on Jewish creativity, independence, and pluralism is unappetizing to the central funding and organizing institutions of the Jewish community. For rarely do bureaucracies welcome the emergence of feisty individuals or groups with their own approaches. In that case, the sharpness and clarity of alternative educational approaches may decrease, and their "alternativeness" may decline into gimmicks.

But meanwhile, the yeast of change in CAJE has brought ideas and approaches originally grown in the hothouse atmosphere of the havurot into the broader arena of the Jewish community. As a result, some interesting educational hybrids have emerged which draw from the strengths of the large synagogues as well as from those of the experimental havurot.

The strength of the synagogue is that it pools enough money to hire professionals and to provide a large and self-controlled space. Getting hooked on the mortgage and dependent on the professionals are its corresponding defects. The strengths of the havurot are its intensity and flexibility. Sloppiness and the limited time and energy it can draw from unpaid volunteers are its defects. There have begun to be attempts to create complementary forms in which the strengths of both approaches can be tapped..

First, internal havurot have emerged in a growing number of synagogues. They consist of pre-arranged groups of twenty to forty people who typically meet one to four times a month to share in some project—study, or tzedakah, or leisurely relaxation. Depending on the synagogue and the havurah, these groups may receive continuing advice, teaching, and help from the rabbi and other congregational staff, or may find themselves on their own after being brought together. The emergence of these synagogue havurot testifies to the growing awareness of some congregational rabbis and lay leaders of the need for a kind of intimacy that is cooler and more variegated than that of the nuclear family, but much warmer and more intense than can possibly be provided by undifferentiated membership in a congregation of hundreds or thousands.

Most of the synagogue havurot that have emerged have been quite different from the original independent havurot. They meet less often, share less of their lives, and develop a less intense Jewish focus. Very few of them have become autonomous groups for prayer; that, it seems, feels too threatening to most rabbis and congregational leaders. Some havurot do *davven* together one Shabbos out of every two or four, periodically rejoining the larger congregation. A number of them have turned out to be social groups with little Jewish cultural content. But a growing number have found deeper vitality in studying together a range of Jewish sources, from Torah to modern Jewish poetry. And some have found themselves becoming *de facto* family-education groups, in which ten or fifteen families help each other celebrate Jewish holy days and observe life cycle events like bar and bat mitzvahs, weddings, and funerals. The main strength of this model is that the paid synagogue professionals—rabbis, teachers, secretaries, executive directors—are available to help the intimate fellowship when they are needed.

Second, a "complementary" approach has been an arrangement in which a rabbi or knowledgeable Jewish teacher helps organize or is sought out by a federation of havurot. Because a number of havurot are acting together, they can afford to hire a professional to be a resource person and teacher. He or she helps the havurot to plan their own programs, trains people to lead their own prayers and groups, suggests readings for study groups to explore, and helps in other ways. Such a federation of havurot does not need a building, except one it can rent for special occasions when all the havurot might want to be together (as on the High Holy Days). On most occasions, meeting in homes is workable. For a group that dislikes high mortgage costs and elaborate administration more than it likes efficiency and having a multi-use space on instant call, such an arrangement may bring professionalism and intimacy into a workable relationship with each other.

Third, in a deeper way than institutional arrangements, the educational approach of the havurot is working its way into the synagogues. They are beginning to understand that people—children and adults—learn by doing, doing what they want to learn. So synagogue children have been learning to study Torah by doing what *yeshiva* students always did: sitting in couples to read a passage together, explaining it to each other, asking help from a teacher only when they get stuck. Synagogue children have been learning to pray by praying: up on their feet, looking at each other, moving their muscles, swaying in the ancient *shukl*, chanting in the ancient rhythm. Synagogue children have been learning Hebrew by speaking it, reading it, writing it, using calligraphy. Synagogue children have been learning about *kiddush* by shaping wine cups out of clay; about mezuzahs by carving the wood and writing the text.

In a few synagogues, the age barriers to learning have begun to dissolve. In Congregation Beth El in Sudbury, Massachusetts, there is one class in which the admission ticket for a child is to bring one parent; for an adult, to bring one child. In many Hillel Houses on college campuses and now in a growing number of congregations as well, adults have been taking on the role and ceremony of the bar or bat mitzvah, either because they never went through the process when they were thirteen years old or because they feel themselves newly growing as Jews. Some adults have chosen to make a special study and a special observance of leading a service, reading the Torah, chanting the prophetic Haftarah.

Some of the newest and oldest customs of the Jewish community have begun to be intertwined. Since more and more Jewish families are headed by a single working parent or by two job-holding parents, child-care centers have become a necessity. Among the oldest customs is the practice of involving small children in learning Torah, even with the reward and reinforcement of a slice of honeyed cake to start with. Now there have appeared a few Jewishly focused child-care centers, with more on the way: centers for three-, four-, and five-year-olds that teach the holidays by celebrating their special practices, teach Shabbos with songs and dances, teach Hebrew with everyday words and phrases. In Philadelphia, the Germantown Jewish Centre (a Conservative synagogue) has become the host for a day-care center for children as young as a few months, in which dolls, crafts, conversation, cooking, rituals, all steep the children in Jewish tradition—simply as the path of normal life.

One way to see these efforts is as a way of reconstituting the extended Jewish family and the Jewish neighborhood—in time rather than space. Where not only the extended family but even the nuclear family has been split, when not only *tantes*, *zaydes*, and *bubbes*, but even mom and dad may be a city or a continent away, when children are often living with one or the other of their parents at a time rather than with both, there is much less opportunity to learn a variety of Jewish skills from a variety of adults. Who will teach the Yiddish songs, the way to make *gribenes* from chicken, the right way to bow and sway in the synagogue chanting, the skeptical Jewish-socialist outlook on world politics, the way to organize an effective neighborhood campaign for the Jewish National Fund, when the uncle who studies Talmud lives in Philadelphia, the aunt who organized a teachers' union local is in Pasadena, the grandmother cooks superbly in a Miami apartment, the older brother who loves to davven is in college in Madison, Wisconsin, and the nearest Jewish neighbor who keeps Shabbos lives three miles away?

Under these circumstances, the havurah, the child-care center, and the school become Jewish "neighborhoods" that gather by automobile to create a Jewish milieu. Of necessity, the new kinds of schools find themselves teaching that milieu and path of life as much as a language, a history, and a literature. At their best, the schools and havurot may even become extended Jewish families—helping mourn a death, provide the "uncle" who is passionately religious or socialist, meshing the many different Jewish roles and skills so that the children can test them out, try them on for size, mix and match them in new ways.

And not just the children. For the process has both grown from reawakened adults, and has helped reawaken those adults. Taking conscious steps to create a Jewish "neighborhood" or "extended family" has different effects from growing up in one as a given. In most cases where families have taken deliberate steps, the act has been self-reinforcing, and not only the children but their elders have begun to study, sing, and pray together.

Meanwhile, the havurot, the synagogues, and boards of Jewish education that were affected by the new atmospheres began to create new forms for the adult education of their own members and of unaffiliated Jews who were much like them. One such new form was modeled on the *Freies Jüdisches Lehrhaus* or "Free Jewish House of Learning" of Frankfurt in prewar Germany, founded by Martin Buber and Franz Rosenzweig. The Frankfurt Lehrhaus was different from older models of Jewish study. First of all, it taught not only in the traditional pattern "from the text to life," accepting Torah as a given and applying it to new life issues, but also in a new pattern from life to the text—that is, from the life-problems that Jews faced every day to the texts of Jewish tradition that might illuminate them. Secondly, it made no rigid distinction between those steeped in Jewish thought and those new to it, but instead treated every teacher as a student, every student as a potential teacher.

In Washington, D.C., the first effort at a Lehrhaus was called just that, and was put together by a young rabbi, Daniel Polish. It lasted for three years and demonstrated that there was a strong and growing community desire for such learning. It also showed that in the absence of some form of congregational support, the burden of planning and organizing such a program was too great for any one person.

A few years later, the Washington havurah Fabrangen created a Jewish Study Center that met the needs of its own members and of unaffiliated Jews who were in education and life style, much like themselves. This second version of the Lehrhaus approach had behind it Fabrangen's cadre of willing volunteers, the psychological support necessary to get beyond discouraging moments, and enough money contributed by Fabrangen to pay for publicity and a part-time coordinator until there were enough students to pay these expenses from tuition fees. That combination worked. The official community—in the form of the local United Jewish Appeal Federation—year after year murmured its interest in helping support the Study Center, and year after year shrugged off specific grant proposals and requests for money. But the Study Center's steady success finally proved to the Jewish Community Center (JCC) that a "market" for its programs, made of young, mostly single Jews, existed in downtown Washington. So, twelve years after the JCC had fled the city for a spot twenty miles into the suburbs, the JCC began offering intown programs again.

It might be imagined that Washington is a special case in that its government and paragovernment jobs attract more than the average number of upward mobile Jewish young professionals who, from a successfully "assimilated" stance in American society, decide to pursue some aspect of Jewish knowledge. Yet, in Philadelphia and on the upper West Side of Manhattan, similar Lehrhaus-style projects met similar needs; and more recently, as the new approaches spread, such a traditional center for adult education as Gratz College of Jewish Studies in Philadelphia has found new students in the new constituency. In many cities, Jewish "Y"s and Community Centers that had provided Western music, Western drama, Western sports—but rarely Jewish culture—have found their audiences thirsty for reconnections of Jewish intellect with the energies of body, emotion, and spirit.

What experiences have made the new forms of learning attractive? Sitting around a table with the teacher in one of the seats, instead of sitting in rows of chairs facing a blackboard. Reading a text together and talking about it, rather than being lectured at. Bringing in everyday feelings and ideas, rubbing them up against the texture of Jewish experience, facing everyday ethical issues in the light of Jewish experience and thought, rather than treating Jewish matters as a bubble, a ghetto, walled off from other areas of life. Having a chance to talk, laugh, look at, make friends with the other participants. The attraction lies in the process of dissolving bits and pieces of the barriers that separate Judaism from the world, thought from feeling, analysis from ethics, teachers from students—and letting the juices flow into new connections, unexpected associations.

It is the regathering of separated sparks that has given new life and liveliness to Jewish learning

Having tasted the pleasures of this kind of learning in small weekly snacks and snatches, people who are involved in Jewish renewal have begun to seek ways of making longer, fuller meals of it. One approach has been to borrow from an ancient custom of the Diaspora who lived in Babylonia, while the Talmud was being evolved in the fourth century C.E. A large part of the Jewish community in that time and place would lay down the tools of their ordinary work during the late summer month of *Elul*—the month just before Rosh Hashanah. They took the month as a time for Torah-study, preparing themselves for the Days of *Tshuvah*, Turning, that run from Rosh Hashanah to Yom Kippur by reconnecting Torah with their own lives. In our own schedule in the American Jewish community, August vacations are a time of flight from regular work, a time to "vacate," empty out our lives of their conventional routines. Could they also become a time of approach toward the new forms of Jewish education, a time to fill ourselves with new and unconventional possibilities?

The answer is beginning—just barely beginning—to be yes. For many years, the campus-oriented Hillel Foundations held a week-long summer institute in which a number of teachers and rabbis worked with college students from all over North America on understanding Jewish texts and improving particular Jewish skills. More recently, the Coalition for Alternatives in Jewish Education has made its annual summer conference not only a professional convention with workshops in methodology, but a time for Jewish teachers to learn Torah—in words, crafts, music—with each other. And the National Havurah Coordinating Committee has found that hundreds of Jews from a range of secular jobs have been delighted to gather for a summer week of exploring in depth such subjects as the Psalms, modern Jewish poetry focused on biblical themes, the structure of Jewish communal life in the Middle Ages, or the meaning and practice of one of the festivals or fasts. These summer institutes have been held on campuses where it was possible to swim, walk, play tennis; where the participants' children could take part in a "minicamp"; where it was possible to sing new Jewish songs, exhibit Jewish pottery and paper-cuts, experiment with Jewish mime and dance; and in many ways open up to "body Judaism" intertwined with texts.

In 1981, havurah people—mostly from synagogues in the South—sponsored a summer institute of their own. It seems likely that Jewish communities throughout the country could organize their own summer institutes, perhaps for the four days of the Labor Day weekend, perhaps for a whole week.

From these new flowerings there have begun to float more seeds of ideas. So far they remain ideas only, but they have begun to spread and may soon have enough adherents to grow roots of their own:

There could be Jewish "family camps" to which children come for, say, four weeks and their parents for one week. That would both provide the separation that children and parents need for growth as individuals, and provide the common experience of Jewish living that reinforces Jewish creativity. Among havurah people there has been a sense of the absence of any summer camp that would reinforce the havurot's unusual mix of concern for Jewish religious tradition, for experiential Jewish involvement, and for cooperation and equality in work. As things stand now, one or another of these might be found in one or another camp of religious or secularist background; but rarely or never do the secular-Zionist and secular-Yiddishist values of hard work, sharing, and economic equality get intertwined with the religious values of prayer, celebration, and Torah-study. The havurot, or congregations with a havurah bent, or an organization like CAJE, could create such camps.

Synagogues that have encouraged havurot could strengthen these groups by restructuring their educational work to fit into the havurot. For example, instead of hiring teachers to teach "history," "ritual," "Bible," and "Hebrew," or "first grade," "junior high," or "Bar and Bat Mitzvah," suppose the synagogue hired "teachers" as resource people for "Havurah Aleph" and "Havurah Beit." The teacher's job would be to help the havurah create learning situations for its children and adults. The parents-co-op model for a school, in which the whole family reinforces and rewards Jewish learning, would be interwoven with the model of a professional teacher. Each teacher would be a kind of para-rabbi for a minicongregation.

And finally, what about new ways of teaching the future teachers and leaders of the community? In 1960, I began by saying, only small children and rabbis received a Jewish education—and both educations were boring. In twenty years a revolution has begun: not only have some children begun to enjoy their Jewish studies, but even teen-agers, college students, young single people in the first burst of their careers, and older adults focused on their families, have all begun to make ways of learning Jewishly, breaking down the barriers between the storehouse of Jewish thought and the needs of their present lives. But the education of rabbis has remained much the same. Are changes possible? Are they desirable?

The major rabbinical seminaries were created in the nineteenth and twentieth centuries by the official "denominations" of religious Jewish life. (In one case, that of the Conservative movement's Jewish Theological Seminary, the seminary more nearly created the movement than the other way around.) Like those denominational structures, the seminaries were products of modernist ideas about how to teach and learn. They imitated the modern universities in which, and as a result of which, it has seemed puzzling that the word "know" could mean "make love." They teach a great deal like graduate or professional schools of law, history, or clinical psychology. Their students attend lectures, take exams, write papers. The seminaries have not yet absorbed some important lessons of the decades of Jewish renewal:

• The lesson that the folk-singing rabbi, Shlomo Carlebach, has probably touched more Jewish souls, sent more unconnected Jews to drink again from Jewish wellsprings of being, than any other rabbi of the generation. The seminaries are not yet teaching rabbinical students to sing, write songs, play the guitar or the flute.

• The lesson that the most exciting and useful Torah-learning of the decade has probably come not from sermons but from round-the-circle discussions. The seminaries are not yet teaching rabbinical students how *not* to give sermons, how instead to ask the right questions, and then wait for congregations to create new answers.

• The lesson that the renewal of intense mime and dance and poetry and drama and meditative exercise, all on Jewish themes, is reconnecting the inner hope and anguish of the Jews with the outer arena of Jewish communal life. The seminaries are not yet teaching rabbinical students to be poets or playwrights or mimes or dancers or storytellers or meditators, let alone to be creative liturgists able to "play" the *Siddur*.

• The lesson that the whole milieu of American professional schools or graduate schools, with their detachment between teachers and students, and their analytic attitude toward knowledge and toward clients, is utterly contradictory to the ancient tradition in which Torah-study was intimate, playful, and profound—a tradition renewed by the Lehrhaus. The seminaries are not yet creating intimate *hevras* of teachers/students in the Lehrhaus style, as a way of teaching how to be a rabbi.

Some hesitant efforts toward changing what it means to become a rabbi have occurred. When Havurot Shalom began one of the earliest havurot, it called itself a "community seminary" and contemplated organizing intensive, long-term study in a communal context even more intimate than the Lehrhaus. It contemplated ordaining new rabbis, and granting an intermediate "degree" or status of *Haver(a)*. But that part of the vision never came to fulfillment.

In 1978, some of the rabbis who had been closest to the havurot—members, guides, exemplars—began discussing the creation of a "Seminary Without Walls." They imagined fusing two models of education—one from ancient Jewish practice, the other from experimental American education of the sixties and seventies. Before the modern rabbinical seminary, new rabbis were ordained by older rabbis after a close personal relationship of study and emulation. Typically, three who already held *smicha* ("connection" to the line of rabbinical learning) could extend it to someone new. This was the ancient Jewish model. The experimental American model was the "university without walls," in which a degree candidate could arrange study meeting certain standards, to be undertaken anywhere in close consultation with a committee of scholars tailor-made to the student's own concerns. The committee of scholars would certify when the candidate had met the requirements and was ready to receive a degree. The university as a whole would grant it. In some ways this experiment was a postmodern effort to reconstruct an educational approach that would connect cognitive and emotional learning, arising from the critique of modernism that erupted in America of the sixties and seventies.

The havurah-oriented rabbis had in mind the creation of a seminary or yeshiva with a minimal central structure, the faculty of which would be a number of rabbis of extraordinary creativity and knowledge, living in many different places. Together they would define a basic set of requirements for granting smicha. Candidates could then study with a committee of three from this faculty, could define a special program for the study, and when the study was completed—in two, five, or ten years—could receive smicha. With the prestige of a more formal seminary behind it, this process might also be able to help the new kinds of rabbis get jobs and acceptance. Thus the planners hoped to bring together the "premodern" Jewish smicha process with the postmodern form of the "university without walls," in order to serve Jewish needs in America.

The rabbis tested out the concept by meeting with a group of prospective students for an extended summer institute of intensive study and discussions. The institute was successful enough to show that the concept could work—and to show as well, how much time and energy and perseverance it would take to make it work. How to set standards that would be open to creative possibilities, without facing the scorn of most existing rabbis? How to keep a sense of shared endeavor and central structure among a group of strong-minded individuals who were also geographically scattered? How to . . . there were many other problems. The effort was put on the shelf.

But some of those involved—especially Rabbi Zalman Schachter-Shalomi, rebbe of a group called *B'nai Or* (Children of Light) and professor of religion at Temple University—decided to go forward with the traditional, preseminary model. Several students received smicha from committees of three rabbis, and the search for new approaches is continuing.

The search received new impetus from the sudden growth of another kind of fusion of American education with Jewish learning: the "Jewish studies" programs in a host of American universities. These programs risked all the problems of the rigidified academicism of their surrounding faculties. But they emerged partly from the ferment of the movement for Jewish renewal, in ways similar to those in which Black studies programs had emerged from the ferment of Black consciousness. So at least in the early years, many of the teachers and students in these Jewish studies programs came into them not for academic reasons in the narrow sense, but because they shared the values of the movement for Jewish renewal and saw most of the seminaries as too stuffy to explore them. Many of their students expected to use their learning either in their everyday nonprofessional Jewish lives or in a variety of jobs attached to organized Jewish communal work. The teachers came from a range of disciplines that had not been brought together before in just such ways: history, political and communal theory, literary criticism and scholarship, sociology and social work, demography, theology and the rabbinate. By cutting across the conventional categories, the new Jewish studies programs offered a framework in which the old dichotomy of "religious" and "secularist" had less meaning. So the new framework was open to unexpected connections and recombinations, and offered route to Jewish learning embodying yoday-ah.

There were even more explicit connections between the Jewish studies network and some aspects of the movement for Jewish renewal. One of the most seminal of the Jewish studies professors, Jacob Neusner of Brown University, was also one of the earliest Jews to perceive the relevance and renewal of the ancient form of the havurah, and to perceive the importance of the postmodern havurot as they began to happen. And as the teachers and students of the Jewish studies departments and centers began to multiply, many of them found their natural nonprofessional homes in the havurot, and greatly enriched the Jewish knowledgeability of the havurot.

Whether the values of the early years will be gradually swallowed up by the modernist tone of the surrounding universities remains to be seen and tested.

Meanwhile, the actual process of learning at the conventional seminaries has begun to change in unofficial ways as students and professors begin to pay attention to the successes of Lehrhaus-style education and to be revitalized by the movement for Jewish renewal. The smallest and newest of the seminaries, the Reconstructionist Rabbinical College (RRC) in Philadelphia, was founded in 1968 explicitly as a critique of the alienated professionalism and intellectuality of the Conservative and Reform seminaries. It restructured rabbinical education around the teaching of five successive Jewish "civilizations," Biblical to Contemporary. Many of its students came because they wanted to see themselves as "resource rabbis" for participatory congregations, rather than as remote priests or scholars. In its early years, RRC had few faculty members who could act out the vision of the founders. In a sense, only the Jewish renewal movement itself could create such teachers. Yet RRC was the seminary most open to pursuing a post-modern version of yoday-ah learning. In 1981 it undertook a more conscious effort to do so under a new president, Ira Silverman, himself a havurah member. Silverman saw the possiblities of reconnecting the College with the broader movement for Jewish renewal and of drawing on the movement's experience in order to train rabbis who could meet the needs of the reawakening American Jewish community.

What is most promising about the new approaches in Jewish education is that many different kinds of people are using them at many different points in the Jewish community—children and college students and rabbis and workers, in campuses and at synagogues and in living rooms. This is happening because an experiment in one place touches someone, releases blocked up energy, leads to an experiment somewhere else. Even the sense of curiosity, surprise, discovery that accompanies the newness of putting Jewishness together with an unexpected piece of life gives new freshness and excitement to the search. So far the changes have needed very little money and have posed few threats to the power of any established bodies. They may begin to—and that is when we will begin to know whether the new excitement is not a merely superficial pleasure, but strikes deep enough into the marrow of the bones of Jewishness to have staying power, to attract support if it were to be attacked.

Meanwhile, the reunification of learning and loving—the rediscovery of the full meaning of yoday-ah—has shown that Jewish culture may be able to transcend the shattering effects of modernism and reconnect the elements that once made it possible for an age-old intellectual tradition to be transmitted with such joyful passion. This renewal of passionate learning is certainly a sine qua non for the reconnection of other holy sparks. For when it comes to questions of money, politics, sexuality, family, peoplehood, God—it is only a passionate wrestling with all the generations of Jewish thought that can regather the sparks into a new holy vessel.

Let us, therefore, look now at how the renewal of passionate engagement with Torah is affecting other areas of Jewish life.

3. Money and Mitzvah

Fifteen people sitting in chairs and sofas around a living room, munching nuts and raisins, looking at a list of projects on a long sheet of paper. The same people had gathered a few days before to pray and chant together and to discuss the Torah, but now a different atmosphere prevails: more businesslike, more tense. No longer Shabbos. Work to do. Money to spend.

The hostess speaks: "Tonight, by our custom, I'll be chair. Who will take notes?" A pause, a hand. "Thanks. The agenda looks like this: some questions about the percentage of our incomes we are giving; committee reports on the projects; a preliminary vote on allocations; setting the time and place for us to meet again. Okay?" A dozen nods. "Okay. Percentages . . ."

One of the group says, "All of us have been giving a flat 2 percent of our incomes into the collective fund we vote on. I've been feeling uncomfortable about that. What about those of us who are living at close to subsistence incomes? For us 2 percent is a much bigger bite than for members with upper-middle incomes. Should we pay less?"

Someone else: "That makes me nervous. After all, the tradition teaches that everybody owes tzedakah to help the poor—even those who are poor themselves. The word itself is from the root *tzedek*, justice, in order to teach us that it is not a matter of noblesse oblige, of graciousness from the rich. It is an act of justice that everyone must do. And in the traditional communities everybody really did give, even the poorest gave something. But I suppose we could have a lower percentage."

"Nuts. We're all middle-class people. Anybody among us who is at subsistence income is just choosing to be. Voluntary poverty isn't the same as real poverty."

"Come on! When one of us is unemployed because the work he or she wants to do is not available, that isn't voluntary. I guess there are other jobs, but some of us are choosing *not* to work for places that don't fit our ethical concerns. In fact, where and how we choose to work may be the most important tzedakah choice we make. Maybe we should talk about our work places—or is that too scary?"

Suddenly the temperature in the room is higher. Money is important. How we spend it and how we get it are easy to disagree about. Somebody else steps in: "Maybe we shouldn't be distinguishing between *people*, setting different rates for different *people*. Maybe instead we could set 1 percent for the first chunk of income at subsistence level for everybody?"

"But our contributions are already fairly low. Traditionally, tzedakah was 10 percent. I know that most of us give on our own, as well as through the collective, but we'll be reducing our collective contribution a good bit this way."

"Well, how about doing the 1 percent thing for the first *x* thousand dollars a year and raise our contribution to 2.5 percent or 3 percent for income over that? That will keep our totals about even."

"Okay, but I want to raise a different question, too. Some of our incomes have risen a lot in the last year. The range among us is much wider than it used to be, and a few of us are now giving amounts that are big proportions of the total. That doesn't feel very 'collective' in a different way. Maybe we should put a cap on contributions from a single household, so that none of us will overshadow the others."

"But why should those of us who have chosen to have cushy jobs pay less of their income to the pool and still have an equal vote with people who pay proportionally more?"

And again the temperature rises. Money is a troublesome thing.

And yet . . . the problems for the moment get resolved. The group takes up a list of projects: A drop-in center for the Jewish poor. A Christian church's plan to help low-income tenants buy their apartment house as a co-op. An absorption center for Russian Jews just arriving in America. Oxfam's fund to feed Cambodians. A summer study institute for havurah people to study Torah. A coalition campaign for the Washington City Council to pass a stronger rent control bill. A shelter for battered women in Jerusalem.

And again the arguments begin. How much for Jewish trouble,

how much for the troubles of the rest of humankind? How much for small projects in a neighborhood of Washington, how much for a worldwide relief effort? How much for direct help to the poor and sick, how much for social action? And again, the arguments get resolved—sometimes to be raised again in six months, sometimes to be gone beyond with a sense of real solution.

The cluster of people in the living room calls itself a "tzedakah collective." The phrase itself is a kind of dance between Jewish tradition and the postmodern world: one part from the language of the American counterculture of the sixties, one part ancient Torah-tongue—a feminine ending on the word for "righteousness" or "justice." The newest and the oldest modes of thought—organically joined in the actions of a group of Jews.

This way of dealing with money is not conventional for American Jews. It does have connections and similarities to the ways Jews used to behave long before there was an America. For in traditional Jewish communities, tzedakah was what connected *mitzvah* and money—mitzvah, "command," the divine commands that were transmitted by the Torah—and the money, the material resources based on work and planning that individual Jews and the Jewish communities had at their disposal to use and to share.

For ages Jews accepted that how they spent their money was shaped, given boundaries, by their sense of mitzvah. The Jewish community heard the mitzvah of tzedakah through Torah, and enforced the mitzvah upon individuals. In order to know how much money it was righteous to give, when, and to whom among the poor and the desperate, Jews wrestled with what the Torah taught about "righteousness" and "justice." From Torah they learned that heart-felt response to desperate need was more righteous than long-range bureaucratic planning; that avoiding condescension or even pride from the giver and avoiding obsequiousness or even gratitude from the recipient were crucial; that it was more desirable to provide the poor with the tools and skills for ending their own poverty than it was to keep them barely alive. And from Torah and from the word itself they learned that tzedakah is not an act of graciousness but one of justice, one of communal obligation.

This sense of limits on the individual use of money went far back to the biblical agrarian society in which the most important property was land and food. The Jews learned, for example, that even the owner of a field did not really, fully own the field—for the corners of the field were left unharvested so that the poor could glean them (Lev. 19:9; 23:22); what the owner missed in first harvesting the crop at once became the property of the poor who followed behind (Deut. 24:19); and in every seventh and every fiftieth year the whole field was restored to God's ownership. In every seventh year, the land's produce was left open to free public gathering without an organized cultivation or harvest; and in the fiftieth year the whole land of Israel was restored to equal family shares (Lev. 25). These commands taught that the concept of private property itself had "corners"—limits in space and in time, so that no "owner" owned in full all of the space, all of the time. And yet these "corners" were not just public property, either. They were on the fringe of private and public—as perhaps the sacred fringes on the four corners of a garment were intended to make clear that not even one's own clothing was wholly private, wholly personal—but merged with the public and Divine.

This sense that no "private" property was wholly private was preserved long after the Jewish people had moved from the Land of Israel to many lands, from the land itself to many cities. The *halakhist* and philosopher Maimonides writes:

It is a positive commandment [mitzvah] to give tzedakah to the poor of Israel, according to what is fitting for them, if the giver can afford it, as it is said, *Thou shalt surely open thy hand unto him* (Deut. 15:8), and again, *Then thou shalt uphold him; as a stranger and a settler shall he live with thee . . . that thy brother may live with thee* (Lev. 25:35–36).

He who seeing a poor person begging turns his eyes away from him and fails to give tzedakah, transgresses a negative commandment, as it is said, *Thou shalt not harden thy heart, nor shift thy hand from thy needy brother* (Deut. 15:7).

You are commanded to give the poor according to what he lacks. If he has no clothing, he should be clothed. If he has no house furnishings, they should be bought for him . . . Even if it had been his wont to ride a horse, with a manservant running in front of him, and he has become poor and has lost his possessions, one must buy him a horse to ride and a manservant to run before him, as it is said, *sufficient for his need in that which he wanteth*

(Deut. 15:8). You are thus obligated to fill his want; you are not, however, obligated to restore his wealth . . .

If the poor person comes forth and asks for enough to satisfy his want, and if the giver is unable to afford it, the latter may give him as much as he can afford. How much is that? In full performance of this religious duty, up to one-fifth of his possessions; in middling performance, up to one-tenth of his possessions; less than this brands him as a person of evil eye . . . Even a poor person who lives entirely on tzedakah must himself give alms to another poor person.

If a poor person unknown to anyone comes forth and says, "I am hungry; give me something to eat," he should not be examined as to whether he might be an imposter—he should be fed immediately. If, however, he is naked and says, "Clothe me," he should be examined as to possible fraud. If he is known, he should be clothed immediately according to his dignity, without any further inquiry.

One must feed and clothe the heathen poor together with the Israelite poor, for the sake of the ways of peace. In the case of a poor person who goes from door to door, one is not obligated to give him a large gift, but only a small one. It is forbidden, however, to let a poor person who asks for alms go empty-handed, just so you give him at least one dry fig, as it is said, *O let not the oppressed turn back in confusion* (Ps. 74:21).

Whoever refuses to give tzedakah or gives less than is proper for him, must be compelled by the court to comply, and must be flogged for disobedience until he gives as much as the court estimates he should give. The court may even seize his property in his presence and take from him what is proper for him to give. One may indeed pawn things in order to give alms, even on the eve of the Sabbath.

A poor person who is one's relative has priority over all others, the poor of one's own household have priority over the other poor of his city, and the poor of one's city have priority over the poor of another city, as it is said, *Unto thy poor and needy brother, in thy land* (Deut. 15:11).

But in the lives of most American Jews, money and mitzvah have now become widely separated. For most, the two main institutions of their Jewish lives are the synagogue which guides their prayer and reading of Torah, and the United Jewish Appeal/Federation complex, which raises money for Jewish community centers, social-work agencies, hospitals, defense organizations against anti-Semitism, and above all for Israel. These two major institutions—the synagogue and the UJA—have almost nothing to do with each other. In synagogue, the rabbi may once a year preach on the importance of giving money to the UJA. In the UJA, the staff and the board of wealthy men may once a year discuss whether to give more money to Jewish schools where Torah is taught. But hardly ever (ever? never!) does the UJA arrive at its decisions by wrestling with Torah, and hardly ever does the synagogue have a study group on what the Torah teaches about help to the poor—let alone insist that such teachings be carried into action by its members in the congregational setting.

Not only is the sense of "command" from Torah now separated from money for most American Jews, but so is that sense of "command" separated from the community—for the community is voluntary, and cannot enforce its obligations. Until the Modern Age, Jewish communities were hermetically sealed, left only through conversion to Christianity or Islam; and those within the community were subject to corporal punishment, fines, and ostracism for ignoring the obligations of tzedakah. Now membership in the community as a whole is voluntary, and membership in any particular subcommunity—any particular path of being Jewish—is also voluntary. So there is no external compulsion to give tzedakah, and the internal compulsions rest on the attractiveness of being Jewish rather than on its necessity.

Moreover, in American society there is not much attraction to viewing one's own private property as in some way also partially "public." The physical power of the government to collect taxes is clear, and its legitimacy in doing so (to the degree it is democratically controlled) is accepted. But taxes transfer money from the wholly private to the wholly public realm. The notion that there might be "fringes" and "corners"—that there might be a noncoercive, nongovernmental, but highly authoritative public claim on the remaining "private" property—this notion is not encouraged by American society. In an age of religious freedom, this notion requires an internal, passionate conviction that God or human decency makes the claim. Even among those who feel the passionate conviction that they owe some of their money to some public use, American mores make it hard to believe that a nongovernmental public has the authority to decide *what* public use they owe it to.

The more typical pattern of belief and practice goes like this: "It is *my* money. Even what the government takes is really my money, and the more they take the more I feel correct in objecting if they use it in a way I dislike. As for what's left, that's *certainly* all mine. I may feel committed to using part of it of my own free will to help other people and to improve the broader world I live in, but of course I will choose *which* other people and *how* to improve the world."

In this atmosphere, the traditional practices by which the Jewish community as a whole decided on the priorities of tzedakah soon broke down. Individual Jews continued the Jewish habit of supporting public projects, but the more money they had, the more they were likely to insist on defining what it went to.

As the Jewish community settled down in North America during the first third of the twentieth century, a helter-skelter of local competitive Jewish fund raising slowly got somewhat rationalized into local federations and welfare funds that did joint fund raising and allocated funds among participating groups. Many local organizations, however, never became part of this process— synagogues, day schools, many of the various Zionist political groups. There were also a number of competing groups doing national and international "defense" work against anti-Semitism, and doing relief and reconstruction work among overseas Jewish communities that were in trouble.

The present massive structures of large-scale fund raising took shape as the Jewish community during World War II responded to the needs of the European Jews whose lives were being shattered by Nazism, the war, and the Holocaust. After the war, as efforts focused on repairing the lives of the few million European Jews who survived, these structures were strengthened. The new massive structures seemed necessary in order to raise and spend intelligently a great deal of money. And more than money was needed; it took elaborate organizing to bring together the pubic-health specialists, teachers, occupational-training experts, immigration workers, lawyers, nurses, agronomists, and engineers, all of whom were desperately needed and all of whom had to be brought to Europe, to the Jewish settlements in Palestine, which were trying to absorb European refugees, and after 1948 to Israel.

As World War II began and the scales of need began to be apparent—even before the Holocaust itself got underway—the two main agencies of support for European Jewish communities and for the Jewish settlements in Palestine, the American Jewish Joint Distribution Committee and the United Palestine Appeal (later renamed the United Israel Appeal) became partners in the United Jewish Appeal. They divided between themselves (and several smaller groups) the growing amounts of money that the UJA collected from the Jewish public for Jewish rescue, relief, and reconstruction outside the United States.

By the 1960s, almost all the Jewish communities of the Middle East and North Africa had resettled in Israel, Europe, or North America, and the communities of Europe had been restabilized. The needs of Israel had grown, partly as a result of the resettlement of refugees from Europe, North Africa, and the Middle East. So UJA funds shifted until more than four-fifths of them were being spent in Israel.

Almost all the money was coming from allocations to the national UJA made by local Jewish federations and welfare funds in about two hundred cities across the United States. These local federations also allocated money to local institutions—community centers, hospitals, social-work organizations, schools—and to such nationwide organizations as the American Jewish Congress and the Anti-Defamation League. By far the greatest power in this constellation was centered in the Large City Budgeting Committee, where the twenty largest local federations consulted closely and came to de facto agreements on how much money they would allocate to various organizations and projects.

By the late 1960s, as the tiny, decentralized, and fluid havurah movement began to form, the Jewish community could take great pride in its creation of one of the largest, most structured, and most effective of American voluntary institutions. The Federation/UJA structure raised more money from more people within its constituency than almost any other nongovernmental body. It met many grave human needs with a fair amount of creativity and very little corruption. As a way of holding together a large Jewish community under the individualist, universalist, and bureaucratic conditions of modernist society, it worked better than any other way except, perhaps, the state of Israel.

Yet problems began to be apparent. In practically all the local federations and in the UJA, power rested with a combination of very large donors and a full-time professional staff. The federations often described themselves as the broadest institutions of Jewish "self-government." They described the contributions they requested as the equivalent of taxes that should be viewed as obligatory. But in few situations, if any, were these "quasi governments" under any form of democratic control or consent by the public they governed. There were no public debates or election campaigns based on conflicting visions of how to spend the money. Thus small or medium givers had no control over the big decisions; they could withdraw their money as individuals, but no one would care. If the big givers chose to withdraw, however, the organizations they supported cared a great deal. So the rich got to decide a great deal about how to spend not only "their own" money, but that of the small and medium donors as well. If this was a government, it was run by a House of Lords.

Moreover, it was a limited "government" within the broader Jewish community. In 1980, the federations collected about $500 million. Of this about 45 percent was allocated to local groups, about 5 to 7 percent to national organizations, and about half to the UJA for international programs. This was only a fraction of the "total Jewish budget"—though it was the most focused and centrally directed. Amazingly enough, no one knows what the total Jewish budget of American Jewry is. The educated guess of Rabbi Wolfe Kelman, executive director of the Rabbinical Assembly, is that the collective budget of the three thousand or so synagogues may be $1.5 billion, and that the day schools, medical programs, political action, rabbinical training, and other Jewish spending may bring the total up to about $5 billion. Perhaps the most important facts are first, that no one does know, and second, that all financial, philanthropic, and tzedakah planning, therefore, goes on in the dark.

Shifts of direction in spending this money do occur. In the late sixties, among organized Jewish students and other "outsiders" there began to be simmerings of concern and anger about the situation of Soviet Jewry—concern and anger that the "Jewish establishment" was doing so little to press the Soviet Union to permit Jews to live more Jewish lives or to emigrate. The issue simmered, bubbled, turned into mass demonstrations and led to the emergence of independent Soviet-Jewry support groups not run by the conventionally recognized community leadership. Slowly the conventional organizations realized they had to pay heed. Energy, time, and money began to flow to the Soviet-Jewry issue. A similar process in the arena of Jewish culture and education may have been started by the havurot and the Coalition for Alternatives in Jewish Education. As "outside" groupings gathered sterength, the "lords" of the federations slowly moved to increase the money going to Jewish education. But there was never a clear and vigorous public debate over the value priorities of the Jewish community.

As we know this Federation/UJA Jewish communal "government" is not really a government in that it is wholly voluntary—and in fact does not collect "taxes" from about half the Jews in the United States. It is hardly surprising that in a society where "taxation without representation" is anathema, Jews who have no representation in the official Jewish community are not interested in giving money; and that Jews who do not feel obligated to give money do not feel interested in struggling over where the money goes. Anyone who feels outraged enough, or bored enough, with the ways that official Jewry behaves can simply not give. And this is what half of all American Jews have chosen to do.

But this structure does not take into account those Jews who have strongly positive Jewish feelings that are not expressed through the Federation/UJA complex. For them, of course, it is necessary to invent other ways of giving money. The Hassidic communities give extraordinary support to their own *rebbes* and organizations, and keep hands off the official UJA campaigns. Reform, Conservative, Reconstructionist, and Orthodox synagogues keep one foot in the UJA process—many of them schedule one Saturday a year as "UJA *Shabbat,*" for example, and raise money for Israel on Yom Kippur— but they also raise very large amounts of their own money independently of the Federation/UJA process.

By the late 1960s, questioning and criticism of this whole approach of the American Jewish community to money began among some Jews who felt it was separated from any sense of mitzvah and either was focused on direct support for the organizations that the givers themselves belonged to, or was given to groups where the larger givers ended up dominating the decision making. Several different directions of criticism emerged. First, some Jewish "outsiders" challenged the separation between the sense of mitzvah and decisions about money, but were not yet ready to propose specific institutional goals or alternatives. Then some others focused on the Federation/UJA complex as the place decisions were made and tried to change the content of those decisions or to create similar groups that would make different decisions. Still others sought to develop new kinds of structures in which the reconnection of money with mitzvah might be easier.

It was the issue of whether Jewish money should be used in a Torah-responsive way that led to the emergence of one of the first groupings of the movement for Jewish renewal. In the city of Washington, D.C., in 1967, a group of young Jews went to visit the rabbi of a leading synagogue to make a request: Would he discuss with one of his congregants her behavior as an owner of slum properties in downtown (Black) Washington and of lily-white apartment houses in the suburbs? The rabbi looked astonished, answered *no*. What did her membership in the synagogue have to do with her business practices?

The young Jews were shocked. They had strong feelings but little knowledge about being Jewish. They were certain that Jews should govern their business dealings according to Jewish principles. They felt, vaguely but strongly, that for Jews there were not supposed to be two worlds to live in—one of matter and one of spirit, one of business and one of prayer—but a single world. So they reacted to this conversation with the rabbi by leafleting the synagogue to ask the question: Should a Jew be expected to carry on the real-estate business according to Jewish values, to prophetic principles? When part of the Jewish community erupted in fury at their disturbing the quiet of the synagogue, they decided to call themselves Jews for Urban Justice (JUJ) and to keep working together.

From JUJ there ultimately grew the Washington havurah called Fabrangen. It is instructive that issues of money and business were the kindling spark. But it is also instructive that as JUJ became a havurah more deeply rooted in religious tradition and practice, it set aside this initial interest in connecting mitzvah with money. Not until years later did Fabrangen return to this basic issue, and then with a more precise focus on tzedakah as the way to connect its own money with its own sense of mitzvah.

Meanwhile, some young Jews decided to confront the decision makers to question their priorities and ask for changes. The decision makers gather once a year at the meetings of the General Assembly of the Council of Jewish Federations and Welfare Funds (CJF). The General Assembly is a meeting, not a parliament. It makes few decisions that directly change how money is spent, but it does bring together thousands of the fund-raising and social-service professionals and lay leaders of the American Jewish community to hear and talk about new ideas. In 1969, a few hundred Jewish students and havurah members came to Boston to picket the General Assembly, to demand changes in the federation approach. Specifically, they wanted much higher priority given to Jewish education and the issue of Soviet Jewry, and they wanted young Jews with new ideas to play a part in federation decisions on funding. The pickets were reinforced by the high prestige of general student activism in the country at large, and by the emergence of a Jewish student movement. There were also some CJF leaders who, sympathetic to their hopes, helped them win an agreement to let one of their number address the full General Assembly. Hillel Levine, a newly ordained Conservative rabbi, member of Havurat Shalom, and Harvard graduate student in Jewish studies, told the delegates that students, scholars, and rabbis—people committed not only to Jewish ethnic-organizational structure and political power but to Jewish culture and tradition—must be added to federation boards and that all federation leaders must begin studying Jewish thought and history. He urged a shift of funding priorities away from the outward-oriented building of large defense organizations aimed against miniscule amounts of anti-Semitism and from the building of large "Jewish" buildings with little Jewish content, toward the inner regrowing of Jewish knowledge and commitment.

The student/havurah initiative helped crystallize some thoughts and hopes that had already been growing in strength among some federation folk. The federations created a "Task Force on Jewish Identity" to decide what to do. After two years of agonizing debate, the Task Force recommended creation of a "Fund for Jewish Life," a temporary miniature foundation that could fund innovative projects. The CJF responded by watering down the recommendation by reducing the budget and by refusing to set up an independent fund outside the CJF. It agreed to support a temporary in-house division called the Institute for Jewish Life, but with a board that included a large contingent of heads of Jewish agencies that had opposed the project all along. The CJF had little money of its own to give the Institute, prevented it from raising money on its own, and could only recommend—not require—that local federations give it amounts based on their budgets. With constant sniping from opponents inside and out who either disliked the criticisms of federation approaches on which the Institute was based or who agreed with the criticisms, but thought their own agencies should be the ones to deal with innovations, the Institute stagnated. Its only fully successful grant, in three years of effort, was $4,500 given to the editors of what became *The Jewish Catalog*.

So through this process, the efforts to affect the existing mechanisms of Jewish funding failed. Money and the sense of mitzvah were not reunited; the changes in people and priorities demanded by Hillel Levine and the student/havurah demonstrators were not accomplished.

One of the lessons of the failure, in the eyes of an energetic and

somewhat unconventional Orthodox rabbi named Irving Greenberg, was that direct approaches need to be made to people who
were in the Federation/UJA complex, on the basis of their own
individual stirrings of Jewish spirituality and culture. Greenberg saw
the greatest possibilities among those in "Young Leadership" groups
in the UJA who had not yet taken charge of, and therefore had not
yet become identified with the old-line programs and practices of
the federations or the UJA. He hoped that if these people were
approached directly as individuals rather than as bureaucrats, that if
they were offered experiences similar to the intense and intimate
involvement with Torah and ceremony that had given life to the
havurot, then they would find the rewards of Jewish renewal in their
own lives great enough to make them want to remake UJA and
federation approaches.

Greenberg recognized that the synagogue as an institution is too
weak in financial and political power and often too watered-down in
spiritual content to be the place where Jewish renewal can begin.
Yet within the synagogues, as well as among the havurah outsiders,
are people who are spirtually strong. Greenberg decided to bring
these people together with the UJA Young Leadership insiders, who
are financially and politically strong. Greenberg founded the National Jewish Conference Center (later renamed the National Jewish
Resource Center) as a nexus for these contacts. In the short run he
expected the wealthy young donors to be able to willingly support
the Center because they were getting something out of it that they
needed for themselves; in the long run, as these newly remade
Jewish leaders permeated the Federation/UJA structures they
would bring a sense of mitzvah from their own lives into the institutional structures, rejoining mitzvah to money.

One major difficulty with Greenberg's approach is that the collective and participatory style of the more spiritually intense havurah and synagogue people has not always meshed well with the
top-down, more bureaucratic style of many of the donors and staff
people of the Young Leadership groups. To some extent,
Greenberg's Center has been caught in the clashing gears. Yet it has
managed to open up a number of the Young Leadership people to

Jewish tradition and celebration, and may have been one of the factors involved in the gradual increase of funding given to Jewish education and cultural development during the late 1970s.

Among the havurah people themselves, there have been efforts to work out new ways to reconnect money and mitzvah within their own communities. In 1973 several of the oldest East Coast havurot began to meet three times a year in weekend retreats, to pray and sing, study various strands of Jewish tradition, share new insights or approaches that had occurred to them, laugh, and meet new friends. In one of the early retreats, there was a workshop on how to do tzedakah. It was led by Sharon Strassfeld, one of the coeditors of the just published *The Jewish Catalog*. In the havurot, she said, the revulsion against traditional Jewish fund raising—against showy UJA dinners and public shaming in the synagogues—was so great that the havurah people were not giving tzedakah at all. What forms would be acceptable, desirable?

Out of that workshop came the notion of the tzedakah collective— a group of people who shared some basic values that would pool part of their incomes and then vote on where and how to give it. They might argue about how much to give to Jews and how much to the rest of the suffering world, how much to meeting life-and-death needs directly and how much to encouraging political change that would end those desperate needs, how much to well-established organizations and how much to small and innovative projects, how much to those who were starving and how much to those who were spiritually thirsty, how much in their own town or neighborhood and how much to those who were half a world away. But their arguing would reinforce their community; their own knowledge and sensitivity would increase; they would become more open to the *mitzvot* of money; and their money would help someone who needed it.

Tzedakah collectives have now been created in a number of American cities. I began this chapter with sample dialogues from the Fabrangen tzedakah collective in Washington. These collectives solve the issues of how to raise and spend money in a thoughtful, conscious way—how to involve a range of medium and small donors in making the decisions, how to teach the process of making morally and ethically informed choices, how to hear, absorb, and balance the predilections and values of others. They solve the problem of getting useful amounts of money to a variety of creative, effective, and democratically operated projects that are responding directly to human needs, have little overhead, and get little support from existing established institutions.

There are two major tests, however, that they have not yet passed. One of these failures is that most of the tzedakah collectives have not fully integrated the process of wrestling with traditional texts and notions of the mitzvot concerning money into the process of making their own decisions about how to spend their money. The tug toward dealing with burning issues, doing research on worthy recipients, and getting the money to its users has been stronger, and the need to act more urgent, than the need to start with the spark of Jewish tradition.

The second unmet test is the one of being able to raise and spend large amounts of money to meet large and complex needs, where long-standing institutions need to be sustained. Some of the tzedakah collectives have resolved this problem by giving some of their money to the UJA, recognizing the contradictions but accepting their own limitations. Some, however, have welcomed the emergence of an experiment in larger-scale fund raising called the New Israel Fund (NIF).

The New Israel Fund began outside the havurah community, though some havurah people were soon attracted to it and became involved. It began as a project of politically progressive rich people, mostly Californians, who cared about Israel, thought that the Israeli government had gotten badly out of touch with the needs of many newly emerging sectors and needs of Israeli society, and felt that there should be the maximum feasible participation by those in need in defining how their needs should best be met. They therefore identified a range of Israeli groups that were beginning to meet hitherto unmet needs: an environmentalist committee, a project for the defense of the legal rights of Bedouin in the Negev desert to water and grazing land, a battered-women's center, an organization of neighborhood activists in a slum community of Oriental Jews in Jerusalem, a project of dialogue between Israeli Arabs and Jews.

Israelis who were involved in these projects, or who knew them well and supported them, were invited to become members of an Israel Committee of the Fund that would share in making key decisions about how to spend the money. The New Israel Fund periodically sent Americans to assess how applicant groups were operating and what new questions should be raised. The Fund used fairly conventional techniques of personal solicitation to raise most of its money. In 1980—its first year—it was able to raise $130,000, which was divided among twenty-four different Israeli groups. By 1983, the money had tripled. Though the overall amounts are small compared to the donations to the UJA, the projects NIF was helping were so tiny that these amounts of money made a real difference to them.

Despite its practical attractiveness to many havurah people who wanted to help independent-minded and alternative groups in Israel, the New Israel Fund clearly did not meet the test of emerging from or encouraging renewed Jewish intimacy or a sense of the mitzvot. Many havurah people continued to search for other avenues. Many of them were fascinated by what started as the efforts of a single person, a lone lamb in the movement for intimate tzedakah.

This loner is Danny Siegel, writer of a number of books of Jewish verse and poetry, who, half by accident, became a *shaliach* or "messenger" for doing good. Once, when Siegel was about to visit Israel, some friends asked him to take along a few dollars apiece to give to the poor. His friends had in mind to help the poor of Israel— and also a superstition that no harm could come to a traveler who was carrying money for the poor.

When Siegel arrived, he took the obligation more seriously than to give at random to one of the *pushkes* sitting at the Western Wall or in many Israeli grocery stores. Instead he began to search out people or small groups that were doing extraordinary work with the poor: a small group that organized older people to do handicrafts that they could sell, a woman who by herself found, bought, and gave good clothing and household goods to new brides and grooms who would otherwise have been threadbare and housebare.

And then, as Siegel kept traveling back and forth to America and Israel, reporting to his friends on what he had done with their money, more contributions began to pour in—hundreds of dollars, thousands of dollars. It became clear that some American Jews were hungry for some way of giving money to Israelis that would bypass bureaucracies and reach projects that someone could touch, see, talk with. Siegel turned what had happened into an opportunity to teach Torah. Jewish schools invited him to talk, havurot asked him to lead workshops. He explained tzedakah, read the passages from Torah on how the poor must be free to glean from the corners of the fields, passages from Talmud and Maimonides on what was owed to whom, what was a good way of giving and what was a superb way. He encouraged his listeners and comrades to work out their own responses to these traditional texts. He wrote articles, then a brief but potent book. And he explained how to train others as messengers of tzedakah.

Meanwhile, quite different kinds of projects in tzedakah were emerging from a quite different set of experiences in the Jewish neighborhoods of a few North American cities. They emphasized direct personal action rather than money. These projects— especially in New York, Chicago, and Montreal—arose out of the discovery that even among "affluent" American Jews there were tens of thousands of desperately poor Jewish people. This discovery was connected with the rediscovery by the broader American society that in the midst of the great American boom of the fifties and sixties there were millions living in destitution. In the early and mid-60s, young Americans began to work with and among the poor in Appalachia, in Black neighborhoods, on Indian reservations—as community organizers and "participatory social workers." Some of these organizers were Jewish—and some of them began to discover the even more amazing fact that there were not only poor Americans but poor American Jews.

Hidden behind the statistics of the every-Jew-goes-to-college generation were old people; workers displaced when their industries moved to find some cheaper, nonunion workers; failed businesspeople. Especially there were the old—"left behind" in old neighborhoods because they could not afford to move when the synagogues, the kosher butcher shops, the Jewish community centers, the younger Jews moved out. Lonely, frightened, poor, they were not the fashionable objects of philanthropy for those who wanted trips to Israel, plaques on hospital walls, even their names on suburban day schools in exchange for their money. How long could a dying Jew remember them?

The same young middle-class Jews who "discovered" Jewish poverty had learned to feel that direct personal contact, the sense of community, was as important to tzedakah as was the money itself. So they used a simple approach—visits from young to old. On the Lower East Side and the Upper West Side of Manhattan, in Chicago, in Montreal, there emerged projects named with words from Jewish texts and traditions—Ezra (Help), Dorot (Generations), The Ark, Genesis. At their heart was direct contact between the Jewish young and the Jewish old. With a skeleton staff, Projects Ezra and Dorot in New York organized younger people to visit elders, go with them to stores, negotiate for them with landlords. In Montreal, Project Genesis brought together poor people from the Black, Jewish, and French Québecois communities, and set up a storefront walk-in service center that helps thousands of the poor get their apartments repaired, fill out applications for pensions, get in touch with a home health service, call the right offices to arrange a bus-stop shelter and new street lights. In Chicago, The Ark provides volunteers who can treat psoriasis, supply twenty cents for a phone call, replace a broken denture, bake or buy a *challah* for Shabbos.

In all these cases, the local Jewish federations and welfare funds were at first reluctant to put up the money for rent and administrative staff so that amateurs could do "social work." Gradually they let themselves be persuaded to assist with small amounts and short-run commitments. Their unwillingness to commit themselves to longer grants, even at low levels, has frustrated and infuriated organizers much more than the limits on money. What the projects need most is the ability to let the old and the young know that they will be around for awhile—that the process can be trusted, that people can open their hearts and expectations to it. Even where the official agencies have reluctantly concluded that volunteerism is both meeting the needs of the old and poor, and strengthening the

Jewish involvements and commitments of the young, energetic, and more affluent, they have not taken the initiative to found new projects. It is clear they would rather raise money from the distantly involved and hire professionals to perform the services—thus controlling both ends of the process—than to encourage volunteer groups that might remain somewhat independent of their structures.

All these efforts at inventing new forms of tzedakah are only at the first stage of experiment. There have hardly even been experiments in other areas in which Jewish tradition considered matters of money to be matters of mitzvah. What work is worthy, legitimate to do— and what work is forbidden? Is the answer different when unemployment is high and jobs are scarce? What does it mean for Jews to buy houses near each other, create a Jewish neighborhood deliberately, gather a collective farm or a cooperative enterprise in the midst of a non-Jewish society? These questions have hardly been asked, let alone answered with even experimental responses.

It is no accident that these questions have been hard to address. Even in the more limited arena of tzedakah, of help to those in trouble, those who have tried to take part in the movement for Jewish renewal have found it hard and painful to reconnect their money with the flow of Jewish thought. It is clear that American society and culture put many institutional and psychological stumbling blocks in the path of those who seek to reconnect money with mitzvah. It is hard enough for the American ethos to tolerate a sense of mitzvah, of being communally and divinely "commanded," at all. In regard to money, all the more so! For the American ethos views money as what every person owns and may use by utterly private choice. So the American ethos is even more hostile to the regathering of these sparks of money and mitzvah than it is to efforts to remake the Jewish path of life by reuniting love and learning, sexuality and spirituality, politics and loving-kindness, the secular with the religious. Yet it is also clear that Jews who keep seeking how to make all these other reconnections, find themselves still wanting to reconnect the fallen spark of money with the fallen spark of mitzvah, with the sense that the community matters and that the

Torah commands. For they keep rediscovering that money is in fact not a private matter. It is born out of human interaction, the work human beings do together, and it affects human interaction, the life human beings live together. So for those who would walk a Jewish path of life, the question of what individual Jews are obligated to do with the money they are temporarily "owning" must remain a communal, not an individual question; a question that cannot be shrugged away if there is ever to be a new pattern, a new holy vessel, of the Jewish people.

4. Does Torah Teach a Politics?

On a Sunday morning early in 1980, as we all stood "schmoozing" between classes at the Fabrangen *Cheder's* Sunday School, several teen-aged boys and girls asked me what I thought of President Carter's new proposal for registration of teenagers in preparation for a possible military draft. They were members and students of the Cheder, a miniature Jewish community made up of twenty-five families who ran their own parent-taught Sunday school, studied together, were friends, argued, started a Committee for Iranian Jewry and a Committee of Concern for the Jews of France (when more formal Jewish institutions were hesitating), and celebrated some holidays and Shabbosim together. I asked the teen-agers what their own feelings were and we started to talk, but were interrupted by the regular classes.

Then another parent who had been listening walked up to me and said, "I hope David [my son] gets drafted, and I hope M. [his son] gets drafted. How can a socialist like you oppose that? Otherwise the Black and the poor fight the wars."

I was stunned. Not by the political logic. Later, when I thought about the politics, I knew I disagreed with his political logic. If I am a socialist at all, it is a special kind of socialist; for I am a decentralist, I care about intimate communities. I don't like big corporations that run from the top down, and I also do not like strengthening big governments that run from the top down—and that is what the draft would do. And I do not think a draft would bring more racial or class equality, either. But none of this occurred to me that Sunday morning. It was not the political logic that stunned me; it was my friend's readiness to have his own son drafted—presumably to be ready to fight, to kill, to die. How could he be so cool about that prospect?

As for me, I felt weak at the very idea—and I suddenly realized that my weakness was localized. My genitals felt turned to mush, dissolved, when I thought about the killing of my own son.

And an unexpected image rose before my eyes as I thought about the other father's question. Why did I oppose the draft? The image was the bris. The ritual circumcision of my son at eight days, when the *mohel,* the sacred circumciser, raised his delicate knife to do the delicate job of cutting away the foreskin of my son's own genitals. The ritual circumcision that went back through the generations to Abraham and his own sons.

Why was it the bris that I remembered? Why this staggering visual flash of the Covenant of Abraham? Why was the bris my answer to the question of my friend?

What is the meaning of the bris? It hallows the genitals that will give life to the next generation. So it reminds us of the living chain that goes back to Abraham and Sarah, back even to Eve and Adam— and forward to Messiah.

And the bris is painful—to remind us that even in the love between the generations, there is pain. The pain of misunderstanding, anger. . . .

But not the pain of death. Not murder. We do not kill our children. God forbid. God forbade.

Except—and I think this was what made the connection for me— when we send them off to war. Our sons and now perhaps our daughters, too.

Why did I remember the bris? Precisely because it lifts the knife. Because it comes close to murder, close to war. And consciously chooses *not* to be a murder, not a war. In the midst of the pain that cuts across the generations, at every bris there is the "chair of Eliyahu," of the Prophet Elijah. Why? Because according to the last passage of the last Prophetic book, Malachi, Elijah comes in the midst of pain and anger to "turn the hearts of the parents to the children and the hearts of the children to the parents." At that heart-stopping moment when the knife descends, Elijah comes to melt the frozen heart that would plunge the knife into the hearts of children: Elijah, who embodies both the memory of the Prophetic past and the hope of the Messianic future.

If we will stop our hatred of the future, if we will stop our war against our children, we can make sure there is no war between the superpowers. Because a war betweeen the superpowers *is* a war against our children, all earth's children. A war to kill and mutilate them.

Let us be clear: That is what it is all about. Legs lost. Arms mangled. Genitals that bore the sign of the mohel's holy knife, blown to shreds of flesh and ashes.

The bodies of Afghans, of Russians, of Americans. Of men and women. Of Jews and Muslims, Christians and Marxists. Mangled.

And other manglings, less terrible, but terrible enough. More of the Bronx lost to fire, rats, and desolation while sleek new missiles slide from our factories.

And manglings still more terrible, God help us. In Washington, in those weeks in 1980, some responsible people in Congress and the Executive had been saying coolly, calmly, that of course the Persian Gulf was worth a thermonuclear war. Even if this were being said in agony, in tears! New York a firestorm, all of Pennsylvania a radioactive waste—all this deserves a tremor in the hands, some vomiting, some tears. Maybe a fast, in bitterness and sorrow. Not calmness.

These thoughts and feelings embody my deepest, gut-level reactions to the question of the draft, out of a preconscious sense of Torah. Is there anything to learn from Torah on these questions at a more cerebral level?

What does Torah teach us explicitly about service in the military? It says (Deut. 20:1–20) that even at the very moment of battle, no one shall be allowed to fight who has built a new house but not dedicated it, planted a vineyard but not yet harvested it, betrothed a wife but not yet made love to her. The act of creation, of building new life, comes first. And if there was anyone who was "afraid and tender of heart," he too was sent back home. Said the rabbis, "Why not just 'afraid'? Why 'afraid and tender of heart'? 'Afraid'—that he may be killed. 'Tender of heart'—lest he may become a killer."

None who are committed to life—to their own lives, to the new lives they can create, or to the lives of others—shall be forced into battle, into the Kingdom of Death.

More. Look at who is most likely to be at the moment of forming new families, planting new orchards, building new houses. Is it not precisely the young adults that modern nations like to draft? In the society of ancient Israel, which counted military age from twenty to fifty, were these provisions not a way of exempting exactly the people that our modern governments would conscript? Were they not a way of making sure that elders would not send the young to die? And were the provisions necessary because the elders were so tempted to send the young to die?

Even the Maccabees, even when the Land of Israel was occupied by idolators and the Holy of Holies had been defiled, carried out the command to exempt those just beginning new lives, the fearful, and the tenderhearted (1 Macc. 3:56). The Maccabees were not pacifists, but they were committed to communities of life, not petrified institutions of death. They shattered the greatest military institutions of their day because they fought in communities of life.

And in communities of life the old and young can volunteer to fight together—Mattathias alongside his sons. When a living community is fighting for its selfhood, the whole community fights—as in 1948 when women and men, old and young, fought to make Israel real. As in every real revolution. When a community fights, it fights from hand to hand, with spear or rifle or sit-in or strike. Not by pressing the button of oblivion, and not by sending the children to die. It is in the wars of petrified institutions that the old send their children to die, that the chiefs press a button to wipe out the future.

Very well. These were my reactions, from gut and head, both taught by Torah. But my reactions could not end there. There were reasons that registration for the draft had been proposed. Real reasons. Real challenges. There is a real world in which Torah must be applied. There are real dangers, real facts to understand, real problems and evils to deal with. Torah teaches us that the feelings within us and the physical events around us are both real. The world of nature, the world of politics, and the world of spirit, are all real. Using this sense of reality, I asked myself, "What are the real problems? What are the reasons that we respond with military gestures to these problems?"

When I began to list these reasons for myself, I realized that some of them are "out there," to deal with outsiders and their hostility—and some of them are "in here," to play out the problems of our own society. Some are so much "in here" that they are not only part of American society but part of our own selves. So I will set out the reasons that occurred to me, in that order: from outward to inward.

First, Russian troops were firing guns at Afghan peasants, dropping napalm on Afghan villages, preventing Afghans from deciding for themselves what kind of government they will have. That is a reason, a *good* reason, to be angry and to seek ways of resisting. Is it *the* reason? The reason we chose the *way* of resisting that we did? Or would there have been other ways to deal with that, if not for the other reasons?

Second, we feared that Russian troops might next be holding the great oil fields of the Persian Gulf, denying to the West the chemical blood of its industry. And for Jews especially, raising the danger of still another pressure upon Israel. That is a reason. Again, a good reason to be fearful, worried, to react. Is it *the* reason? The reason that our reaction took the form it did? Or would there have been other ways to deal with that, if not for the other reasons?

Third, Americans were already in a state of shock and outrage at their own helplessness in the face of the Iranian capture of the United States Embassy and United States diplomats. That is a reason. (A good reason to be outraged.) Was it *the* reason? The reason that our outrage found the outlet that it did? Would there have been another way to deal with it?

Fourth, an American President was lower in public esteem than any since at least 1932, was facing an imminent election, and needed to redirect attention from an unraveling domestic economy. Would there have been another way to deal with that?

Fifth, certain major institutions that had been on the defensive—like the armed forces, the intelligence agencies, the complex of military contractors, some of the labor leadership—saw the opportunity to win back public support and money for what they saw as their necessary functions at a level which would probably continue even if the immediate crisis were resolved. Would there have been another way to deal with that?

Sixth, not only major institutions like the press, but also large parts of our own selves would like to distract our attention from our deepening morass of daily problems—how to pay the rent, how to do a decent politics in the midst of a spiderweb of crises, how to love our families, how to feel at peace in the world. It is easy to distract ourselves by focusing upon an Enemy outside. Would there have been another way to deal with that?

Seventh, with some part of ourselves we *want* to murder our children. Like Abraham when the knife was already descending to kill Isaac, we are so dead set upon our deadly mission that it takes two Callings of the Voice to stay our hand. We are often sick at heart, frightened of the future, furious at those who are the future. We would sometimes rather destroy the future than face it.

So at those times we are ready to send our children into death, and—if that is not enough to stop the future—to send ourselves as well. Better the clean, clear flash of thermonuclear light than a muddled, murky dimness in our future.

These reasons move from those officially proclaimed to those unofficially admitted, to those we all indignantly deny. I do not think that one set are the "true" reasons and the others are "false." I believe that all of them are operating in us—the clean, bold, heroic ones about resisting attack from outside, and the dirty little secret ones about our own inadequacies and desperation. What is more, I believe that we are acting as we are only because all of them are operating in us. I believe that we would be dealing with our secret despair in other ways if the Russians had not attacked Afghanistan—leaving us feeling outraged and frightened. And I believe, were it not for our interior despair, we would have responded differently to the Russians' attack.

These reasons operate within our enemies as well.

But it is easy to see this, and then throw up our hands in frustration. It is the simplest of formulas: All our hands are dirty. The Enemy is Them and the enemy is Us.

But it is not so. The enemy is neither Them nor Us. The enemy is a way, a path, we have of being us, they have of being them. The enemy is one false way we choose to deal with real problems.

I think the crucial process could be called petrification. Within every society, within every person, the crucial danger is petrification. There are real human needs—living, bubbling, rising from deep roots. The issue is whether they will be met in living, fluid ways—or frozen. Frozen socially by erecting a petrifying institutional structure in order to meet them. Petrified personally, individually, by freezing our fluid hopes and fears into a life pattern that holds us rigidly.

For example: We can take the direct, living, decent, fluid indignation of the young at the Soviet invasion of Afghanistan—and petrify it in the draft. We can take all their desire to act, and channel it into the bureaucratic compulsion of a tax on their lifetime. We can create a rigid bureaucracy of conscription to administer this lifetime. We can strengthen the rigid institutions of the military so as to control this lifetime. We can pour more money into the hardware of ships, planes, tanks, that armies need.

And so we would petrify the young—who otherwise would flow and change as their life-patterns grew, as they grew new interests and new skills, as they deepened their world views. And we would further petrify both our government and our economy—which are already too locked-in to rigid patterns and large-scale useless hardware. For it is true that all bureaucracies are rigid—but the stoniest of all are the bureaucracies of death, as death itself is the ultimate petrification.

And what is not worst but saddest, most ironic—we would petrify into a still more stony rigidity the already great stone face of Soviet society—the stony face whose hardness we already rage at.

How do we turn the different "reasons" into the response of war fever? And how could we turn them into life-sparks?

What could our youth do with our help, if we wanted to help them live more fully instead of ordering them to die? For example: The chief "external" reason for our war fever was the fear of a Soviet attack on the Persian Gulf, and of our losing oil. What if our government had taken the energy problem as the real issue, and instead of reviving the cold war against the Russians had called for a much tougher "moral equivalent" of war on the real front—the energy front? What if we had asked our youth to put in six months of their time over an eighteen-month period in applying conservation techniques: weatherizing houses and office buildings, putting up "solar walls" that conserve heat, replacing cars with bikes? What if we had done this on a voluntary basis—paid decent salaries for those who entered a "Conservation Campaign," and mobilized for them all the rewards of media attention and approval? Would the payoffs in reduced dependence on Persian Gulf oil, increased versatility in our economy, new skills and training for our youth, and a deeper sense of shared community have been more—or less—than the gains we imagined from a military buildup and a draft?

Another example: We wanted to weaken the Soviets' ability to move militarily. Could we have used some of the people-to-people techniques that the Soviet-Jewry movement has pioneered in? What if we had launched direct citizen-to-citizen contacts with Muslim leaders in the southern Soviet Union, undertaken efforts to reach the parents and wives of the Russian soldiers patrolling Afghanistan—and being shot at? What if we had offered most-favored-nation status in our trade relations if the Soviets withdrew their troops?

Are these specific ideas good enough? *Probably not.* The stone face of the Soviet state is not easy to soften. Just as it took the Soviet-Jewry movement years to invent approaches that brought some success, even limited and temporary success, so we will have to experiment. What we can learn from the Soviet-Jewry movement is that it is possible to use techniques like these in a closed society— even though it is hard. And every time they are used successfully, they help open up the Soviet Union a little more.

The opposite will be the effect of escalating military confrontation, or a new cold war. For that will help the Soviet bosses reunify their country in fear and hatred of America. Indeed, the worsening of the cold war since the invasion of Afghanistan and the "tough" Carter-Reagan response has already been linked with a toughening of Soviet policy toward Soviet Jewish emigration. At the beginning of the Reagan administration, some Soviet-Jewry activists warned that an American policy of all sticks, no carrots, would probably worsen the lot of Soviet Jews. And they turned out to be right.

This is a way of applying recent Jewish experience to the problems of how to deal with the Soviet Union. Can we also draw on our own Jewish experience to understand better what is happening in Islam? We might, if we pay attention to our own national and religious renewal in the past two generations.

Out of our own experience we might come to understand that Islam Resurgent is not a pawn between the superpowers, but an authentic and powerful fact on its own. We might even come to see Islam Resurgent as an opening door—neither of diabolical fanaticism nor of utopian perfection, but of useful as well as disturbing possibilities and new directions.

Out of the welter of struggle in Iran, even now, might there still emerge a new synthesis of spiritual and political reconstruction that is an advance beyond Marxist materialism and Christian ethereality? Out of the Muslim southern regions of the Soviet Union, can there emerge the pressures that open up the locked-in Soviet state—a parallel to the Soviet-Jewry movement but twenty times as big?

We Jews have a special stake in understanding Islam Resurgent—understanding it in the spirit of the Hebrew word "yodayah," where knowledge requires intimate and empathic interrelationship. Wherever possible we should be facing Islam not as its enemies or as academically "neutral" observers, but as empathic coparticipants in the struggle to reconnect religious traditions with modern social needs—and as those who deeply hope to see first peace and then friendship between Israel and Islam.

In all of this, our goal should be to strengthen the real communities of life and growth in every people—and to weaken the petrified institutions, encased in steel and concrete, that are the juggernauts of war.

The whole effort to approach international politics in the way that I have just laid out is an experimental case study of what it might mean to address modern political problems both by struggling with Torah and by drawing on the history and experience of the Jewish people. It is, indeed, only an experiment, an exploration. The effort must be made to bring Torah to bear in a far richer, more sophisticated way. I am not suggesting that by wrestling with Torah we will come to a single, agreed "Jewish position" on such issues. We will not, any more than the Talmud did on many similar issues. But we will learn, both more Jewishly and more profoundly, what the deepest issues are. And we may arrive at some new answers.

This process, even on an experimental basis, has not been the way Jewish politics has been developed in the past generation. Both Israel and the leading Jewish political groupings in America—the Anti-Defamation League, the American Jewish Committee, the American Jewish Congress, the American Israel Public Affairs Committee—have operated without regard to Torah when they were deciding what Jewish interests were. Even the religious institutions, when it came to general public policy other than "personal" moral issues like abortion, developed Jewish policy more from an automatic sense of liberalism or a "self-interest" attachment to conservatism than from an encounter with Torah. Some Biblical verses might get quoted, in an effort to Judaize a liberal or conservative politics. But rarely or never was discussion of Torah put first in the process when it came to the draft, the military budget, regulation of business, labor law, energy policy, health insurance, the welfare system. On abortion, yes; on these others, no.

Why? the answer may lie in the fact that for two thousand years the Jewish community as a community has had limited political power—limited power to shape its own political economy or that of the society in which it lived. Questions like abortion were still subject to communal decision; war and peace, the use of natural resources, the choice of private or public investment of capital were not. Especially since the beginning of the Modern Age, with the shattering of the vessel of Jewish community and the scattering of the sparks of Jewish vitality, the Jewish community became unskilled—and uninterested in doing what it could not do.

But no more. The project of the last generation of the Jewish people was the invention of institutions with political clout. The project worked. But no one hurried to fill these institutions with Jewish content. That, like the other aspects of the regathering of the sparks, has been an effort of the movement for Jewish renewal.

As the Jewish renewal movement first took shape in the late 1960s and as it has grown and changed since then, the relationship between Jewish thought and political action has been one of its main concerns. There have been three main waves of Jewish-renewal political activity:

1. From 1968 to 1971, there were two sharply distinct groups. First, those people of the early Jewish-renewal movement who wanted and expected to live in America concerned themselves mainly with the hottest American issues of the Vietnam War and racism in American society. They brought to these general issues an explicitly Jewish presence—but little uniquely Jewish in perspective. Second, those Jewish-renewal people who wanted and expected to live in Israel focused very strongly on political and social issues current in Israel. Many soon moved there, and thus removed themselves from American politics.

2. From 1973 to 1977, there was among Diaspora-oriented Jews who intended to live in America a wave of critical concern for Israel—both strong support for its survival and strong criticism of what seemed to be the self-destructive aspects of its government's foreign policy. This period was the time of birth, meteoric rise, and collapse of *Breira* ("Alternative"), an organization that urged mutual recognition and negotiations between Israel and some valid representative of the Palestinian people, looking toward guarantees of peace and security for Israel and guarantees of self-determination for the Palestinians. In this period there was a uniquely Jewish concern for Israel and little involvement in more general public issues.

3. From 1979 on, there grew in the broader Jewish-renewal move-ment both a mood and an organization—New Jewish Agenda—that wanted to address both a number of general American and world-wide issues *and* a number of special "Jewish" problems (like Israel and anti-Semitism). Many Agenda people wanted to do both these things not only *as Jews* but also from the standpoint of Jewish tradi-tion and Jewish values. It was this attitude that came closest toward "regathering the sparks" in the sense of bringing back together the texts, ideas, and approaches of Jewish religious and secular culture with the political ideas and organizing approaches of the modern world.

This progression itself has much to teach about the process of Jewish self-development. First the activists discovered simply the fact of their own Jewishness, the comfort of sharing that discovery with other Jews, and the pleasure of reaffirming their half-abandoned culture and identity. Second came their discovery and desire to act on the special political problems of the Jewish people—especially those rooted in the relationship between the Jews and other peoples. And third came their discovery and desire to act on the internal agendas of the Jewish people across the generations. It is a rhythm of turning inward, outward, and inward again—and both its logic and psycho-logic is that once the movement for Jewish renewal has absorbed and grown comfortable with a sense of Jew-ishly based practices and values, it will act vigorously to bring those values into the mainstream of American politics.

That mainstream is clearly changing. It is flowing now in eddies, rapids, whirlpools, perhaps great waterfalls. The basic social, eco-nomic, and military upheavals since World War II have, like earth-quake after earthquake, torn apart both the comfortable liberalism and the comfortable conservatism we were used to. Jews especially have felt themselves afloat without direction. Even before 1980 that sense was growing among many Jews, and it was intensified by the results of the 1980 elections. For the elections not only defeated, but killed the kind of liberalism that had dominated American politics since 1932—and broke up the liberal coalition in which American Jews had found a comfortable place.

One glue that held Jews, Blacks, and "ethnic" Catholics together in the New Deal coalition was the sense that all of us were outsiders. We did not feel part of America. One result of our success, these fifty years, is that "America" changed. The Jews, the Poles, the Italians do feel ethnically part of America. Only the Blacks and Hispanics are still outsiders, and even they are—as ethnics—far less outsiders than before. (Economically we may all still be outsiders—even the "prosperous" Jews.) It may be that, to the New Right all of us are still really outsiders; we shall see. The New Right certainly does not like the ethnic style of most American Jews—brash, experimental, "liberated," sardonic. We shall see.

I am not saying that the coalition of labor, Blacks, Catholics, Jews, and morally committed liberal Protestants will never come together again. It may, but in new ways and with new approaches for dealing with the problems we face.

One instance of a new approach: perhaps an alliance of "ethnic outsiders" will never come together again on ethnic grounds. But there are spiritual roots to our ethnic peoplehoods, and the spiritual needs of Americans are urgent. Urgent enough to take political form, because these spiritual needs require some kind of social fulfillment.

It was no accident that in the great political and cultural eruption of the sixties, the Southern Black churches were the seedbed and a Black preacher was the central national figure. It was no accident that the "spiritual" issues of dignity, community, and ecstasy became "political" issues. And is no accident now that the "Moral Majority" and a certain religious approach are important ingredients of the New Right.

What are the crucial differences between the religious politics of the sixties and that of the eighties?

One is that in the sixties there was a strong sense of religious fulfillment through inclusion. Blacks and whites together. Americans and Vietnamese together. Women and men together. In the New Right religious world, there seems to be a much stronger sense of condemnation, exclusion, separation, as the basis for defining community. Can our own special religious traditions be the basis for reaching out, as well as for turning in?

Another, extremely important (and closely connected) difference from the sixties revolves around the issues of sexuality and the roles of women and men. The New Right has mobilized most strongly of all around these issues. These issues are very strong in their pull on most human beings, and our feelings about them are closely connected with how we shape our "spiritual" lives. Indeed, the message of the "Moral Majority" is that an authentic religious life requires the subordination of women and the repression of sexuality.

Does it? Certainly traditional religious practices are built upon these approaches to questions of sex and the sexes. Even traditional Judaism, though certainly less repressive of women and sex than, say, traditional Catholicism, leaned hard in that direction.

Is it possible to create a fulfilling spiritual life that includes not only the formal equality of women, but also the full expression of women's spiritual experience, and the celebration of sexuality as fulfillment—rather than as commerce or as routine? Is it possible to make real the spiritual life of the Song of Songs? If not, there is a great danger that the religious politics of the eighties—and the winning politics of the eighties—will continue to be anti-woman, anti-sexual, and pro-military, pro-top-down.

So this is an important question for us to put to Jewish tradition. By invoking the Song of Songs, with all its weight of biblical and rabbinic tradition, I am suggesting that the question of a more fluid and joyful sexuality is not only a concern of modernists, but is also an important question that Jewish tradition puts to us—if we will listen.

There are also other questions that the age-old tradition puts to us sharply:

How shall we deal with an economic pie that is no longer growing bigger? Shall we—Jews, Blacks, labor union members, Third World shanty-dwellers—keep fighting over subshares of the limited piece of pie we have been assigned? Or decide to share out the whole pie, including the parts of it that we have never seen? What does the tradition teach about the economy?

How shall we deal with earth, air, and water that are being poisoned? How shall we deal with irreplaceable sources of energy that are now being used up? Where shall we turn for energy to run a technological society? What is technology for? What does the tradition teach about the environment?

How shall we deal with the collapse of our sense of community in our neighborhoods and families? This collapse is murderous—literally. It leads to violence against children and women inside the family, against "neighbors" on the street, and teachers and students in the schools; to drug and alcohol addiction; to murder. What does the tradition teach about community?

Who cares what the tradition teaches? Do we?

I believe that we should work out our approach to such issues by wrestling with Torah. By "Torah" I mean the entire biblical and talmudic traditions, including rabbinic and modern commentaries on them—even commentaries that call themselves "secularist," so long as it is the biblical and talmudic tradition they are using as their wrestling partners. To wrestle with Torah means coming, fully as who *we* really are, to fight-and-make-love-at-the-same-time with Torah as who *she* fully is. We are not just a mirror image of Torah, nor should we make Torah a mirror image of us. It is out of an authentic encounter between our different selves that renewed truth will emerge.

Why do I argue this? In good Jewish fashion, for one particularist and one universalist reason:

1. Because the wrestle with Torah is precisely the authentic Jewish process for working out how to live. This is what the prophets did; it is what the rabbis did when they were talking and then writing the Talmud; it is what Kabbalists and Hassidim and Reform Jews and often secular Zionists and Bundists did. It is even apparent that the Torah itself interlaces several strands of wrestling with Torah. And even when different Jews and different groups of Jews have disagreed over what Torah taught, they have stayed together as part of the Jewish people because they shared a common process of argument. In our own generation, when the Jewish people has succeeded in creating institutions with great political clout, it is important to make sure those institutions become and stay seriously Jewish by working out their political positions through struggling with Jewish tradition.

2. Because Torah carries teachings that are crucial if humankind is to survive its present profound crisis and to transform the world rather than destroy it. What is more, these Torah teachings are different from much of what we find in modern secular ideologies—whether nationalism, liberalism, individualism, socialism, capitalism, science, or industrialism. All these ideologies—products of the last four hundred years of human history—have basic flaws if we are seeking guides on how to grow past the crises we are in, because the crises are themselves products of the last four hundred years and of those ideologies.

This second reason is crucial not only to the method of generating a new Jewish political agenda but also to the content of that agenda. For it is clear that the present crises of America—simultaneous depression and inflation, grotesquely swollen military systems and a collapsing foreign policy, a poisoned environment and rotting cities, an energy crisis and enormous oil-company profits—are all inter-related. There is one overall crisis—and to pin it down to a single aphorism, I would say that the crisis stems from the fact that in the last five hundred years the human race has celebrated no Shabbat, no *shmitah*, no Jubilee. We have for five hundred years taken no rest from the race for more production and more consumption—the race for explosive economic development. We have in five hundred years not paused to catch our breath, to contemplate our purposes and intentions. We have in five hundred years not shared our wealth.

Torah teaches that the six workdays of economic development are worthy and desirable, but that one-seventh of our time must be spent in meditation, contemplation, prayer—in not working. Torah teaches that once a generation we must interrupt our amassing of more property, and share out again to every family its equal share of the land—and recognize that all land belongs to God. Torah teaches that every seventh year we must let the land be fallow. In short, Torah teaches that the rhythms of the natural world, including the human life cycle, have analogues in the rhythms of a human social system—and that if we ignore these rhythms, we will bring destruction on ourselves.

I believe that out of this approach to the economy and the environment we could work out a postmodern political program. It might include a continuous recycling of investment capital to small family, co-op, workers' collectives, and neighborhood enterprises. It might include a periodic moratorium on technological research and development while we reassess where we are and what we want to become. It might include the encouragement of neighborhood-level production and control of energy from the sun, wind, and water. It might include the encouragement of noncommercial, wholly volunteer festivals at the neighborhood level and the periodic shutdown of all commercial activity for seasons of celebration and self-examination. It might . . .

The point is that there is something special in the content of Torah that is peculiarly appropriate to our era and to meeting the dangers posed in our era of modernism run riot. At the same time, the upheavals and conquests that modernism has already achieved require us to wrestle again with Torah as powerfully and profoundly as the Hellenistic upheavals and conquests forced us to wrestle in order to create the Talmud. The emergence of a great new era of Jewish peoplehood, wrought by the encounter between Torah and those modernist Jews who are Jewish enough to wrestle with Torah, will be a joyful step forward for the Jewish people. It will also contribute toward solving the universal crisis of the human race.

5. *All My Bones Shall Praise You*

Said the prophet Ezekiel, "Dry bones, hear the word of the Lord! I will put breath into you, and you shall live again." Bones, breath: these are the physical aspects of the self that need to be reunified. For generations, the Jewish breath has floated not within the body but above it, in the form of words and songs—breath blown across the tongue and lips to make for "spiritual" exaltation and for intellectual meaning. (Our word "spirit" is from the Latin word for breath; to be dispirited is to be breathless, lifeless.) Jewish bones and muscles have been dry, dispirited. The body drooped lifeless, while all its liveliness was focused in the head.

What would it mean—to use Ezekiel's phrase—to put breath deep *into* the body? What would it mean to infuse every bone and muscle with the meaning that has been blown away in words?

What would it mean for Jews who were trying to reunify the sparks of community—passion and study, politics and Torah, money and mitzvah—to look within themselves to reunify the sparks of personhood—the separated sparks of "breath" and "bone," of meaning and body? As Jews in the havurot began to gather together the scattered aspects of their congregations and communities, they grew more open, as well, to sensing inside their individual selves the scatteredness that made them not quite whole persons. And they grew more open to seeking Jewish ways of regathering these other scattered sparks. They began to search for Jewish dance, Jewish theater, Jewish therapy—the literal embodying of Jewish meaning.

One of the first manifestations of this search was the forms of prayer and Torah-study, flooding every muscle with meaning and devotion, that Jews of the havurot all across North America began to create.

Sometimes the impetus for experiments came from dancers who brought their own best selves to Jewish celebration; sometimes people who were committed to Jewish spirituality found their bodies choosing new ways to celebrate. Early in the seventies, for example, in the Washington havurah, Fabrangen, a young dancer, Rivka Nurit Stone, began to dance-improvise at unexpected moments in the Friday-evening service, simply expressing her prayers in swoops and leaps and gestures—her own body language. At first Fabrangeners were startled, a little shaken; then a number began to "get it," started to improvise brief dances of their own, and finally asked her to teach them how to choreograph a psalm.

Together a group of eight or ten people worked out the story "behind" Psalm 115, and together they tested out dance and mime that would tell the story and express the feelings it called forth. Finally they danced the Psalm at a service—as if they were collectively the cantor, leading the congregation in prayer as its messenger to God. The congregation was deeply moved and the dancers were deeply taught. They reported that for the first time a psalm seemed to be coming from deep inside them—from their legs and guts and arms, not just their brains and tongues.

A little later, the Fabrangen became aware of Liz Lerman, the choreographer and artistic director of the Dance Exchange, a leading avant-garde dance group. She was drawing on Jewish dance motifs in Eastern Europe, on the forms of motion of semi-assimilated American Jews, and on the existential quandaries of a searching, questioning Jew, to choreograph *Ms. Galaxy and Her Three Raps With God*. In order to create a dance on cancer, pollution, and the Earth, Lerman decided to read the prophets and consciously draw on their deepest motifs and thought patterns. As Fabrangeners absorbed the implications of these uses of modern dance, they invited Lerman to recast a Shabbos-evening service into a dance.

She taught Fabrangeners to act out the rigid motions of the six workdays and the flowing motions of Shabbos, as a way of doing the

Kabbalat Shabbat service, and to develop body motions to express the themes of creation, revelation, unity, and redemption in the structure of the evening service. As Lerman and Fabrangen learned more from each other, she experimented with dancing an entire Torah portion by having each Fabrangener choose one person or object in it—Moses, the rebel Korach, Miriam, an almond branch—and acting out that creature for a while. Meanwhile all around them others were moving, acting out their chosen parts—and changing when they chose. And so the portion came to life, a dream kaleidoscope of Torah.

Moving in the other direction, some "artists" of Jewish liturgical commitment began to use body language in new ways. In New York, a rabbinical student named Lynn Gottlieb began to draw on the body consciousness she had learned from a mother who was a puppeteer. She acted as rabbi for several congregations of deaf Jews, "signed" the Siddur as part of the davvening, turned the expressiveness of signing into a dance-of-the-hands, and used it in midrashic storytelling sessions with many kinds of audiences. Then, for audiences of hearing people, she started telling biblical stories of the women of the Bible by using signing as dance and mime. Ululant chant, trance, dance, all reappeared in her work.

In Philadelphia, Zalman Schachter-Shalomi—rebbe of a neo-Hassidic movement called B'nai Or, who was already drawing on Buddhist and Sufi and Gestalt-psychology practices for Jewish purposes—asked people at a *Simchas Torah* retreat to do the traditional Torah dances in a new way. They divided themselves into seven grouplets, each to plan how to do one of the *hakkafot*—the seven dancings of the Torah—in accord with one of the seven mystical *S'phirot*. Since the S'phirot, or emanations of God, are as different as Loving-kindness, Power, Sexual Unity, Compassion—the hakkafot came out in remarkably different forms of dance, song, and readings. The seven dances, in particular, were shaped in extraordinarily expressive ways: flowing and relaxed for *Chesed* or Loving-kindness, sharp and vigorous for *Gevurah* or Power. Suddenly the Sphirot came alive to the celebrants—not "before their eyes," but in their bones.

Are these body-expressions of prayer and Torah utterly new, un-heard of? No. For generations, Hassidic Jews have stomped and clapped and chanted. And for generations before that, Jews have mimed moments of their prayers: Knees have been bent in the *Alenu* as we pledge allegiance to the King of Kings; heads have been bowed in the Bar'chu; bodies have turned toward the setting sun in welcoming the Shabbos Queen with *L'Cha Dodi*. And for millenia, Jews have praised God each morning for reawakening their bodies: *Every mouth shall praise you, every tongue swear loyalty to You, every heart revere You and our innards chant Your praise—for it is written, "All my bones shall say, 'Adonai, who is like you?'" and "All that is within me shall bless God's holy name."*

Indeed, the morning service begins with blessings of the God Who opens eyes from sleep, frees limbs from their nightly cramp, makes footsteps firm on the firm earth. Most Jews have chanted these blessings as words alone. But in the havurot members have overcome both their sleepiness and their embarrassment in order actually to move their bodies in tune with the meaning of the bless-ings. And only in the havurot have Jews begun to use the paragraph *Elohai neshama*—"My God, the breath you give within me"— not only as a hymn to breath but as itself a breathing exercise. For the paragraph includes more than a dozen words ending in an "ah" sound, some of them emphasized to end in "ahhh." Said lovingly, with care, the paragraph slows down into a rhythm for exhaling and inhaling. In blessing the God who "restores breath to deadened bodies," we open up our own bodies to receive that breath.

And so there emerges what is new about the sense of body in the havurot. Where the tradition has clearly *understood* the bodiness of prayer, the havurah Jews have *acted it out*. Where for generations Jewish men have shaken, "shuckled," rocked back and forth in a tense, sharp rhythm, as they chanted prayers, havurah Jews— women and men—have moved far more fluidly, expansively.

Why is this happening now? The change may have something to do with the sociology of the Jewish people. The Haggadah teaches that we "recline" on Passover to express our freedom. But the re-clining that meant freedom in the age of Roman banquets no longer carries that same overtone. We need to invent new ways of physically expressing and acting out our freedom. When most of us were shepherds and farmers exhausting ourselves each day on a dry and sandy soil—or tailors working from dawn to dusk to make a living—then reclining, simply leaning back, may have been the best expression of our freedom. But now we are more likely to be pinned to desks, doing over and over some rigid, repetitive motion with a stack of papers, or standing in a schoolroom where our muscles vibrate in emotional tension. Now our body's freedom may lie not in a Shabbos nap, but in free and flowing motions of the largest muscles. Walking. Skipping. Dancing.

Was it true, as some scholars say, that *Pesach* ("Passover") originally meant a hopping, skipping dance—a dance that "passed over" a step, skipped over a step?

Four strands of recent Jewish history are now intertwining to renew the Body Jewish:

1. The Holocaust and the nightmares it has stimulated in most Jews (and here I mean literal nightmares as well as figurative) are about rending scars on the individual and collective Jewish body. There has arisen from the Holocaust an intense need to experience and celebrate the Jewish body.

2. The collective version of this has been the focus on *Eretz Yisrael*, the Land of Israel in its physicality, and on the farming, working, fighting, dancing bodies of Jews involved in it. This focus has then evoked images and stimulated muscles in individual Jewish minds and bodies, outside Israel as well as in it.

3. Where the ghetto offered Jews two kinds of body-process—hard, grinding toil and/or the bodily withdrawal into Torah study—the new free citizen Diasporas like American Jewry (as remarkable a departure from the past two thousand years of history as is the state of Israel) have offered Jews a chance to experience and use their bodies in new and freer ways—in dance and athletics, especially.

4. The full involvement of women alongside men in davvening in the havurot, the newest congregations, and in some synagogues, has intensified a sense of body in the davveners. The sexual awareness that the tradition used to dread, for fear it would lead to spiritual

degradation, has instead led toward a reunion of body-and-spirit and the desire to involve the body more fully in prayer. Even the physical arrangements of the havurot—the circle, open space, movable chairs and cushions, have encouraged movement. Who could dance in bolted pews of rigid seats?

It is especially notable that almost all the new body-prayer energies are coming first from women—though some men have responded warmly and strongly. Perhaps American Jewish women, who in American culture have been encouraged in a "woman's" role of dance, are now beginning to carry that specialty into the heart of Jewish culture. The very Talmud that says, "The woman of sixty runs to the sound of music like the girl of six," discourages the teaching of Torah to women—perhaps seeing dance and Torah as different spheres of life. In our own generation, women who have entered the world of Torah have refused to leave dance behind, and men, who have Torah as a patrimony, are beginning to discover dance.

Perhaps the time has come for all our bones to learn to praise the Holy One. The time for us to unify and free our body-spirits. Perhaps, just as the biblical era of Jewish celebration focused on the body-event of sacrifice and the Rabbinic era on the spirit-event of prayer, the era into which the Jewish people now is entering may synthesize them through dance.

What are the *tzaddikim*, the righteous ones, doing in Heaven? According to the Talmud, they are dancing in a circle around the Holy One, pointing their fingers at the Presence in the Center.

During the same time that body-sensing was spreading among the havurot, there was growing among a group of Jews who were already body-conscious—those in the theater—a desire to explore their Jewishness. The two sets of motion converged when the first Jewish Theater Festival was held in New York City in the summer of 1980. From all across North America and from all the currents of the modern theater—realistic and surrealist, expository and symbolic, in the styles of Broadway and of the radical opposition—came Jewish theater groups exploring the most troubling themes of modern Jewish life.

Three days of immersion in the Festival stirred me to some new thoughts and feelings about the relationship of acting, action, to ritual and prayer. I was especially struck that just as the most ancient forms of theater—among the Greeks, for example—were expressions of religious feeling, growing directly from religious ritual and storytelling, so now these forms are reappearing in our generation.

I was especially shaken, moved, opened, by these events:

• A workshop led by Suzanne Benton, who had sculpted two dozen metal masks of biblical women and used them in telling the stories of these women—so that the "telling" became an acting out. Her masks were open, could be seen through. So just as midrash, reinterpretation of the Torah, always lets you see the original Torah text beneath, just so her own face acted as a kind of original text, visible through the midrash of the masks—themselves, of course, a midrash on the texts. The stories Benton told were taken mostly from the traditional midrash, but her choices and her own tones expressed strong anger at the demeaning of these women in the traditional texts and tales. She reported that the masks themselves had become sacred objects to her, and that the mask making and acting were reopening Judaism as a possible religious experience for her—after years of feeling excluded, along with other women, from Jewish thought and practice. When Benton invited her audience to hold the masks, wear them, and use them to generate their own gestural expressions of these women, the masks took on a sacred aura for many other participants as well.

• A workshop led by Rabbi Everett Gendler and Michael Poznick, an actor who taught how to enrich a blessing with breath control and fragments of dance and gesture. They drew on the *kabbala* of Abulafia concerning the proper breathing and head movement for the various Hebrew vowels; and then asked the participants, in clusters of two and three, to create gestures that would express each of the words of the *brocha*. Each cluster then taught its word-gesture to the whole group, and thus the brocha as a whole became a dance. Since they taught the blessing *boray pri ha-adamah,* "who creates the fruit of the earth," and the session ended by a meditative eating of fresh peas, carrots, celery and lettuce (seed, root, stem, and leaf), the workshop itself was a "real" religious event—not just a preparation or a lesson.

• A surrealistic "play" using masks, mime, and clowning by A Traveling Jewish Theater. The play, *The Last Yiddish Poet,* presented an encounter between a post-Holocaust despairing Jew and the long-dead Hassidic rebbe Nachman of Bratzlav. On the one side the desperate Jew invokes Jacob Glatstein's poem: "At Sinai we received the Torah and at Lublin we gave it back; the dead do not praise God." On the other, Nachman's Torah of the void: Enter deeply enough into death, stare it hard enough in the face, and you are freed into life. The play used elements of ritual and the midrashic method in such a way as to seem itself a passage of modern Talmud leaping off the page—that is to say, a modern version of the rabbis' anguished debates as they were recorded in the Talmud, here with the audience present for, and almost part, of the conversation.

• *Children of Night,* a play by Gabriel Emanuel of Nephesh Theater Company about the Warsaw Ghetto—focusing on the work of the teacher Janusz Korczak and of *Judenrat* president Adam Czerniakow, addressing the fate of a dozen orphans in Korcza's school. The children present a play within the play—a Passover pageant for the ghetto's grownups, reenacting the liberation from Egypt— which is interrupted by a Nazi order to speed up deportations from the ghetto. The play's audience in 1980 becomes the ghetto audience of 1942 as actors rise in the audience to bewail the deportations, seek work permits, demand resistance. The "play" thus became a kind of collective reenactment and reexperiencing. "We, not our ancestors alone, suffered in Egypt."

• A one-person theater piece, *The Survivor and the Translator,* in which Leeny Sack presented the impossible conversation between a Holocaust survivor and her daughter. She acted out first the jagged fragments of raw reality in both generations: terror in Maidanek, cynicism and affluence in America of the seventies, switching back and forth with gut-wrenching intensity. Then she did an incredible flip—physical as well as dramatic—and became a survivor who finally tries to bridge the abyss in language, that is, to "translate" the jagged events into hearable words. Obsessiveness, forgetfulness, anxiety became the tone of the toned-down report. The "audience" became tense, angry, sad, fascinated, bored, anxious, guilty, compassionate—became the children, the real heirs, the real hearers, of a real survivor.

These Holocaust pieces raised for me some troubling questions about the limits of "theater" and the ways in which theater might be brought *inside* the Jewish body. For even theater, with all its physicality, can be held at arm's length through the conventions of the Western stage. For instance, at the end of each of these Holocaust pieces, most of the audience applauded and—after some hesitation—the actors appeared for curtain calls. For me this pushed the meaning away, blew the breath outward rather than letting it come into my bones, dissipated the intensity and violated the profundity of the experience. And I was not alone; I could see others in the audience sitting quietly instead of clapping. When I talked later with some of the actors and directors, they said they had debated, and still felt conflicted, over whether to do curtain calls. One suggested that individuals would have to decide whether their experiencing was theatrical or religious. Another said that for her the theater *is* religious or spiritual experience. Still another said that the audience needed to show it felt part of the experience—by clapping.

Are such pieces "theater"? Is clapping the only way for an "audience" to affirm its participation? I think the applause and curtain calls are a way of saying that it was, after all, only a "play"—playing around. The actors are not really in the Holocaust, nor are we. It *was* our ancestors only, not we, who suffered in the Ghetto.

We do not applaud at the end of the Passover Seder, or at the end of reading *Eikha*—the Book of Lamentations—when on *Tisha B'Av* we recall the destruction of the Temple. We may afterward say quietly *Yasher Ko'ach* ("Right on, and more power to you!") to the person who led the service on behalf of the community. But this is an assertion that he or she was *part* of the community, speaking to God—not separate from the community, speaking to it and play-acting for its entertainment.

Why did I feel the applause inappropriate? Why are these theater pieces *not* just plays?

Theater began not as "pretend" but as reality. Religious ceremonies affect the real world. They liberate whole peoples. They make real crops grow. They help real people fit into the real cycle of their life histories and the real spiral of social change. There is a magnificent teaching of how "theater" can change the world in the weekly Torah portion that we had read just before the Theater Festival:

First, we are told, in order to restore to the community those who have become taboo, uncanny, by contact with death, a red heifer is slaughtered and burned with red wood, red spice, and red dye in a great cloud of red smoke *for and before the eyes* of the priest—a spectacle, literally, of redness for him to stare at hard. When he blinks he will see the green of life.

Second, God tells Moses to speak to the rock so that, *for and before the eyes* of the people, it will turn to water. If they stare hard at hardness, dryness, deadliness, unchangeableness, it will turn to flow, to giving life.

And finally, God tells Moses to cure the people of the plague of fiery snakes by raising before them a brass, serpenty serpent, a *nahash n'hoshet* (a "super-serpent") for them to stare at.

Look hard into the face of death, the face of fear, and you will be freed to life. This teaching is about the content of the Holocaust Theater, and also about its medium. For this is spectacle, theater, but not a play. *It works*—in the real world. And so does the seder, so does Eikha on Tisha B'Av.

When our gaze is clear enough, intense enough, theater is real—not merely play. It becomes religious event, religious experience. It *embodies* meaning.

When the life-experience of a people is at white heat, that people creates new ritual—real ritual, real participatory spectacle that changes the real world. When the life-experience cools down, the ritual becomes a crystal of experience, cooler but still capable of renewing the feelings and changing the world.

Twice in Jewish history—in the experience of slavery-and-liberation in Egypt and in the experience of the *Khurban*, the Destruction of the Holy Temple—the heat of life-experience of the Jewish people has been so intense as to melt down old forms and shape new ones. Even less hot moments—like the expulsion from Spain—have led to such creations of new ritual as what emerged from the Kabbalists of Safed. It is in such moments of life-quake that Jews meet again the Root of Roots, the Rock of Ages. When they do, they need new forms of speaking, learning, seeing the Holy One.

Now is just such a moment—perhaps one as profound and "hot" as the moment after the Destruction of the Second Temple. There are at least two sources of the heat that is melting down old forms: the Holocaust and the sense of outrage-leading-to-liberation that is coming from women who assert the fullness of their share in the tradition. And perhaps a third source of heat is the modernist emphasis on the individual person. For example, the effort in both the Benton and Gendler-Poznick workshops to get individuals to explore their own religious feelings in all their rich idiosyncrasy, and only then contribute them to a communally shared experience is quite different from the traditional practice of communal Jewish prayer, in which individuality is submerged.

The intensity of changing life-experience that the Jewish people has felt in the last two generations is beginning to affect the practice of prayer and midrash. Gesture, dance, mime, masks, acting out, are becoming "hot" again. In this process, the conventional categories are melting into each other—as they should:

Prayer becomes dance.

Midrash becomes mime.

Theater becomes religious experience.

How can this melting process become more effective in making contact with the Holy?

The Jewish community could invite the new theater groups to do their work in places like synagogues and havurot, at times like Passover, Tisha B'Av, *Yom Ha Shoah*—even Shabbos, or *Ois-Shabbos* (Saturday night), as part of *M'laveh Malkah*—the farewell to the Sabbath Queen.

The community could consciously and communally decide that

certain forms of "theater" are not to be treated with the conventions we use for "plays." Thus any theater that immerses us in the Holocaust ought to end with silence. Or far better, with singing *Ani Ma'amin,* the reaffirmation of hope in the coming of Messiah "despite all this" which thousands sang before they died in Europe. But not with clapping.

The community could bring together liturgists, midrashists, dancers, and dramatists—and perhaps also those political activists who have skillfully used "street theater" to change public policy (like the prophet Jeremiah, who carried on his back a heavy ox-yoke to warn the people they must accept the yoke of foreign domination as recompense for rejecting the yoke of God's Torah), and those psychotherapists who have skillfully used Gestalt "exercises" to express and transform feelings. Together, across the conventional categories, fusing the conventional expertises—they could address directly and consciously the issue of how best to express the volcanic feelings that are welling up. To express them as holiness, to express them to Holiness.

The community could set up a Department of Jewish Theater and Arts within a rabbinical seminary—and redefine the rabbinate to include art, drama, dance.

And Jews could "look" more at themselves and at each other, at the gestures they use and the faces they make when they feel most deeply moved, so that they can, like the ancient Israelites, stare death, fear, anger, in the face and turn them toward life.

So far we have talked about the renewal of Jewish personhood as it might take place through the "embodying" of religious ceremony and through the "reheating" of theatrical intensity. But in our society there is another arena in which breath and body are sometimes reunited, in which the person tries to become whole. That is the arena of psychotherapy—literally, in Greek, "the cure of souls."

In American practice, it rarely occurs to a psychotherapist that it might be seriously necessary to cure the soul. But traditional Jewish thought assumes as much. For example, the prayer for healing that is recited on behalf of one who is sick pleads not only for *r'fuat haguf* ("healing of the body"), but also *r'fuat hanefesh* ("healing of the soul"). For of course the rabbis knew that even when someone is sick in body, a "healing of soul" is part of what is needed.

But does Jewish tradition go beyond this prayer for healing in accomplishing the cure of souls? Many modern congregational rabbis see themselves as pastoral counselors, but they usually draw not on Torah but on Freud, Carl Rogers, Fritz Perls for the techniques of healing. Would it be possible to draw a psychotherapeutic process from the practices of Torah? Would there be any value in doing so? Why bother? Are not modern therapies adequate?

If they seemed adequate to me, I do not think I would have found myself hearing in Torah the sparks of a psychotherapy. But the modern therapies I have experienced and read and heard about have felt tantalizingly almost-good-enough to me. Out of this sense of their inadequacy, I have been intrigued, made curious, when every year, as we read through the Torah we come to the descriptions of the Temple sacrifices: I find myself feeling partly repelled, but even more attracted. I find myself wondering whether this—presumably the most outmoded and abandoned of all traditional Jewish practices—has a great deal more to say to us than we are ready to hear.

The Torah text describes "offerings" intended to deal with a great range of mind-and-feeling-sets. Some extraordinary acts of blood and body seem to have purged the people of guilt and sin. Do we have anything today that does it so well?

Others, *shalem* offerings, were evidently to be brought out of a sense of utter harmony, peacefulness, "well-being." Certainly these offerings were intended to express that wholeness of shalom, which means not only "peace" as the absence of international or interpersonal war, but "peaceful harmony." But perhaps they were also intended to restore the people to a more normal state of consciousness in which they were released from the exaltation of shalom—and could do their normal work again. Do we have anything to channel our moments of exalted harmony so well—and bring us down from them? Still another exercise, a plunge into the waters of the ritual pool or *mikveh*, came to release people from the taboo, the eeriness of *tumah* (which we usually translate as "defilement" or "impurity"). This eeriness comes from dead bodies, seminal emissions, menstrual flows, sexual intercourse, childbirths, and certain skin eruptions. Are these "impurities"? Or rather, as Rachel Adler has suggested, are they moments on the edge of life and death—and therefore moments that are uncanny, eerie, taboo? In any case, plunging into the waters of mikveh is how we dealt with them, and also with the eeriness of writing God's Holy Name in a Torah scroll, or preparing for Shabbos. Do we have any exercise today that helps us deal with the eerie edge between life and death? Still another exercise helped release people from violent fits of jealousy. Another, when the high priest emerged from the Holy of Holies on Yom Kippur and the people flung themselves flat on their faces—as if they themselves had died—helped them become reborn again, forgiven all their misdeeds.

For our generation's ears—at least for mine—these practices take on a new dimension when we call them "exercises." I am deliberately using a word from the jargon of Gestalt therapy because that therapeutic approach cares a great deal about the connection of body and spirit. Cares a great deal about *acting out, embodying* emotional charges and binds. And so these practices of Torah, all of them involving the body in powerful ways, seem to me most cognate with this aspect of Gestalt.

There are, of course, important differences between Torah and Gestalt. One is that the sacrifices were not *simply* psychotherapy in the modern secular sense. They involved always the economic life of a society that had a shared economy—for they required a lamb, a sheaf of barley, a loaf of bread, a bowl of wine. The body politic and economic, not only the body personal, brought the offering. Since they included the self and went beyond the self, they could be "offerings-up" even beyond all selves, beyond all seed and fruits to the Root of all Being. They were the cure of *souls*, souls that had a trans-human reality, souls of human beings who were cast in the Image of God. To cure human beings required making contact with the Shaper Who gave them shape. Of this, most Gestalt therapy has no inkling.

And the second—perhaps connected—difference can be seen most clearly from a saying of Fritz Perls, the cofounder of Gestalt therapy: "I am not in the world to meet your needs. You are not in the world to meet my needs. If we meet, it's beautiful; if not, it can't be helped." This sounds a great deal like, but also a great deal unlike, that saying of Hillel: "If I am not for myself, who will be? If I am for myself only, what am I? If not now, when?"

Indeed, the difference between these two aphorisms might in itself teach us to create a Torah therapy—one that rejects both the tyranny of Selfishness and the slavery of Otherism. For Torah seems to teach that it is precisely the encounter between Self and Other that is the heart of the matter. What is more, the Torah teaches the pattern by which this drama can take place, if it is to be healthy. The pattern is a process over time, with four basic phases that are represented by the four basic festivals of the year:

Pesach (Passover)—birth, spring, sprouting, freedom, the emergence of a new identity.
Shavuot (Sinai)—the encounter of this new identity, now mature, with an Other.
Sukkot (Harvest)—fulfillment of the relationship achieved at Sinai: fruitfulness, peacefulness.
Sh'mini Atzeret (Hibernation)—inward contraction, withdrawal from the Other, a seeming retreat and death, but preservation and transmission of whatever has been the most crucial forward step in the previous process; from full-blown fruit to tiny seed, ready to be sown to reach toward the next spring.

These four play themselves out in many forms. Look at the very shape of the Hebrew letters in the name of God, as aspects of the Tree of Life: *Yod* is the tiny seed, *Hay* the expansive rooting, *Vav* the tall trunk reaching up, Hay the expansive foliage and fruitage of the Tree of Life—out of which comes Yod to start the process over again. Yod is the scarcely visible Sh'mini Atzeret, Hay the expansive Pesach, Vav the thin, tall Shavuot, Hay the expansive Sukkot. The Holy Name of God is not linear but circular or spiral:

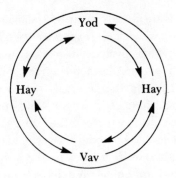

And the process of human spiritual growth and healing follows the same phases:

1. Emergence of a new direction, a new caring, a new aspect of identity.

2. Reaching out to the other in relationship, encounter.

3. Fulfillment of the new encounter in a harvest of work and love.

4. Absorption of this new truth as an old truth, outdated, dying, deadly; abandonment of all except its useful central core; mourning; transmission of the central core as the seed of a new growth.

If this is the basic pattern of a healthy process of spiritual growth, how could a therapeutic approach that assists it be developed? The festival pattern itself—the holy circle of the year—is one such therapeutic approach. A wholehearted celebration of the holy days, the *acting out* and *embodiment* of their practices, is intended to draw human beings through the growing, healing process. The very extremes of different points upon the circle—hilarity and drunkenness at *Purim*, solemnity and fasting at Yom Kippur—encourage the fulfillment and emptying out of these impulses, and the continuous restoration of a harmonious equilibrium. We need to explore the traditional celebrational cycles of the day and of the human life-span to see whether they too are so structured as to heal, restore wholeness, to the human spirit.

These patterns are "normal" processes, intended to keep souls healthy rather than to heal sick souls. What of deliberate interventions when souls are already disturbed, shaken, out of orbit? This is, after all, precisely what can be expected in a modern world where the observance of the holy cycles is itself likely to be disturbed—and the cycles in their ancient form no longer fulfill their functions adequately. It is because the "normal" patterns of keeping souls healthy are no longer followed that the word "psychotherapy" and the professions that do it have emerged to deal with widespread disturbance. Yet it should be noted that even when the cycles were presumably operating well in ancient days, the off-cycle "guilt offerings" and other exercises seem to have been necessary for individuals who got out of kilter.

We can try to imagine how a Torah therapy might work. Since one of the values of therapy is that it concentrates and crystallizes the teaching of "real life," we might work out a time pattern for a day or a weekend or a week that would take people through the four-step process, in effect training them in the whole yearly cycle. Or, if in any particular person only one of the phases seemed to be seriously disturbed, the therapy might then get that person to act out, embody, practice, that phase.

How could a Torah therapy embody the training in particular phases? Perhaps by drawing on particular moments of acting out in Torah. For example, in the first phase of emergence, the "birth" of freedom and of Israel in the Pesach story is connected with a night of "thick darkness," as is the birth of Eve and the beginning of the covenant between God and Abraham. A "thick darkness" seems to be a kind of simultaneous sensory deprivation (no-seeing) and sensory totality (all-touching). Could this be translated into an experience or exercise of "thick darkness" that is adequate to give us a sense of rebirth? Might a plunge of total immersion into water (as with Jonah or the mikveh) be such an exercise—a version of this "thick darkness" because for a moment it fuses sensory deprivation with sensory totality?

God is described as breathing life into Adam and (in Ezekiel's vision) into the dry and scattered bones of Israel; as feeding Adam and Eve, and clothing them; as wrestling with Jacob. All of these seem to be connected with the second phase, the "encounter" mode.

Are these translatable into exercises for training people in making contact with each other? One person breathing into the other's mouth, feeding the other, clothing the other, wrestling?

What are analogous moments, practices, exercises for expressing the other two phases of the cycle—fulfillment and withdrawal?

In these areas, the gathering of sparks has only begun; it has not yet produced even a tentative Torah-based therapy. It is time to gather our selves to explore these questions. Perhaps as we reach beyond the single self toward healing the most intimate relationships of couples and families—perhaps as we struggle to infuse these relationships with Torah—the effort to heal relationships will force us and teach us more profoundly how to heal our individual selves.

6. *Mishpacha: New Jews, New Families*

A thirteen-year-old girl, sitting at the table in the midst of the Passover Seder, firmly says "She" and "Her" at the points where the printed Haggadah reads "He" and "His" for God. The table vibrates. Boys giggle uneasily. One man snorts, "Just another form of sexism masquerading as equality." The girl flings her long hair: "You didn't compain when it said 'He'!" The vibrations diminish, but they do not go away.

A thirty-year-old woman on a Shabbos morning, reading aloud the Torah portion that describes trial by ordeal for a woman suspected of adultery. "Not for men!" she almost shouts, her voice cracking with rage, and hands the text to someone else: "I won't read it!"

On another Shabbos, a man begins to read the passage that commands that women, during their menstrual period, must be separated from the rest of the community. In the English translation he is using, the period is called a time of "impurity." He remembers the times he and his wife have made love while she was menstruating, the times he has held her close and rubbed her belly and her back to ease the cramps. He looks at his twelve-year-old daughter, on the verge of her first period. His voice falters, drops; he will not hand on the book for her to read, to be forced into proclaiming her own "impurity," her own demeaning. He reads the passage to the end, flushed and angry.

And all this in the circles where women and men are already "equal." For this is at a havurah service where women and men count equally in the *minyan,* the quorum that must be present for some deeply powerful prayers to be said. Where women and men walk up naturally and equally to read the Torah and lead the service.

Where women as well as men are studying to be rabbis. Where some single women and single men accept their singleness as a valid path of living—not as a tormented, temporary gateway into marriage. Where some single women and men celebrate their sexuality instead of hiding or repressing it; where they do not conceal from the community that some of them are lovers and do not intend to marry.

All this! But even in these circles, the relationship with layer after layer of Jewish tradition that seems male-dominant is tense. Can men and women who feel women and men to be equal ever feel at peace with Jewish tradition—or will there always be a core of it that troubles them? Can women and men for whom sexuality may sometimes be joyful and holy outside marriage and sometimes sad and unholy inside marriage ever feel at peace with Jewish tradition—or will there always be a core of it that troubles them?

And what about the arenas of Jewish life that are more distant from the ancient patterns of Torah—the secular institutional forms of daily life in which many Jewish lives are lived out? Are these places comfortable with new kinds of Jews? And are new kinds of Jews comfortable within them?

Already in our ordinary institutions and relationships, the ground is shifting. Already the first stages of change in the economic and legal relationships of women and men have wrought basic changes in the nature of marriage, the family, sex, and child rearing, and have called into question the structures of the synagogue, volunteer communal work, and the Jewish bureaucracies.

Changes in values, in economic patterns and expectations, and in such technology as the availability of cheap and highly effective contraceptives have interwoven with each other in such a way as to create new social patterns. Men and women are becoming much more like each other in education, jobs, and sexual behavior. Both are more likely to marry later and get divorced sooner, so that there are many more single people in their twenties, thirties, and forties.

These changes are affecting American society at large, but they may be affecting the Jewish community more strongly in less time because proportionally more Jews are in the white-collar professional and semiprofessional strata that tend to change sooner. The breakup of Jewish neighborhoods, the emergence of large numbers of single Jews, and the entrance into the job market of large numbers of Jewish women (single and married), all create difficulties for many aspects of Jewish institutional life that had been geared to the older patterns:

1. Synagogues and other Jewish organizations are not oriented to single people. Their membership rules, as well as their forms of social life, prayer, and celebration—all assume married couples and families.

2. Hadassah and many other Jewish organizations were built on the assumption that there were many Jewish housewives with time to spare for volunteer work. Many of these women have taken jobs. Now what?

3. The national and local structures of Jewish professionalism were built for Jewish men who did not have to spend time raising children. Now what?

4. The old patterns of Jewish celebration are not geared to single people, or even single-parent families. The traditional pattern assumed a man who prayed and understood Torah, and a woman who shaped it into daily life. Without the one, Torah becomes a headtrip; without the other, it becomes a mindless rote. Now what?

5. The old patterns of begetting, bearing, and rearing children into Jewish life-practice are not geared to single people. Where will new Jews come from? Where will Jewish Jews come from?

6. The breakdown of Jewish neighborhoods makes it harder for Jewish men and women to meet each other, so it leads to fewer Jewish marriages and families. The reduction of Jewish marriages helps to break down Jewish neighborhoods. Now what?

7. The breakdown of Jewish neighborhoods, the chilliness of synagogues, and the delay and reduction in number of Jewish marriages creates emotional, sexual, and spiritual problems among many people who lack intimacy, community, commitment, ecstasy, mirth, and meaningful mourning in their lives.

These are the breakdowns. One response to them is trying to restore the old patterns. But it is hard to see how some of the economic, technological, and cultural changes can be reversed.

Many of them have pleased many people, who have become their established constituencies. Suppose the old world is dead? Really dead? What then? What now? Can these changes be woven into a Jewish community that takes on new institutional forms?

In particular, what new forms of mishpacha—of Jewish families that nurture Jewishness—might we bring into being?

Let us look at several possibilities that would involve different levels of accepting or going beyond the new men-women patterns:

1. We could simply accept that many fewer Jews will become couples than did before. For some individuals, permanent single-hood may be workable and joyful; for those who do not choose it freely, however, this solution may mean more unhappiness. For the Jewish people it may mean fewer Jews and less Yiddishkeit, but this danger could be lessened. Elizabeth Koltun and Rabbi Laura Geller (in an essay in Koltun's book, *The Jewish Woman*) have made specific suggestions of "new" mitzvot for single people, parallel to the traditional ones for couples. Several possibilites:

• Teaching Judaism to children could be seen by single people as a parallel to begetting more children. Since many formally Jewish children have in the past two generations had no or little Jewish upbringing, strengthening the mitzvah of teaching Judaism diligently to children might even result in the next generation's having larger numbers of "Jewishly Jewish" grownups—even if the total number of Jews is smaller. Rabbi Rebecca Alpert calls this "spiritual parenting" and sees it as an obligation for single people.

• Single people could decide to have or adopt children and raise them Jewishly. I know of one seriously Jewish single woman who decided, after long discussions with a rabbi, to have a child through artificial insemination.

• Judaism has traditionally taught that the pleasures and joys of sex are holy in themselves, even if not intended for procreation, if they have been hallowed through marriage. For people who are single and continue to find joy and holiness in their sexuality, it may be necessary to work out new ways of hallowing sex. Such ways might (as Rabbi Arthur Green suggested in an article in *The Second Jewish Catalog*) recognize that all freely chosen sexual relationships have some holiness in them—the more holiness, the more they partake of honesty, caring, commitment, and love.

All these efforts to bring Jewish values, practices, and approaches into the formerly "alien" territory of singlehood—any effort to develop "new mitzvot" for single people, for example—will probably succeed only if there are communities of single people who together think them out, work them out, and help each other carry them out.

2. We could consciously create new forms of Jewish life that make it easier and more attractive for single people in their twenties and thirties (and divorced people in their thirties, forties, and fifties) to decide to get married. These new forms would not be keyed to family life, as the synagogues are. But they would also not be just "singles clubs," where people feel the only purpose is pairing off. They would have Jewish tasks to perform—and in the process some of the members might decide to pair off.

The havurot of the past ten years, especially those outside the synagogues, have to some extent fulfilled this function. They tend to attract single people who have a lot of energy to give and who seek a kind of intimacy that is comfortable and lukewarm rather than intense. Their focus is on the tasks to be performed: celebrating Shabbos and festivals when there is no hired rabbi to make them happen; initiating projects of social service and social justice. The intimacy grows from sharing the work.

Some synagogues have been sponsoring "singles services" in the hope both of enriching the Jewish lives of the single participants and of helping those who wish to meet possible spouses. They have been encouraging nonmembers of the synagogue to attend and have been using more fluid, more participatory forms of song and prayer. In several synagogues, monthly singles services on Friday night have been regularly attracting about a thousand people. Some synagogues have then encouraged those who attend to meet in each other's homes for Shabbos dinner in groups of a dozen or so. Could these grow into havurot? How will havurot that begin with mostly single people deal with the changes that emerge when some of their members marry? Are other forms desirable?

3. Some observers claim that the fluidity of our society and the

breakup of strong subcommunities like ethnic neighborhoods weaken the ability of many people to mature in such a way as to form strong marriages and families—or for that matter, healthy lives as single people. And some have suggested that women's consciousness-raising and support groups have become a means of doing this. If so, we could create among men (or among women and men together) the same kinds of consciousness-raising and maturity-developing groups that there have been among women. Could this become a function of the havurot? Could they provide, in a Jewish context, for groups where men and women can more openly wrestle with whatever troubles them?

4. We could decide to focus attention on making marriages possible and in order to do so revive the role of the *shadchan* (matchmaker). For example: suppose a lively, intelligent, Jewishly knowledgeable, and psychologically sensitive couple in some given city or neighborhood were to begin inviting a dozen or so single people to Shabbos dinner (or Saturday-night M'laveh Malkah), once a month perhaps. At such a dinner the single people would have a chance to meet each other and arrange to meet again. But they would also be enjoying a pleasant meal and conversation, celebrating Shabbos, perhaps studying Torah. Would it make sense to pay the expenses of the shadchan-couple? A fee as well? Would it be possible to gather the names of those couples who would be willing to do this, and of single people who would like to take part, and then to put them in touch with each other?

5. We could accept that marriages may begin later and end earlier—so that at any given moment there are fewer married Jews and more single Jews than there used to be—but we could nevertheless encourage these shorter-term married couples to have children and raise them Jewishly. That would require us to insist that job patterns change so that people in midcareer do not have to abandon their work in order to raise children. And it would require us to meet the Jewish-child-rearing needs of single parents and two-working-parent families by setting up child-care programs that are Jewishly focused and that teach Jewish life-styles to children.

Such child-care programs could teach Hebrew as a living language

for conversation, prayer, and studying Torah; could celebrate the
holy days with all their wealth of foods and ceremony and meaning;
could teach both boys and girls to light Shabbos candles and both
girls and boys to hallow the Shabbos wine; could, in the ancient
Jewish way, teach the children how to use the Bible and Talmud
stories as prisms by which to reflect light on their own changing and
growing life concerns. In short, such centers could play a major role
in raising Jewishly the next generation of Jewish children.

6. There have been some very tentative suggestions for making
more radical reexaminations of what a marriage is. In one semipublic
discussion, a "creatively traditional" rabbi suggested that perhaps
under some circumstances, an "open" marriage ought not to be
automatically rejected as irredeemably antithetical to Jewish values.
In the same discussion, a respected Jewish writer—a woman and a
feminist—suggested that the ancient Jewish openness to plural marriage (abolished only one thousand years ago and only in the West)
be reexamined. She suggest that in the present atmosphere in which
women have independent social and economic power and a strong
sense of sisterhood, plural marriage might not be denigrating to
women as it almost always was in the past. Most of those present
doubted that these ideas were desirable, or workable. Yet the fact
that they were put forward suggests how shaky the traditional
ground has come to feel for some of those who stand on it.

Most of these approaches, coming from their different angles,
point nevertheless in the same direction: the importance of the
rather small and intimate circle of people sharing a task as a way of
either making marriages more possible or a "single" life-style far
more Jewishly rewarding. They point toward patterns of Jewish
community that do not depend on the old-form Jewish family, with
its strong distinctions between male and female roles, to generate
and regenerate Yiddishkeit.

They may even be hinting in the direction that the havurot, the
new participatory and intimate congregations, may themselves become or may nurture new forms of mishpacha, new forms of extended family which might meet the needs and desires of their
members for sexual expression, emotional intimacy, child rearing—
perhaps even for economic help in times of trouble.

All of these new developments and new possibilities in the "Judaization" of new kinds of men-women relationships are connected with the emergence of women who have the intellectual, economic, and emotional power and determination to share fully in Jewish life.

Such women have already begun to reshape Jewish institutions in the ways we have described. They have also been finding that the symbols and practices of traditional Judaism need to be reshaped in order to meet their own spiritual needs and in order to explain, celebrate, and make sense out of the new institutions and arrangements. To reshape Jewish religious symbols and practices in this way is not easy; for not only were almost all of the traditional writers and interpreters men, but in many ways the focus of their work was male human beings and the "male" aspects of God. So to create a "feminist" or "androgynist" Judaism requires a heroic effort to unveil and rediscover the deepest most hidden truths of Torah.

Is there any hint in the tradition itself that such an unveiling of a deeper layer of Torah might meet the needs of women? Arlene Agus, in Koltun's *The Jewish Woman*, has suggested that there is. Her work is an excellent example of how women, once they begin to study Torah in the traditional way, may bring a perspective that transforms how women and men understand Torah, and even transforms how Torah is studied. Agus draws on a strange and little-known strand of Jewish tradition that sees the changing moon in a somewhat eerie light. Says the Prophet Isaiah (30:26), "The light of the moon shall become like the light of the sun." And the Talmud (Hullin 60a and Sanhedrin 42a) expands on this unsettling notion:

[When God created the sun and moon, the two great lights,] the moon said to the Holy One, "Sovereign of the Universe! Can two rulers wear one crown?" He answered, "Go then and make yourself smaller!" . . . Rabbi Simeon ben Lakish declared, "Why is the he-goat offered on the New Moon [for a sin offering] distinctive in that only of it is written 'unto the Lord'?" Because the Holy One said, "Let this he-goat be an atonement for Me [for My sin] in making the moon smaller."

Rabbi Akha said to Rabbbi Ashi: In the West, they pronounce the following blessing: "Blessed be the One Who renews the moons." Whereupon he retorted: "Such a blessing even our women folk pronounce." [Let there be added] . . . "The moon He ordered that she should renew herself as a crown of beauty for those whom He sustains from the womb, and who will someday, like her, be renewed and magnify their Maker in the name of the glory of His Kingdom."

These texts express an ancient tradition that when Creation began, the moon was equal to the sun; that God reduced its brightness just as the Shekhinah (God's Presence in the world, a nurturing, female aspect of God) went into mourning exile; and that the moon will again become equal to the sun when the Messianic redemption comes and the Shekhinah returns to Her full glory in the days of love and justice. Agus has suggested that we read this strand of the tradition as a veiled comment on the possibility of a profound change in the relationships of women and men in Jewish religious life—with the moon symbolizing women and the sun, men.

The Talmud promises that the moon will be made bright again in Heaven when those who are like her on earth are restored to their rightful place: those whom God has sustained "from the womb" but whose splendor God has dimmed. Who are these? According to rabbinic and mystical tradition, these are the people Israel—who almost disappear from history and then return in unexpected glory; disappear and return, over and over. Today, we can both accept this tradition that the redemption of Israel is meant by the passage, and believe that the passage should be read to mean as well the redemption of women—who also, like Israel and the moon, have been pushed to the shadowy side of history.

For it would not be surprising for the moon to be a symbol of women. The "moonthly" and menstrual cycles have in many religious traditions been seen as echoes of each other. And the imagery of God as Midwife and Mother who sustains "from the womb" would fit well with God's concern for those people whose wombs move and change with the moon.

What else in the tradition might suggest this outlook?

The tradition explicitly connects women with the moon. It teaches that God gave the women of Israel an exemption from work on Rosh Hodesh—the renewing of the moon at the beginning of the Jewish lunar month—because they refused to give their jewelry to the making of the idol Golden Bull-calf at Sinai. This, it seems to me, can be understood as a kind of anthropological field observation with a religious dimension.

If so, the story might run this way: The Israelite men, under pressure of travail in the wilderness and Moses' long absence, reverted to the male fertility rites they had known in Egypt, and so cast the male fertility idol of the Golden Bull-calf. Women, who in Egypt had not been part of the Bull-calf rite, turned for their own solace to a moon ceremony instead. When Moses returned and furiously denounced the Bull-calf as an idol, questions were raised about whether the women's moon rite was as idolatrous as the men's calf rite. But God, Moses, and the Jewish community confirmed women's right and affirmed their desire to continue celebrating the Moon, which symbolized female spirituality because her ebb and flow seemed akin to the menstrual cycle.

There are more hidden hints at an ancient connection between strong-spirited women and a ritual of the moon. The Jewish Patriarchs Isaac and Jacob, according to tradition, married into a family of strong women—the family of Rebekah, Rachel, and Leah. It was, by the way, the family of Lavan—a name for the pale-white moon, in Hebrew *levana*.

These women had strong associations with a well—and of Rebekah there is a traditional midrash that when she met Abraham's servant Eliezer at the well, the water rose to meet her.* When would water do this? When it is attracted by the moon. Is it possible that the household *teraphim* which Rachel took from Lavan's household when she left with Jacob were sacred moon symbols, and it was no mere accident or trick that led her to conceal them from Lavan by explaining that she could not move since she was in the time of her menstrual flow? (Gen. 31:19, 31:30–35) Was it necessary for those women to become the mothers of Israel precisely because they carried a strong "feminist," moon-centered religious tradition—but were not moon worshippers?

Strong women are also crucial to the process, laid out in the first

---

* Bereshit Rabbah LX:5; in Soncino English ed., vol. 2, p. 529. This midrash was called to my attention by Ruth Sohn.

four chapters of Exodus, by which the liberation of the Israelites from *Mitzrayim* begins. It is women who take the initiative and teach men the process of freedom, because the women know the mysteries of birth. Since every birth brings newness, unpredictability, into the world, the birth of a new person is the biological archetype of freedom in the historical-political arena. Thus it is midwives—experts in birth—who resist Pharoah's royal decree, in order to save the Israelite baby boys from death; the Israelite Miriam and Pharaoh's own daughter form an international feminist conspiracy to save Moses; Moses must flee to seven women and a well, marry Zipporah, and *have a child* before he can experience God in the Burning Bush; and Zipporah must complete the birth by teaching him to circumcise his son before he can reenter Egypt to become the liberator. Zipporah was not an Israelite. She, like Rachel and Rebekah, was associated with a well. Was she a celebrator of the moon?

And strong women are crucial in some of the most Messianic, future-oriented stories of the Bible as well as in some of the tales of earliest beginnings. The Book of Ruth goes out of its way to assert that Lot's nameless daughter (the mother of Moab), Tamar, and Ruth the Moabite were necessary elements in the genealogy of King David (and therefore the Messiah). All these women were non-Israelites, and they all broke the normal law and custom in radical ways to claim husbands, become mothers, and build up the families that led to David. Perhaps the most Messianic of all Biblical books, the Song of Songs, which the great Rabbi Akiba called "the holy of holies" among the Holy Writings, affirms and celebrates not only an assertive woman, but a mode of open, fluid spirituality that flows from the life-experience of women and is quite different from the more guarded, structured, time-bound spiritual patterns that have been celebrated by most of the men of Jewish history.

Thus at a number of moments of great mythic power—crucial points in the earliest stages of Jewish peoplehood and in the progenitorship of David—women, and symbols of women like the moon and various wells were absolutely crucial.

To read the tradition this way would mean that these texts preserve both a dim memory of the past and a shadowy prophecy of the future:

A faint memory of a time in the early history of the people of Israel—perhaps even before it viewed itself as Israel—when women and the symbols of their spiritual experience (such as the moon) were equal to men and their symbols in the religious life of the people. A prophecy that someday, in Jewish practice, not only women but also the symbols of women's spiritual experience will be restored to equality with men and their symbols.

When that "someday" comes, women will not simply take a numerically equal place in the traditional forms of Jewish religious practice; the forms of practice will themselves be transformed as women's spiritual experience is discovered, uncovered.

I think "someday" is now, if we will make it so.

I am suggesting that in the fragments of mystical thought quoted above and in some other fragments of the tradition are hints toward a feminist transformation of Torah—expected and invited by Torah herself, as part of the unfolding of the oral tradition.

What would it mean for God and the Jewish people now to restore the former brightness of women and their spiritual experience?

It would mean that women and men come to understand the Jewish feminist movement as a process in which there must be several levels of change. One necessary level is the demand that women must count in the minyan, be called for aliyot to read the Torah, become rabbis—and that men must rear children, care for households, feed the hungry. In short, the demand that *all* the mitzvot, all the commandments, apply fully to *all* adult Jews.

It is true that this demand has not yet been accepted even in theory in some areas of Jewish life. It has not yet been carried out in practice even in most of the areas where it is accepted in theory. So Jewish feminists must continue to press this demand. Yet there are other levels of change that Jewish feminists need to pursue as well—the changes involved in the brightening of "the moon"—that is, the forms by which women can more richly express their spiritual experience.

These deeper levels of change are necessary because the Jewish people—women and men—need more than the inclusion of women in the same kind of Jewish life the rabbis knew. We need the *renewal* of Jewish life—its becoming as fresh, creative, and new in its response to Torah after the earthquakes of the last generation as it was after Sinai, in the wilderness; as it was after the First Destruction, when it gave us "the Prophets"; as it was after the Second Destruction, when it gave us the Talmud.

And in our generation we need this renewal to include the lessons of the life-experience of women. Some aspects of the special life-experience of women may be biologically rooted. Most are culturally rooted. What is biological and what is cultural does matter, but what matters much more is being open to the lessons women might teach—whether these lessons are rooted in biology or culture. It is true that some men experience in some degree the elements of a life that we often think of as especially part of women's experience. That is, men experience the moon, water, life cycles, feeding, parenting, rearing children, caring for households, nurturing families and communities, even *nekevah* sexuality—open, pierced, and receptive. But all these are, for biological and cultural reasons, *more* fully experienced by *more* women.

Now we need to reclaim and renew this "women's element" in Judaism.

Some feminists have been concerned that focusing on the "womanliness" of these aspects of life may encourage old stereotypes of women's roles, and thereby assist in the resubjugation of women into these roles. My own view is that women can draw on these elements of their own past special experience without fear, if two conditions are met: if women and men are clear that both men and women can draw on the whole spectrum of life-experience, even if perhaps to different degrees; and, most important, if women hold enough power in our culture to control how these symbols and roles are used—enough power to make sure that they are used in the service of a broader "feminization and humanization" rather than resubjugation. That is why the demand for equality for women in Jewish institutions cannot be separated from the demand for a feminist transformation of those institutions.

Why do we need to pursue these intertwined issues at this moment of Jewish history? We need to do this for the sake of those women who have been excluded and whose life-experience has been ignored—and for the sake of justice toward them. We *also* need to do this for the sake of giving health to a Judaism that is now suffering from the exclusion of much else in life. In this sense we may see the restoration of the moon more broadly still: as meaning the Messianic liberation and redemption not only of women and of the Jewish people, not only of the poor, the weak, of all who have been excluded, diminished, demeaned, but also as the reemergence of all that is valuable *within* each human being, but has been repressed.

For Isaiah and the Talmud to see even the moon as a diminished equal who will return in splendor to her place, as the weeping Shekhinah will return to hers, can be seen as a metaphor for all *tikkun:* all repair of the world.

In this way there would emerge as part of the Jewish feminist process what might be called a "feminist Judaism"—a Judaism informed and transformed throughout its fabric by the feminist consciousness. Such a feminist Judaism would mean not only the restoration of women to their almost forgotten equal place in life, but also the "return of the repressed" in other spheres. For example: the reawakening of the repressed sense of sexuality that is celebrated in the Song of Songs—and that was pushed underground by the tradition even when the tradition elevated the Song of Songs. For example: the reawakening of music and dance, the celebration of our bones and muscles, that was repressed when the Temple was destroyed. For example: the celebration of the earth through the cycles of Sabbatical and Jubilee Years—years when the land lies fallow and the wealth is shared, years of a kind of body cycle writ large, a kind of menstrual cycle of the Shekhinah expressed in the land and the society. For example: the celebration of equality that is expressed in a circle-dance (where everyone must sooner or later stand in the footsteps of everyone else) and the circle of recycling the wealth from the rich to every newly equal family. For example: the repressed sense of God not as a separate Other, "out there," but "in here," in process, immanent, everywhere.

What specific actions could we undertake in order to effect a feminist transformation of Judaism?

First, strengthening moon and water symbolism in our liturgies. This has already begun as women and men have developed various kinds of liturgies for Rosh Hodesh, the Renewing of the Moon. As these spread, and especially as groups of women develop more and more expressive ceremonials, they need to be shared with and taught to the Jewish people as a whole. So do rituals of water, old and new—wells, rivers, seas, mikveh, *tashlikh,* the bitter-water/ sweet-water ceremony of reconciliation developed for Slichot by the journal *Menorah,* perhaps a reworking of the water pouring that was celebrated at the Temple for Sukkot.

Second, encouraging circles in space. The fluid and circular seating arrangements of the havurot seem to owe something to the (unconscious?) influence of women who fully participated in forming havurah practice. For the biology of women's inner life space, as contrasted with men's outward life-projection, seems to be congruent with the circular seating where God is felt as being present in the center, not far out along one dimension. These havurah circles have taught us that when we look for God, what we see is not the Ark or the Rabbi—but each others' faces. And the circles have encouraged a sense of equality, participation, and community that may also stem partly from the life-experience and needs of women. What would happen if all Jewish meetings—for prayer and for discussion—were held in circles small enough for us to talk with each other, instead of in rows where we see only the back of each other's heads, plus the face of one Grand Master? If we *talked* in circles, we could stop *going* in circles. If we do not live out the circle, the circle lives us: Zero.

Third, encouraging circles and spirals in time. We need to strengthen our sense of the cycles in our bodies and in society. For example, we need to see the holy days as not simply individual events but parts of the spiritual cycles of the month and year. The social-political cycles of Shabbos, the shmitah, and Jubilee need to be renewed, accentuated, made much more real. These cycles alternate hard work toward economic development, with contemplative rest; swift piling-up of wealth and power, with an equal sharing of all wealth and power; doing, with being.

Fourth, celebrating, honoring, and materially supporting the life-moments of sexuality, sexual intercourse, menstruation, giving birth, nursing, parenting, and grandparenting much more richly and thoroughly than we do now. For example, in an era when the over-whelming proportion of Jewish women ignore *niddah* and abhor the mikveh as a demeaning of menstruation, what if there were *one* or *two* days of sexual separation around menstruation, precisely to celebrate it without treating it as a time of "impurity?" For example, what if there were ceremonies around first menstruation and meno-pause? Around beginning to nurse and weaning? Could such cere-monies include men, even at some remove, as *bris milah* did women? Could we create ceremonies to mark the shift that occurs when children leave home—away from parenting, toward the pro-vision of wisdom to a wider world? Ceremonies to honor the link with an older culture that is represented by those who are grandparents—either in their own bodies or in a cultural, gener-ational sense? And what if we honored all these processes in the "workaday world" by making time (and money) available for workers to care for children, pausing during menstrual periods, grandpar-enting?

Fifth, as I have suggested in the previous chapter, enriching the Jewish sense that the spirit *is* the body, that the spiritual and the physical fuse, by encouraging dance, mime, body movement, breathing, the arts and artisanship, and theatrical "acting" as part of prayer, Torah-study, and midrashic storytelling. Already many women and some men are renewing this process.

Sixth, developing that element of Jewish theology, already present in Kabbalah and Hassidus, that focuses on God *within* the world, the "still small voice," the Shekhinah.

These six will be enough to begin with. For on the seventh day Queen Shabbos, the Bride, will teach us how to continue.

These midrashim—these unfoldings, unveilings, of the meaning of a Torah in which the spirituality of women was hidden away to be discovered later—can bring us back to where we began, the institutional need for new forms of mishpacha in which new kinds of Jewish women and men can live creatively and well. For a Judaism of cycles, spirals, inner space, and the indwelling presence of God accords well with the life-experience of the havurot and of those new forms of mishpacha that might emerge from it. In a feminist or androgynist Judaism, the havurot might find their "theological" expression; and in the new kinds of havurah and mishpacha, feminists might find a fitting life-practice.

In this confluence, the theory of Torah and the theory of feminism would also flow together. For Torah is not simply a set of Grand Ideas, but a path of practices and ceremonies. Indeed, one of its Most Grand Ideas is precisely that daily life-practice and ceremonial are crucial to the Holy Root of Being. So in this way Torah, like feminism, teaches that the personal is political.

But there remain some important questions. Why should feminists bother to reconstruct Jewish life—either at the institutional or the theological level? Why should women who seek an equal share of power to control the situations that control their lives not simply shrug off the sexist institutions of conventional Judaism and refuse to let these institutions any longer control their lives? Why should women and men who share a feminist vision of a transformed society bother to transform the one minor subculture in which, it has been argued, the vision and practice of patriarchy may have been born, and may have been most forcefully transmitted across the ages from civilization to civilization? Why take the trouble?

For some personal and some public, political reasons.

The personal reasons are that for some Jewish feminists, specific strands of Jewish memory, ceremonial, community, and practice still have a powerful appeal. Whether it is identification with the oldest, longest-lived resistance movement against oppression that is known to human history; or a sense of fulfillment from participating in such a ceremony as the Passover Seder; or a strong rush of feeling about a foggy mental picture of pioneer kibbutzniks in the Land of Israel—for *some* Jewish feminists (by no means all) it is there. So if this tug is real, and if "the personal is political," as feminists remind us, then the turf of Judaism must be struggled for.

In itself, however, this tug might or might not be enough to "go with"—enough to spark a growing fire of interest in Jewish renewal. But these personal responses are not casual, not accidental—they do not in fact simply exist "in themselves." The personal response is a symptom, a sign, of the powerful public, political truths within Jewish tradition.

Some of the truths-toward-change that already are fermenting in the tradition not only accord with feminist perceptions of the world but might even—at the very moment when patriarchal power was defeating the ancient matriarchies—have been smuggled into Torah from the insights of some ancient matriarchs, the moon-celebrators we have talked about. They may have been smuggled into, around, and underneath the patriarchal surface of the Torah. And some of these are insights that modern secularists, even feminists, need to hear—insights that secular liberal, socialist, and feminist thought may not supply.

To some extent, it is the struggle of modern feminists to raise some profound questions that has brought to the level of audibility some unheard proto-feminist concerns that lay beneath the surface of Torah. It is as if the voice of modern feminism reawoke a sleeping beauty in the Torah, a wisdom that recognized her daughter's voice.

What are these truths of Torah that our world-on-the-brink-of-dissolution needs to hear? I have already mentioned two of them, and here want only to point out that they may spring from the proto-feminist roots of Torah.

One of these is the necessity of rhythm, of making Shabbos, of pausing to take a breath, to rest, to meditate, to contemplate. Especially the necessity of periodically pausing from incessant, explosive economic development—not to *end* development, but to pause long enough to sense again its limitations, its purpose, its Owner. The sense of biological and social rhythms—the week, month, year, Jubilee—may very well have come into our tradition out of some matriarch's close sensing of her body and of Mother Earth. We need to hear that Teaching.

The other is the necessity of acting consciously to keep ourselves from murdering the next generation. Over and over, from the story of the binding of Isaac to the command that we celebrate the bris of circumcision, to the biblical horror at the offering up of children through fire to Moloch, to the rigorous restrictions in Deuteronomy against the old sending the young to kill and die for their wars—over and over, the Torah teaches that there is a serious danger that the older generation will want to kill the younger; that especially fathers will want to kill their sons; and, most important, that we must create law codes, rituals, and stories that train us to struggle against this danger. Elijah will come, says the last passage of the last Prophet, before the great and terrible day of the Lord—to turn the hearts of the fathers to the sons and the hearts of the sons to the fathers. This too is a feminist teaching. One commentator on the Torah, David Bakan,* has even said that the Torah comes precisely to "motherize" men—to teach men to act loving and caring of the community, as mothers have to act if their children are to live. And in our time, when the human race stands poised upon the possibility of destroying not a son here or there or even one whole people but the entire next generation—this Teaching stands between us and the danger.

But it is now also clear that the Teaching as we have so far understood it is not yet strong enough to keep us safe from the overarching dangers of destruction. If Torah bore within herself a secret feminist guerrilla victory smuggled into an obvious patriarchal triumph, then the secret victory has oozed away and lost its power. The feminism must be made explicit and public. Torah must be transformed and the feminist element in it strengthened. The modern feminist "daughter" must revitalize the sleeping feminist "mother."

It is *because* there is powerful truth in the tradition's resistance to power, in the multilevel poetry of its ritual, in its sardonic view of the transitory idols of convention, in its commitment to the creation of counterinstitutions reaching toward equality and community, that feminists feel tugged toward the kibbutz and the seder. The truths of the tradition have kept on having the power to work toward justice, community, holiness in the world, even when women and their deepest truths were kept on its margins. But all this is not

---

The Duality of Human Existence (Boston: Beacon, 1971).

enough. There is good reason for feminists, both men and women, to struggle for a major forward step in the tradition.

What is extraordinary about the reopening and renewal of the relationships among women, men, and Torah is that these most intimate and "in-here" kinds of issues bear such meaning for the macrocosm, for the larger context of Jewish and human life. If there is to emerge from the movement for Jewish renewal a new pattern of life, a new holy vessel, then feminism will be one of the most important strands in the new life-pattern—perhaps along with the strands of a spiritually open secularism and Jewish mysticism. We will therefore examine how these other elements of Jewish thought and practice are now working and what intertwinings they may come to have with feminism. First we will look at secularist Labor Zionism and Diaspora liberalism, and then at new versions of Jewish mysticism.

7. *New Israel, New Diaspora*

The changes that we have been describing have been happening among Jews in the intimate lives of face-to-face local groups, individuals, and families. They began around 1967, and around 1979 began to be visible and sometimes mildly influential in the lives of the larger and more formally organized Jewish communities. But what about the next larger sphere, the fourth concentric sphere, of Jewish life—the life of the worldwide Jewish community? Does the movement for Jewish renewal have any implications for this wider sphere? To understand the implications of those changes for the future, especially for the overall patterns of the worldwide Jewish people in the next generation, it is necessary to look at what has been going on in that wider Jewish world. To do this, I will have to change the way I am writing in this book. I will have to step out of the process of describing the intimate life events of individuals and groups, and shift into looking at more overarching processes and using more abstract words for broader historical events.

The most important fact is that the basic world views out of which organized Jewish communities acted, from about 1945 on, have begun to disintegrate under the pressure of historical change, from both inside and outside the Jewish communities. From 1945 into the late 1970s, the behavior of most Jews and of the organized Jewish community in America, Israel, and most of the rest of the world, was guided by two major world views: secular Labor Zionism and secularized Jewish liberalism. One dominated Israel and the other, American Jewry. There were some strains between them, but there were more important ways in which they meshed with each other.

Labor Zionism was the carefully worked out ideology and practice of the governing party of the Jewish settlements in Palestine and then of the state of Israel. It included a commitment to a Jewish state led by the Jewish working class organized into unions and political parties working toward socialism; the abandonment of religious Judaism; and the elimination of the far-flung Jewish settlements of the Diaspora through the gathering of their people to the Land of Israel.

Jewish liberalism was the much fuzzier, less explicitly articulated working mind-set of the organized Jewish community in America. This "Jewish liberalism" was not the same thing as the religious philosophy of "liberal," "progressive," or "Reform" Judaism—but it included a watered-down version of this religious approach in its generally secular view of Jewish life. Jewish liberalism was a Jewish variant of social-welfare liberalism that defined the Jewish community as only a mildly special variant of American and Western culture, with a different formal religion but the same basic view of religious pluralism under the First Amendment; with a special concern for social justice but the same basic vision of American politics or society; with a special attachment to Israel but the same basic view of having a secure place in American society and the same basic vision of the desirable international order as one of self-determining nations, precarious peace, and collective security through the United Nations.

Beginning in small and almost invisible ways in the late 1960s, then with such more public events as the shifts in Israeli voting patterns in 1977 and American Jewish voting patterns in 1980, this meshing of Labor Zionism and Jewish liberalism as the operating world views of the organized Jewish people has been breaking down. It is not that these two ideologies have fallen into conflict with each other; rather, each of them has been eroding in its own bailiwick. They have begun to falter and fail not only as descriptions of the world but also as movements, organizations, and structures that can act to change the world. Although there have been efforts to rethink and rework some aspects of Labor Zionism and Jewish liberalism, these efforts have not yet been effective enough to deal successfully with new historical developments. The reformulation of a Jewish world outlook is therefore an urgent task for the Jewish people.

Let us first examine what happened to Labor Zionism. It defined the greatest need of the Jewish people to be its reconstitution as a nation on the territory of the Land of Israel—a whole nation with a Jewish working class, a nation led by its working class organized into labor unions, co-ops, and a labor party (or parties), a nation able both to fight for its territory and to make peace with its neighbors, a nation that in its own land could abandon the religion that had been useful for a long time but was an ultimately self-deceptive form of national consciousness.

Labor Zionism succeeded in several ways. The most obvious was that it built the crucial social, cultural, economic, and political institutions of Israel. At a deeper level, Labor Zionism before 1940 offered one of many ideological possibilities through which the Jewish people might have dealt with its entry into the modern industrial-scientific world and the dissolving effect of that world on traditional religious ideas. Before 1940, Labor Zionism was only one such alternative. It competed for Jewish allegiance with the Jewish Labor Bund, a strong movement that was socialist, antireligious, and anti-Zionist because it was committed to the Diaspora—especially Yiddish-speaking Eastern Europe; with Simon Dubnow's version of Diaspora Jewish nationalism; with Reform Judaism's religious liberalism and its anti-Zionist universalism; with efforts by such people as Martin Buber, Franz Rosenzweig, and Mordecai Kaplan to renew Jewish religious life through one or another version of God-covenanted Jewish peoplehood, and of course with efforts to preserve or modernize Orthodox Judaism.

But after 1945 this conflict and competition ended. In the wake of the Holocaust, Labor Zionism had two great advantages over all competing Jewish ideologies.

First, it had not only argued for but worked for and actually built a defensible Jewish community in the Land of Israel. To meet the immediate desperate needs of refugees from the Holocaust, and to meet the desperate crisis of self-confidence of the Jewish people, the State of Israel under Labor leadership was necessary.

The second advantage was that the secularist, antireligious bent of Labor Zionism had some attraction even to Jews who preserved their attachment to synagogues. For the Holocaust left the surviving

Jews of the world bereft of the largest and strongest God-oriented and religiously fertile part of the Jewish people, and, even more profoundly, bereft of their own sense that God cares deeply for the Jewish people and would protect it from the worst outrages against the human spirit and the Image of God. Given what had happened, an explicitly nonreligious or antireligious ideology of Jewish peoplehood may very well have been absolutely necessary to the recovery of the Jewish people from the social, psychological, and spiritual destruction wrought by the Holocaust.

Labor Zionism not only won wide respect, it did great deeds. It not only created Israel, but led it effectively through its early crises. But there were certain historical facts, even from the beginning, that were not foreseen by Labor Zionism and were never really dealt with in its ideas or its actions. Gradually over the years, these factors have become more and more important. More and more they have undermined Labor Zionist policy. So in the years since the formation of the state of Israel, Labor Zionism has increasingly failed to account for, understand, and act effectively in the light of these unexpected factors:

1. The Holocaust and its effect of utterly cutting off Israel and Zionism from what had been their primary human, political, and cultural bases in Eastern European Jewry.

2. The defeat of democratic socialism and social democracy in the West after World War II, the resurgence of capitalism in Western Europe, the onset of the Cold War between triumphantly capitalist America and bureaucratic-statist Russia, and the pressures from both to choose sides.

3. The rigidification of tension into a seemingly permanent war between Israel and the Arab states.

4. The emergence of the Palestinian people as a separate nationalistic component of a broader Arab people (rather than its digestion into general Arab peoplehood) and the ability of this Palestinian nationalism to win political support in some circles in some Arab states and in the Third World (even at the same time that some Arab governments were massacring Palestinians in camps and villages).

5. The creation of a Sephardic/Oriental Jewish majority in Israel.

6. The survival and renewal of religious feelings and ideas and of Orthodox religious institutions in Israel.

7. The survival and renewal of strong Diaspora Jewries in a number of countries, especially the United States, and the reassertion by some part of their leadership of a desire to see these Diaspora communities as authentic parts of world Jewry *in addition to* their role as supporters of Israel.

The interaction of these factors, and the failure of Labor Zionism to respond creatively to them, produced a social and political situation that steadily weakened the Labor parties and resulted in the defeat of the Labor Alignment in the Israeli elections of 1977. Let us look at these problems in more detail.

First, the effects of the Holocaust. Labor Zionism expected European anti-Semitism to continue and grow, but did not predict the utter destruction of the heart of its own political and cultural base, Eastern European Jewry. The Holocaust may have impelled the world in 1945–1948 to encourage and accept the creation of Israel and may have made Zionism the leading world view about the Jewish future within the Jewish people itself; but it also deprived Israel and Zionism of the rich interplay between traditional Jewish religious life, Diaspora nationalism, Jewish socialism, and devotion to the Land of Israel that gave form and would have given added growth to the ideas and practices of Labor Zionism. Instead, the new state of Israel found itself utterly cut off from its roots and, traumatized by the "sheep to the slaughter" image of the Holocaust, even more hostile to the Diaspora Jewish culture, especially religious culture, than it had been before the Holocaust. This separation has made it much harder for the evolving Israeli culture and identity to be fulfillingly "Jewish" in Israel, and to build organic connections with the Jewish cultures of the Diaspora.

Second, Israel found itself squeezed by the Cold War. It partially chose and partially was forced into a path that made it more and more dependent on the greatest capitalist power, the United States. An imaginable alternative—neutralism—was made much harder (and probably impossible) by growing hostility to Israel from the neutralist Third World, occasioned by a combination of Third World sympathy for Palestinian peoplehood and an opportunistic desire of some of the Third World neutralists for alliances with the Arab states. Social democracy and socialism turned out to be weaker in Western Europe after World War II than many Israeli Laborites had expected; so this imaginable ally was also unavailable. The only strong support available to Israel was triumphantly capitalist America.

The result was the slow erosion of the labor movement, socialism, and social democracy inside Israel under the pressure and seductions of the world market and United States and American Jewish aid. The Labor Zionist constituency lost more and more of its ideological edge as well as its material base. The result was the growing smell of demoralization and scandal inside the Labor Party (though by American standards both were penny ante).

Third, the long-term war between Israel and the Arab states probably was the most important factor in providing continuing political support for the Ben-Gurion policy of centralizing power in the state, thus weakening the grass-roots energies of Labor-Zionist groupings, local communites, and the like. This policy tended to rigidify Zionist education and culture as well as to reduce independent reassessment of basic government policy. The permanent war also drastically limited the money and imaginative energy available for social reconstruction.

Fourth, the unexpected emergence of a separate Palestinian nationalism, more and more intense from the 1920s forward, became a more and more baffling problem for Israel, especially after 1967. For the military victory of that year, swallowing the West Bank and Gaza with their Palestinian population, dissolved the Labor Zionist adherence to partition of "Palestine" as the only way to maintain a Jewish state. This element of Labor Zionist thought was not sufficient to outweigh the strategic and economic enticements of holding onto the West Bank.

As a result, Israel had to deal both directly and in world politics with an indigestible Palestinian nationalism that had political weight even in Arab countries whose governments massacred Palestinians. The increasing desire of Labor Zionists to annex the West Bank threw increasing doubt on the premises of Labor Zionist ideology—its focus on Jewish labor, a Jewish state, and democracy. Clearly, one or more of these premises would have to go if the West Bank were to be annexed. For either the Palestinians would have to get full economic, cultural, and political rights, in which case the "Jewish" state would become binational—or they would have to be governed against their will or forcibly expelled, in which cases democracy would be drastically limited or denied. But Labor Zionism was not able either to reject annexation or to revise its own assumptions.

Yet Israel was able to win itself a strong military alliance with the United States that disguised the erosion of its internal political self-confidence and of its external political support. What emerged therefore was an extraordinary brittle situation: seemingly strong, but in danger of being shattered.

Fifth, Labor Zionism proved incapable of building a political base among the most obviously working-class element of Israel—the Sephardic/Oriental Jewish immigrants. Since Labor was responsible for and controlled the "establishment" institutions of the state, it was unable to act vigorously and insurgently on behalf of the working-class interests of the Easterners; both in its gut and in its head it rejected their culture as Levantine and regressive. The Eastern Jewish working class therefore increasingly defined the Labor establishment as its class and cultural enemy, and turned to the right for access to Israeli politics. As Eastern numbers grew, so did the number of Likkud votes.

Sixth, the major groupings of Labor Zionism rejected religious Jewish thought, culture, and practice on principle—and viewed Labor Zionism as the demystified expression of Jewish peoplehood. Labor Zionism was not prepared for the survival and revival of Jewish religion and did not expect what in fact happened: Jewish tradition made deep appeals not only to the formally religious but to some of those who had been sundered from their traditional culture by the destruction of European Jewry and their transplanting from Europe or the Arab countries to Israel. Moreover, one version of religious thought (embodied in Gush Emunim) provided one of the few ideological rationales and militant commitment to continued Israeli possession of the West Bank—at a point when the need for such a rationale and such militance was deeply felt.

To all this, Labor Zionism had as an answer only the short-run expedient of making political bargains with religiously defined Orthodox political parties. It did not open itself up to religious thought and reexamination, did not try to rethink its roots in or connections with Judaism, and did not encourage the emergence of creative or progressive religious thought that might have incorporated Labor Zionist ideas and approaches (except in such tiny ways as the kibbutz cultural magazine *Shdemot*). Quite the contrary—for its political arrangements with the National Religious Party precluded this, and indeed gave a monopoly over religious expression to the most rigid and regressive religious institutions that then trained a generation of Orthodox youth who were contemptuous of this very coalition with Labor.

Thus those Israelis who felt themselves to be in covenant with God, or who were deeply moved by the traditional religious celebration of the life and nature cycles, or who viewed their attachment to the Land as religiously based, or who found the traditional practices helpful in protecting their sense of family and community—all these were ignored by Labor Zionism. They had to choose between utter secularism and a frozen Orthodoxy. More and more of them chose the latter.

Seventh and finally, Labor Zionism expected Diaspora Jewry to wither away—first ideologically, then physically. It expected the Diaspora to redefine itself as simply and entirely a support group for Israel, and its members to choose either to migrate to Israel or to assimilate into the non-Jewish community. But the leaders of the American Diaspora (and others as well), while taking on the role of support for Israel, increasingly insisted that theirs was also an authentic and self-standing Jewish community.

To cope with this development, Labor Zionism would have had to be prepared to view the Diaspora as not only a political and financial resource, but an intellectual and ideological partner. That is, Labor Zionism would have had to affirm the Diaspora as in principle a desirable special aspect of Jewish peoplehood, with its special role to play in building Jewish culture, giving political advice, making political decisions, and so on. But the strain this would have put on Labor Zionist ideology—especially on the negation of the *galut*, the Exile—would evidently have been too great. So the Diaspora was treated as a useful support in money and political power, but all decision making was reserved for Israeli institutions and the Diaspora was told that its main purpose was to support Israeli decisions—in effect, to support the Labor Zionist government's policies.

The problem this created was that when Labor Zionist policy got out of touch with reality (as in the areas noted above), the Diaspora was systematically not encouraged to present serious criticisms or force reconsideration, let alone empowered to take initiatives in policy that would affect Israel.

Of course, the treatment of the Diaspora in this way would not have been possible had the Diaspora not acquiesced. In regard to the American Diaspora (by far the most numerous, wealthy, and powerful) this acquiescence was rooted in the absorption of most of the community into "Jewish liberalism" as its ideology-in-practice.

"Jewish liberalism" is not a formal Jewish ideology like Labor Zionism, religious Orthodoxy, or Bundism, but it nevertheless gives basic impetus to American Jewish behavior. It stems from an American-style political and cultural liberalism that views modern capitalism as a basically creative and productive social system, but looks for checks and balances to correct the excesses of corporate capitalism. Among these are limited social interventions by the national government. Jewish liberalism views organizations of workers and consumers as useful both to strengthen this check-and-balance role of the national government and to confront corporate excesses directly in nongovernmental action. It views the broad American culture that is communicated by family child rearing, mass media, and the schools as basically useful in strengthening individual talents and self-fulfillment; but also views a plurality of ethnic and religious cultures as a necessary corrective to the most violent, alienating, uprooting, and competitive aspects of the general culture—by providing some sense of "roots," community responsibility, and spiritual wholeness. The tendency of Jewish liberalism to celebrate this arrangement is strengthened by—or perhaps originally was based on—its perception of American freedom of religion as an unprecedented offer from a non-Jewish culture to see Jews as full citizens.

Within this basic liberal framework the Jewish-liberal community sees its own Jewishness as exactly one of the "necessary correctives" to the general culture and the general polity. Culturally, it provides moments of spiritual awe and celebration and connects individuals to their family histories. Politically, Jewish liberalism tends to read Jewish tradition so as to strengthen an anti-military, anti–big business, pro-labor, pro-consumer, pro-poor people, pro-social service orientation. The defense of Jewish rights and Jewish interests through united community political action is seen as a fulfillment of American liberalism on the level of both individual rights and pressure-group self-assertion.

For about one generation from the mid-thirties to the mid-sixties, this ideology of "Jewish liberalism" both encouraged and justified most American Jews in their remarkable upward social and economic mobility, which was not so much communal as multi-individual; provided them with a socially and politically more acceptable world view than the previous generations' Jewish socialism or intense religious Orthodoxy; and made it possible for them to make useful political alliances with labor, Black, Catholic, liberal-Protestant, and middle business blocs. Thus it was successful in American life for about the same period in which Labor Zionism was most successful in Israel.

Jewish liberalism also proved successful as an explanation for the relationship between American Jews and Israel. Using this model as their Jewish "orientor," most American Jews have seen Israel as a more intense but basically similar acting out of "Jewish liberalism". Its Jewish culture was seen as a more intensely Jewish variant of Western culture—but basically a part of Western culture. Its Labor Party government (in power till 1977) was seen as a much more vigorously pro-labor, pro-social service variant of Western capitalism—not as a revolutionary threat to capitalism. Israel's self-assertiveness among the nations was seen as a stronger version of Jewish self-confidence as a legitimate pressure group among all the American pressure groups. Moreover, the American-Israeli alliance closed the circle of American Jewry's ability to see Israel as a more vigorous version of itself—and therefore as a reinforcement, not a threat, to its American liberalism. Indeed, this sense of Israel as a more intense and vigorous version of American Jewry, combined with American Jewry's sense of its own Jewishness as marginal to and integrated into its Americanism, encouraged most American Jews to define their Jewishness chiefly through Israel and their support for Israel.

But by 1977 there was a growing sense that this ideology was failing. First of all, Jewish liberalism was failing in its ability to explain or improve American life. By the mid-sixties the United States was carrying on a war that most American Jews found repellent. Racial integration had proved both extremely difficult and unsatisfying. Cities were rotting. In 1968 the combination of Vietnamese, Black and white youth uprisings, assassinations, police riots, and the gold/dollar crisis cracked the optimistic assumptions that underlay Jewish liberalism. By the mid-seventies at least one halfhearted effort toward presidential dictatorship had been dismantled, but no permanent institutional changes or safeguards had been achieved. The permanently unemployed had become a sizable part of the society; the environment was becoming increasingly poisonous and lethal; most incomes were rising more slowly than prices so the average standard of living was falling; more families were collapsing and violence was increasing. Yet the profits of global corporations continued or rose. Federal social-service programs, labor unions, Black political organizers, ecology activists, campus intellectuals, public interest lawyers—the mainstays of liberalism—all seemed incapable of turning the tide. The whole New Deal approach to federal action seemed more and more useless or even dangerous. The one continuing forward wave of liberal motion—the women's movement—seemed to be reaching a dead end, if measured by traditional liberal yardsticks. For example, equal access to jobs became a dead end as it became clear there were fewer and fewer jobs; equal access to social services became a dead end as service organizations went bankrupt.

Second, Jewish liberalism was failing as an orientation for particular Jewish rights and interests. A general sense of social, cultural, and economic limitations, of narrowed horizons, led to a more defensive ethnic response. The combined effect of a belief that the social and economic "pie" was not increasing and the demand from the Black community for a larger slice of the pie was a fear that the Jewish slice might be reduced and that the structure of individual rights of opportunity based on merit—a structure that had benefited Jews—might be undermined. So major Jewish organizations and media began pointing away from a social-service orientation toward a more conservative one, away from alliances with the Black community, the more militant labor unions, antimilitarist organizations, and vigorous environmentalists. And the fear of danger to Israel under siege led, slowly and with great ambivalence, toward support for a larger military budget. Feeling threatened by an upsurge in Klan and Nazi organizing, some Jews questioned their commitment to such an embodiment of Jewish liberalism as the American Civil Liberties Union. Feeling threatened by affirmative action on behalf of Blacks and Hispanics, some Jewish organizations mobilized against some of the main goals of Black and Hispanic organizations.

And finally, the incorporation of Israel into Jewish liberalism became increasingly questionable. The victory of a coalition made up mostly of conservative businessmen, expansionist nationalists, and Orthodox institutionalists in the Israeli election of 1977 made the decription of Israel as a more vigorous version of American Jewish liberalism somewhat harder to accept—though many viewed the election as simply a demonstration of the strength of Israeli democracy in permitting the old Opposition to take power. The increasing sense of collision between the policies of the American and Israeli governments made many American Jews uneasy not only in their sense of self-defense but also in their deeper sense of "rightness" and "order" in the world. And even the first serious possibilities of a stable peace in the Middle East, arising in 1977, raised qualms in the hearts of some American Jews about how their Jewishness and their support for Israel would be played out if the permanent war emergency were to end and the conventional campaigns of financial and political support became less important.

Thus many American Jews began to feel themselves more and more uneasy both about the directions of United States government policy toward Israel (and even policy affecting American Jews, in matters of race relations like affirmative action) and about certain aspects of Israeli government policy—especially the religious, economic, and foreign policies of the Likkud government.

Even more troubling, they also found themselves more and more uncomfortable about what ground to stand on in order to think about and criticize these policies—

Their ground as Americans or as liberals? But this was inadequate in the light of their special concern for Israel. Indeed, if they consulted *only* the national interests of the United States or the values of universalist, individualist liberalism, they uneasily felt that they might find answers that would not be acceptable in the light of their special concern for Israel.

Then their ground as Jews? But what ground would this mean?

Secular Jewish nationalism? But what legitimacy did they have to criticize the views of Jewish national interests held by the government chosen by the citizens of the Jewish state? And if this were the basis for their critique of United States policy, why should the United States government care?

One or another version of religious Judaism? In theory this might have been an authentic platform from which to address and criticize both the United States and Israeli governments, but in fact Judaism rarely governed their "secular" thoughts, and certainly was rarely brought to bear on politics. Even the methodology to do so was lacking.

In short, American Jews found a vacuum at the heart of their Jewish liberalism—a vacuum that left them no adequate basis to understand or to act upon the social problems affecting either Israel or the United States.

What should be where the vacuum is? What are the crucial functions to be fulfilled for American Jews and for Israel by an ideology that might incorporate the best insights of both Labor Zionism and Jewish liberalism, and go forward to meet the needs that these ideologies are not yet meeting?

The first question to be met by such an ideology is whether there is any point to having it. Would a united Jewish peoplehood serve the needs of real Jews in their many various life-situations? From the standpoint of normal social analysis, there is no way to answer this question simply yes or no. (From a transcendent standpoint, there is an immediate answer, but we will take this up later.) The only way to answer is conditionally. "*If* we make Jewish peoplehood meaningful, it will be." Most Jews in the present world feel that there are some positive, some useless, and some negative aspects to conscious, united Jewish peoplehood. To the extent that an ideology of Jewish identification meets direct needs, it will have a point. Those who feel that a reformulation of Jewish peoplehood has no point may very well be reacting to the present deficiencies of Labor Zionism and Jewish liberalism in meeting real needs.

Even accepting the necessity of a conditional answer, we must recognize that the most poignant aspect of this question is whether any ideology at all can unite a people when that people is in the strange situation of being *both* concentrated in its own land and dispersed into many other lands, *both* able to rule and shape its own society and subject to the rules and shapes of many different societies? This question may be called the problem of the "horizontal" dimension in unifying the Jewish people.

The most obvious need that arises from this strange concentrated/dispersed reality of the Jewish people is the need for collective Jewish defense. Many Jews believe that in different parts of the world, Jews are under attack largely because they are Jews, and therefore will find their best help from other Jews. This belief may be the most primitive, but is almost certainly the most widely held and most strongly expressed element of a desire among Jews for a strong, united, Jewishly conscious Jewish people. If Israel were to secure a stable peace, this need would be considerably reduced— but would probably not disappear.

But to go on forever with anti-Semitism as the chief reason for reasserting Jewishness seems to many Jews a profoundly boring and deadening way to exist. To them—and they are likely to be the most creative and life-seeking Jews—it is important to know whether there is any internal, intrinsic usefulness in being a Jewishly focused Jewish people.

It is relatively easy to find among particular groups of Jews one or another aspect of Jewishness that feels intrinsically rewarding, but it is harder to find one that is widely shared. Yet there is one profound need that is widely shared. There is a universal human need to have values on which to act. Jews, simply as individuals, have that need. And if there is a Jewish people at all, even to act in self-defense that people needs to have a source of the values out of which to act. If an ideology of Jewish peoplehood can suggest a Jewish source of such values, that ideology will make itself useful to Jews as individuals and to the Jews as a people. Moreover, it will create a reason for there to continue to be a Jewish people.

Indeed, there is one major arena in which the need for a Jewish source of Jewish values is paramount and urgent: the arena of political action and governmental policy. That arena is paramount precisely because the newest fact in Jewish life is that the Jewish people has entered the political and governmental arena, as a people, in ways unheard of two generations ago. The Jewish people has a sovereign national state; the American Jewish community is vigorously active in American politics and policy; yet there has been little effort put into developing the policies of Israel or American Jewry from a Jewish source of Jewish values.

So the second major question of Jewish peoplehood, what may be called the problem of a "vertical" dimension, is whether there is any Jewishly rooted source for values by which the Jewish people can shape its own behavior, institutions, and policies, and by which the Jews of any country can judge the policies of any government—that of their own country or of Israel, or of any other.

Let us first examine the "horizontal" question: What is to be the relationship between that part of the Jewish people which governs itself in the land of Israel and controls a national state there, and those parts that live in the Diaspora as minorities among other peoples? It would be easy for these radically different life situations to draw such communities more and more apart, especially if the need for mutual protection becomes less intense because peace is built in the Middle East and none of the Diaspora communities comes under a threat to its physical existence. What, therefore, will hold these different parts of the Jewish people together?

The first requirement is that all the parts respect each other as authentic, vital, and necessary parts of the Jewish people. The differences between them must come to be seen as fruitful and useful. The state of Israel and the Diaspora must come to see each other and act toward each other as dialectical and complementary parts of the Jewish whole.

What is the nature of this complementarity?

In Israel, Jews control their own institutions and have been able to create an atmosphere in which the social calendar, the dominant symbols, the language, and other social forms do not run counter to a Jewish culture—and sometimes give positive encouragement to it. On the other hand, precisely by controlling their own institutions the Jews of Israel have involved themselves in the classic problems of institutional establishments—the rigidification and blindness of those institutions, their rigidification in basically the same shapes they had when they were set up or when they won control over their own turf. Indeed, the rigidity of Israeli institutions and culture has even narrowed the vision of most of Israel's critical and oppositionist groups—for where the Zionist State already exists, it is harder to call for, or even freshly imagine, the Zionist Revolution.

In America, Jewish institutions are much weaker and Jews have to swim against the tide to shape their own lives Jewishly. But it is also true that American Jews, precisely because their Jewish institutions do not have the greater power over their lives that Israeli institutions have over Israeli lives, have not had to deal with powerful, rigidified Jewish institutions. They are therefore able to be much more fluid, to reshape Jewish institutions or to create new Jewish forms outside the institutions. Moreover, in a postghetto Diaspora like that in America, this fluidity and creativity are increased by the constant encounter of the Jewish community with universalist Christianity, liberalism, and radicalism. The trade off is assimilation—but the payoff, and sometimes the direct result of the shock of feared assimilation, is greater social and intellectual creativity, invention, and reinforcement within Jewish life.

These two kinds of Jewish socieities—the one based on stability/rigidity and the other on fluidity/looseness—may very well complement each other in meeting the needs of the world Jewish people. Indeed, as complementary forms the two may very well need each other—not temporarily or for tactical political and financial reasons—but permanently, organically, and in principle. If they can both come to recognize this reciprocal need, instead of seeing one form as the definitive shape of the Jewish future, it will be possible to build a new kind of relationship between the Diaspora and Israel, and for both to benefit in new ways.

But complementarity cannot be felt or experienced unless the "other" is perceived as sharing deeply some aspects and identity of the "self." A worldwide Jewish people requires a texture of Jewishness, an agreed-on process for making decisions, a shared language in the figurative sense of a set of basic ideas for dialogue, discussion, and analysis, and perhaps a shared language in the literal sense as well. What is this "Jewish texture" of the world Jewish people to be?

This question can only be answered in the vertical dimension. What Jewish source of values can there be through which all parts of the Jewish people can simultaneously meet the universal need for values and recreate the Jewishness of individual Jews and of the Jewish people?

It seems to me there is only one such possible source. That is the world view which asserts that the Jewish people stands partly outside the boundaries of all nation-states (even its own) *not only* because of its geographical and political distribution *but also* because it stands in a covenant with God and in a continuing wrestle with the Jewish heritage. That world view holds that all authentic expressions of Jewish peoplehood (including "religion," "culture," and "nationality") are expressions, interpretations, and constant reinterpretations of the people's collective covenant with God. That world view holds that even if individual Jews do not see themselves as standing in covenant with God, they can still see the whole Jewish people doing so, and can even contribute to the process of wrestling with the Jewish heritage which claims a covenant with God.

I am not suggesting it would be easy to reunite the Jewish people on this basis. There are profound historical reasons why that world view—which did unite the Jewish people three centuries ago—is not now shared by all Jews. But I am suggesting that it is the only *possible* approach; that it should be encouraged by Jews who see the absence of any source of values as a major human problem afflicting many Jews; that it should be encouraged by all Jews who desire the revitalization of Jewish peoplehood.

To renew Jewish peoplehood on this basis would require the reappropriation and reincorporation of both secular Zionism and Jewish liberalism as "macromidrashim" on Jewish tradition—neither more nor less. In the sense that ordinary midrash is a deeply serious though sometimes playful piercing of the surface of a particular Torah text, so these whole sets of ideas should be seen as a midrashic development from a certain strand of Jewish tradition.

Some might argue that it is precisely the secular bent of Labor Zionism and Jewish liberalism that has encouraged the present ideological vacuum and the present weakness of the Jewish heritage as a source for Jewish values—especially in the political sphere—and that Labor Zionism and Jewish liberalism are in principle not able to be reconnected with the religious tradition and process. I do not agree. Indeed, I think these ideologies sprang from the tradition even as they rejected it, and can be reconnected with it despite their secularist biases. What is more, it is necessary to reconnect them because they have successfully shown that it is possible for Jews to act effectively, as a people, in the world and national political arenas. Rather than reversing our steps three centuries to a period when the religious tradition informed all of daily life but Jews had little impact on public policy, we must go forward by incorporating what secular ideologies have accomplished or celebrated into a renewed Torah process. "Make *new* our days *as of* old."

Let us test out the possibilities by looking at Labor Zionism in this way. A major strand of the prophets, beginning with Moses and continuing with Isaiah, Jeremiah, and Ezekiel, looks forward to God's restoration of the Jewish people to the land of Israel, the recognition of God and the abandonment of idolatry by all peoples, and the onset of God's age of peace and justice. Drawing on and extending the humanist line of Jewish thought that might be said to descend from the line in Psalms, "The Heavens are the Heavens of God, but the earth He has given to the children of Adam," Labor Zionism secularized this prophetic tradition. It ignored other elements of the tradition—its insistence on the hallowing of time as well as place, on the hallowing of everyday life, on the importance of prayer, ceremony, and symbol. Thus Labor Zionism focused with almost a single-minded vision on restoration of the Jewish people to the land, there to create a state of social justice so clear that it could act as a model to all nations.

What distinguished Labor Zionism from what were in their time such other new departures in Jewish thought as Maimonidean philosophy, Kabbalah, Hassidism, and Reform Judaism, was that it refused to see itself as a midrash on the Bible and instead saw itself as a substitute for the Bible. Not that Zionism ignored the Bible; it drew on the Bible but not in the Bible's own terms, as Divine revelation—but rather as a record of the people's most intense and triumphant moments. In this way Zionism could stand outside the Bible while at the same time drawing directly on its intense energy. For as Simon Rawidowicz has pointed out, the Labor Zionist attachment to the prophetic texts and their sense of direct revelations from God gave force to the Zionist vision that "superhumanly human" energy could transform the world, redeem the land, and free the Jewish people.

In reaching back in this special way to what Rawidowicz called the "first house" of Jewish thought, Labor Zionism utterly rejected the "second house"—the Talmud, the archetypal "macromidrash" of Jewish thought. The Talmud was the work of the rabbis who had to deal with the collapse of the ancient Israelite world under the onslaught of Hellenism. What they did was develop and hallow a process of Torah-study and midrash by which God's word was sensed through human discussion of the meaning of direct revelation in the Torah. On the few occasions when direct Divine revelation intervened among the rabbis of the Talmudic Period, they firmly put it aside—and voted among themselves instead.

This approach to God's will sacrificed the explosive intensity of Sinai and Isaiah, but carried great staying power across the boundaries of time and space. Indeed, the Talmud became the "portable constitution" for the Jewish people, enabling it to stay united across all political and cultural boundaries. But precisely its usefulness in Exile made it unpalatable to Zionists who intended to end the Exile. Indeed, many of them saw the Talmud and rabbinic tradition as precisely the embodiment of the contemptible, servile, enervated "galut mentality" they intended to root out. Its staying power did not seem to them a useful trade off for the explosive energy they knew was necessary in order to build the Jewish state. And they believed that since the Talmud presents the Bible through its own midrashic screen, any use of the Talmud was bound to screen off the direct energy of the Bible from their direct access.

The Zionists saw one truth—the need for the direct intense energy inherent in the Bible. But they did not see (or perhaps did not care about) a second: that the development of an authentically Jewish culture after the creation of the Jewish state would require renewing the Jewish people's connection with the Talmud and with the midrashic, halakhic, and aggadic processes that stem from the Talmud. What they feared was imprisonment within the Talmud; in order to escape that, they thought it necessary to smash the Talmud. They did not imagine the possibility of drawing on the Talmud without being imprisoned in it. And indeed, when Labor Zionism was being crystallized this may have been an impossible notion—since all Talmudic thought also assumed that if one used the Talmud at all, it provided the only path to the Bible.

Now, after a generation in which Conservative Judaism has helped to open new perspectives on Talmud and the rabbinic tradition, it is possible to imagine a triangle of energy: the Jewish people today, the Bible, and the Talmud. With such an approach it might be possible to develop a new macromidrash sensitive both to the raw God-energy of Bible and the mediated God-energy of Talmud, and especially sensitive both to the Talmud's process and method for responding to biblical text in the light of a transformed society, and to the Talmud's open-ended content of defining a Jewish culture. In such a macromidrash the best insights of Labor Zionism could be subsumed, at the same time being reincorporated within the Torah process in a broad sense. And in this way Labor Zionism would find itself having to struggle with God and with how to renew Jewish culture in its connection-making between God and work, the family, food, and so on.

Where would such an approach lead liberalism? It would replace liberal individualism (on the one hand) and liberal statism (on the other) with a focus on community. At the heart of American Jewry's concerns there would be the intensification of the communality of the American Jewish community (not chiefly its strengthening as an externally oriented political pressure group). The two major contributions of American Jewish liberalism to Jewish practice—the element of pluralism in forms of Jewishness and the element of the desirability of individual fulfillment—would need to be reincorporated into Jewish tradition in the way I have suggested the useful elements of Labor Zionism would be reincorporated. Individualism and pluralism would cease to be seen as autonomous values. Instead, one aspect of the new macromidrash would be a fruitful tension between Jewish pluralism and the united Jewish people, betwen individual self-fulfillment and communal obligations—all seen as part of the Torah process of renewing and reinterpreting the covenant between God and the Jewish people.

The reestablishment of the vitality and communality of the Jewish community as its chief concerns would benefit American Jewry both in its relation to Israel and its relation to the problems of American society. Vis-à-vis Israel, the entrance of American Jewry into the midrashic process of reexamining all aspects of Jewish practice and policy in the light of biblical and rabbinic sources would strengthen ties with the Jewishness of Israel (and strengthen what is most creatively Jewish within Israel). It would also provide an authentic Jewish basis from which to judge whether particular policies of the Israeli government are wise.

For example, what does the Jubilee tradition teach that modern Jews in a Jewish state might do in regard to concentrated wealth alongside grinding poverty? In regard to the land, the earth itself? In regard to the family and the clan? In regard to the cycle of the generations? In regard to the stranger residing in the land? What would an open encounter with the sources on tzedakah teach about the nature of Israeli social services? What should be the behavior of a Jewish army—toward officers and soldiers, toward civilians, toward enemies, toward prisoners?

Vis-à-vis America, the new outlook would provide a base from which to reexamine perhaps the most critical failing of American society: the absence of community and its low priority as a social goal. In regard to specific social issues, the new outlook would provide a process whereby the Jewish community could wrestle with the deposit of Jewish tradition, biblical and rabbinic, to decide on its own stance toward particular proposals and developments in American politics and society.

For example, how would we view the issue of "affirmative action" if we saw it in the light, not of increasing Jewish upward mobility, but of strengthening Jewish community life and the community life of other peoples in America? We might say that the strongest need of American Jewry is now the internal strengthening of Jewish culture and of the community's ability to use it and wrestle with it. We might say that to this end, we should encourage the brightest young Jews to integrate Jewish knowledge and culture into their professional work and to pursue Jewish cultural studies and creativity wherever possible, instead of encouraging them to pursue swift upward "social mobility" and financial affluence away from Jewishly focused life. We might therefore argue for training Jewish M.D. candidates in consciously Jewish situations and with a deliberate aim that they learn as part of their physicianship Jewish tradition; or we might urge them to seek more Jewishly focused professions. Such an analysis would then come back to the affirmative-action issue from a new standpoint, perhaps seeing the needs of Black, Hispanic, and Jewish communities as complementary rather than competitive, discouraging the upwardly mobile track for all three of them.

What approach toward the problem of American neighborhoods and cities would we learn from an open-ended encounter with Jewish tradition on these issues? How would unemployment be dealt with? Nuclear energy? Nuclear weaponry?

I am not suggesting that I know what answers would emerge if we asked these questions—or even that Jews would agree on the answers, any more than they did in the debates recorded in the Babylonian Talmud. But there could be majorities achieved and decisions taken—and they would be based on authentically Jewish sources and processes. Thus American Jews who had joined in the process of creating new Jewish life-paths from wrestling-together of Jewish sources and the modern Jewish situation would be able to face any public policy issue with an authentic response as Jews. If the issue were one in which Israeli and American policy collided, Jews would respond not as "overseas Israelis" facing America, nor as "American liberals" facing Israel, but as Jews—with a responsibility to the whole Jewish people, to the whole Jewish tradition, and to God, weighing the policies of all governments by that measure.

The process I am suggesting is analogous to what the seven centuries of Jews from 200 B.C.E. to 500 C.E. did when they acted out and wrote down the Talmud. Why do we need to undertake such a profound responsibility? Because the earthquake we feel, the result of the modernist upheaval, is similar to the earthquake they faced in the life of the Jewish people—the Hellenistic/Roman conquest, culminating in the destruction of the Temple, the decimation of Judaeans, and the dispersion of the surviving Jews.

In the last generation, the victory of modernism culminated in three radically different events for which the community and its traditions were utterly unprepared: the Nazi destruction of the people and the culture that were the seedbed of the largest, most devoted, and most knowledgeable community of traditional Jews; the creation of a modern nation-state controlled by Jews and located in the land of Israel; and the flowering of a totally new kind of Diaspora in which Jews seem to have full permission to be both citizens and Jewish.

Moreover, our world is one in which worldwide annihilation of the

human race and life itself are achievable; in which instant communication between any two human beings anywhere is possible; in
which . . . fill in the blank with almost anything.

The world we live in is thus so utterly different from that in which
the Talmud was our portable constitution that it is clear we need a
new such effort. Not only the content but even the process of our
"Talmud" will have to be different; for example, not an elite of
rabbinic adepts but the whole community will be part of the discussions that work out our new life-practice. But in a higher sense,
both the content and the process of the Talmud is what we need: the
content in many areas where the very texture of Jewish culture
grows from Talmud, and the process in the sense that encounter
between our life situation and the Bible is the Talmud's most basic
process.

8. Kings, Prophets, and the Children of Abraham

It was early morning on the second day of Rosh Hashanah in 1982. I was having a cup of breakfast tea at a farm and retreat center outside Philadelphia, where more than ninety Jews had gathered to celebrate the birthday of the world. The rabbi who had gathered these retreatants together beckoned me aside.

"Somebody in the kitchen went into town this morning and ·bought the Sunday paper," he said. "He read it and then he brought it to me. Look."

And I started to read a long, long article, the lead on page 1, the first news of the massacre of hundreds of unarmed Palestinians at the camps of Sabra and Shatila in West Beirut. The story described how Lebanese "Christian" Phalangists had murdered infants, women, old men, teen-age boys. Described it graphically. Said Israeli soldiers, with military control over the camp area, stood in earshot and eyeshot of the camps, and did not intervene until hundreds had died.

I began to tremble. The rabbi said hoarsely, "We have to deal with it. It would be a *chillul haShem*, a hollowing-out of the holy Name of God, to ignore this on Rosh Hashanah. Yesterday was Shabbos so we could not blow the shofar. This noon, when we get to the second round of shofar blowing—for *Zichronot*, Remembrance—I want to deal with this. Will you begin it, explain about it?"

I thought. On Rosh Hashanah we read from the Torah two passages: One story on how Abraham at God's command sent out into the desert his older son Ishmael, ancestor of the Arab peoples. How Ishmael and his mother Hagar almost died of thirst, were saved by God at the last moment. And the other story on how Abraham, at

God's command, took up onto a mountaintop his younger son Isaac, ancestor of the Jewish people, and raised a knife to kill him—until at the last moment God intervened to save him. I thought. I remembered that my name in Hebrew, the name by which I am called up to read the Torah, is "Abraham Isaac Ishmael." I thought how within myself there are the almost-killer father and both almost-murdered sons: all the actors, Jew and Arab. So I agreed.

And when the time came to blow the shofar for Remembering, I said that "Remembering" required faithfulness to the facts. I read the newsstory—all of it—as part of the service. By the time I read the eighth paragraph, people were crying. At the end I said that the shofar was a wail, a cry, to Heaven—and that if we could wail and cry, then and only then would God cry with us—instead of crying out against us. I said we could do midrash for hours, but midrash was not the point. I stopped.

The rabbi spoke. He said he was ashamed—ashamed that he was too polite to scream. He said that the dead child with the crushed skull in Shatila could have been his year-old son—and then he began to cry, and finally indeed to scream: "Gewallt," a scream that shattered walls.

We talked. Someone said that if, as Jewish mysticism teaches, all souls renew their lives and live again, then these dead were not really dead. We did not need to cry so bitterly. The rabbi stirred: "Maybe," he said. "Maybe. But you are trying to jump over the pain, the grief, the rage, the scream—to consolation. Do not jump. Scream first. Then maybe there will come consolation. Maybe."

Someone said the story was all lies, lies from a world seething with hatred for the Jews. "You will see," he said. "They, the world, will blame us, not the Phalange. Our soldiers are heroes of decency— heroes of protecting civilians. We did not do this thing, did not condone it. But they will blame us."

We talked about what it would mean for all of us to add "Ishmael" or "Hagar" to our names. We talked about what it would mean to say the mourners' Kaddish for these dead and to add, where the prayer asks that God send peace "for all Israel," that God send also peace "for all Ishmael." We talked about what it would mean to see the

Shatila and Sabra massacre as a pogrom, like the pogroms that Jews used to suffer from Tsarist police and Russian mobs. We talked about how we could deal with anti-Semites who might twist whatever we might say to fit into their hatred of the Jewish people. We talked about what it would mean for Jews, for us, to meet with Palestinians and Arabs here, in America. We talked about what it would mean for American Jews to take more responsibility for encouraging Arab-Israeli reconciliation. We cried. We prayed. And we blew the shofar.

In the middle of the next week, in the midst of the Days of Turning between Rosh Hashanah and Yom Kippur when Jews are supposed to turn away from their misdeeds and turn back to the path of decency and holiness, the Israeli Knesset voted to uphold the government's refusal to create an independent judicial commission of inquiry into the massacre. But all over the Jewish world, spontaneously, Jews rose up to demand an independent inquiry. In Israel, about 400,000 people—about one-fifth of the entire adult population—marched to make the same demand. So the government reversed itself.

Never in the state of Israel's history had there been such events. And never in the age-old history of the Jewish people had there been such a Days of Turning—ten such days of agony and pain, efforts to understand, efforts to know what repentance was authentically required and what was only being demanded by those who had no love for God, Torah, or the Jewish people

During that ten-day period, the days when Jews as individuals have for thousands of years confronted their own misdeeds, made restitution to those they have hurt, and sought forgiveness from others and from God—in that period in 1982, the Jewish people as a collective body had to confront the questions: Had they *as a people*, through their chosen representatives, done or condoned dreadful misdeeds? Did they *as a people* need to make restitution and to seek forgiveness?

The Days of Turning in 1982 lit up like a great flash of lightning issues that most Jews had hitherto been experiencing in the dark. The issues go to the heart of what it means to regather two sets of holy sparks: the set of sparks that is involved in the ancient dialectic between kingship and prophecy, and the set of fallen sparks that were involved in the separation of Abraham's two sons from one another.

The timing of this trauma had a certain midrashic ring of truth about it. In 1982, the festival of Shavuot which commemorates the Giving of the Torah at Mount Sinai fell on May 28. The joyful fast of Yom Kippur, celebrating reunion with God after a period of painful self-examination, fell on September 27.

Between the two of them came Israel's invasion of Lebanon, the seige of Beirut, the Israeli government's instantaneous and total rejection of the American government's Reagan plan for making peace between Israel and Arabs, and massacre in the Sabra and Shatila camps. During this period there also occurred unprecedented mass demonstrations critical of the Israeli government by tens—even hundreds—of thousands of Israelis, and unprecedented public disagreements with the Israeli government by large American Jewish organizations. These events precipitated one of the deepest self-examinations and some of the most painful disagreements within the Jewish people in centuries—possibly millennia.

This period from Shavuot to Yom Kippur, according to the earliest memories of the Jewish people, was precisely the time of our archetypal internal agony—the agony of choosing between idolatry and holiness. That time span commemorates the Revelation at Sinai, our wandering into worship of the Golden Calf, our return to the path of holiness, and—on Yom Kippur—God's forgiving gift of the second set of Torah tablets.

So it was fitting that in 1982, in the period from Shavuot to Yom Kippur, the Jewish people experienced a major event in our evolving historical consciousness, a great internal agony to work out the meaning of our peoplehood. A great choice between Torah and idolatry.

One way to describe the "event" of 1982 is that the government of the Jewish state took a series of actions that a large minority of the Jewish people, in and out of Israel, viewed as unprecedented violations of Jewish ethics and Jewish good sense. The other is that a large minority of the Jewish people, in and out of Israel, took a series of public actions to criticize Israeli government decisions—even though the government saw these actions as unprecedented betrayals of Jewish solidarity and good sense.

Why do I put the story in both these ways? Because there is agreement among almost all Jews that the summer was extraordinary—but disagreement upon how to see its extraordinariness. Some have focused upon the pattern of the actions of the Israeli government as the extraordinary fact—extraordinary because they violated the usual norms of Jewish life; others have focused on the opponents' protests, describing *them* as the "event," the extraordinary fact—extraordinary because they violated the usual norms of Jewish life.

But neither "event" carries its special meaning without the other. It is the tension *between* the government and its opponents that is now the important event in the life of the Jewish people.

That tension is important not only for 1982 but for the whole next generation—perhaps for longer—because it recreates in a new way one of the most ancient tensions of Jewish peoplehood, the tension between King and Prophet.

This is not the tension between "politics" and "religion," or between "security" and "justice," or between "means" and "ends."

It is rather the tension between *two different ways* of seeing the interconnections of politics-and-religion, security-and-justice, means-and-ends.

One of these ways says that politics, security, and means are one sphere of life—the sphere that belongs to the King—and religion, justice, and ends are another sphere, the sphere of the Prophet. But this way of separated spheres is idolatrous. It is sometimes—but not always—the path that is walked by Kings.

The second path asserts that politics-and-religion are *one* sphere, security-and-justice are *one* sphere, means-and-ends are *one* sphere. This is the path of Torah. In it, on it, the Prophet and the King live not in separate spheres but in dynamic tension with each other. This second path is the one that is held by some Kings and all true Prophets.

In the postmodern life of the Jewish people, the creation of the nation-state of Israel represented the rebirth of the kingly attributes: the rebirth of an institutional form in which a leader (or a small group of leaders) could demand and enforce loyalty, support, and obedience from the whole Jewish people. The legitimacy of that demand for loyalty, support, and obedience came chiefly from sensing that the people willed it.

In ancient times, this popular mandate was asserted when David fought and worked tribe by tribe and region by region to wrest military and political support away from Saul. In our own generation, the popular mandate is asserted when the government of the state is elected.

Since 1948, the prophetic attributes have not been manifested or embodied with a clarity or strength comparable to that of the kingship. This is not to say there have been no prophetic voices. There have been—among small groups. But until 1982, large numbers of Jews had not moved themselves into the prophetic mode, into readiness to criticize a major governmental act on grounds that stand outside the popular mandate. And for that reason, the prophetic mode had, these almost forty years, not carried much weight in the public life of the Jewish people.

It is true that in the days of David and Ahab and Jezebel, the Prophets were few, unorganized, and stood on their own. But in those days even Kingship was far less mechanized and institutionalized, far more individualized, and far narrower in its scope of control over people and society, than it is today. So today a prophetic voice may have to call out from a larger base than a single person for it to be not only heard but listened to by the people. That may be true even though the irreducible individual is still the channel through which the prophetic insight enters the world.

The crucial relationship between King and Prophet is that both recognize each other's role as legitimate. The Prophet subjects the King to transcendent values, and does not accept even the excuse that the King has the support of the people to violate those values. But the Prophet knows that the King must govern.

It is true that one of the earliest prophets—Samuel—reminded the people that God is King, and that to have an earthly King is both idolatrous and self-destructive. When the people insisted, God and Samuel acquiesced. But the condition of their acquiescence was that the king be subject to God's will and to prophetic correction.

As for the King, he must respect and respond to the Prophet—without relinquishing the complex, constantly ambivalent tasks of governing. A bad King is not necessarily one who sins, but one who ignores the Prophet's challenge or treats the Prophet as a traitor. King David sinned when he sent Uriah to his death; what then made David the model of a good king was that he heard the Prophet Nathan's challenge and turned back to the true path.

If we are to learn from the analogy of King and Prophet, we will have to wrestle with one important change inside our own heads. We, as modern democrats, are used to thinking that a king may be a tyrant. But is it possible for a democratically elected government to be guilty of a dreadful public sin? And what if, through elections, the people endorse a dreadful act? Is it possible for "prophets" to speak, and be right, against the people's will?

Jews will face new questions, and will need to find new answers to such questions. Meanwhile, let us look at our recent experience in more detail. In 1982, the Likkud-led government of Israel gave a series of different reasons for sending first the air force and then the army into Lebanon: This was done, they said, . . . to retaliate for the terrorist attack on Ambassador Argov in London; to stop Palestine Liberation Organization (PLO) shellings of northern Israel; to stop all terrorist attacks on Israelis in and out of Israel; to break up the PLO; to liberate the Lebanese from Syria and the PLO so they could choose their own government; to achieve a peace treaty with Lebanon; to break the power of the Soviet Union in the Middle East by shattering its allies.

To do these jobs—all among the more or less normal tasks of kings—they created the context in which by Yom Kippur about 320 Israeli men and some undetermined number of Palestinian, Syrian, and Lebanese men, women, and children went to their deaths. (The number of dead continued to rise after Yom Kippur. If the number of Israeli dead alone were translated into American terms, it would mean about twenty-four thousand men killed in three months.) This also—this sacrifice of lives for political and diplomatic advantage—is about the normal behavior of "Kings." It was not ordinary behavior for the government of Israel, because never before had civilian populations suffered so greatly from Israeli actions, and always before, one of the reasons for risking Israeli lives by going to war had been the perception that the very existence of Israel was at stake. Nevertheless, one could argue with reasonable accuracy, and some did argue, that it was previous Israeli self-restraint that was remarkable and that the Begin-Sharon government did little or nothing more than many governments—Arab, Soviet, American, British— had done before.

But this argument did not appeal to the Jewish critics. Instead there were several levels of "Prophetic" challenge to the actions of the Begin-Sharon government of Israel. Tens of thousands of Israelis, in mass public rallies and hundreds of letters and conversations, argued that in the absence of any credible threat to Israel's existence or even any threat to sizable numbers of Israeli lives, there had been no sufficient reason for the deaths, or for risking the two most crucial Israeli security assets—the peace treaty with Egypt and the alliance with America. These critics argued that the real reasons for the invasion had been to break all Palestinian nationalist aspirations so as to make possible the annexation of the West Bank and Gaza and to establish Israeli control over Lebanese politics.

And what was wrong with these goals? The critics said that the Jewish people ought not to rule over another people—Palestinian or Lebanese—and that the Jewish people ought to have a decent respect for the opinions of humankind.

Ought to. For the sake of the Jewishness of the Jewish people. A transcendent reason, not embedded in ordinary kingly decision making. Not that the critics ignored political reality: they argued that ultimately, in the long run, the violation of these transcendent values would bring down on the heads of the Jewish people a harvest of ruin; what we sow, we shall reap. But they grounded their critique in a sense of Jewish obligation—that Jewish "Kings" ought not to act like other Kings.

When the Reagan plan was proposed (for a peace settlement in which Israel would trade most or all of the West Bank and Gaza for a peace treaty and security guarantees from Jordan) the Begin-Sharon government rejected it instantly and totally, refusing to treat it even as a basis for negotiations. There was another "prophetic" response—this one with even less precedent than the response to Sabra and Shatila. Such "establishment" American Jewish organizations as B'nai B'rith and the American Israel Public Affairs Committee (AIPAC) simply said that the Reagan plan *was* a useful basis for negotiations. The degree to which this was a break with the past should not be overlooked. B'nai B'rith and AIPAC did not criticize the Begin-Sharon government explicitly, but their own actions said loudly that on an issue which the elected government of Israel defined as a vital security question, American Jews were entitled to disagree in public—obligated to disagree, if they saw Israel's security in a different light. After that, who could honestly shout "treason" or "heresy" at any Jew who out of love for Israel debated what was best for Israel, concluded its government was deeply in error, and said so?

Yet even then, the tendency among many American Jews had been to close ranks in solidarity with the Begin government. On Rosh Hashanah, a high proportion of American rabbis directed their sermons only against the lies of the American mass media in criticizing Israel—not against the lies of the Israeli government, which clearly also falsified its motives for stage after stage of the invasion and which also issued falsified reports of low casualties, while the media were falsely reporting high casualties. And few of the rabbis spoke about, let alone against, the emerging Begin-Sharon policy toward Lebanon, the West Bank, and the Palestinian population in both places. Those sermons, with all their defensiveness and apologetics, were being given—as we later learned—at the same moment that hundreds of defenseless Palestinians were being murdered in Shatila and Sabra.

In response to that mass murder, the prophetic mode did finally swell to a mighty chorus. We must honor those who responded in this way; but we must also say, in all clarity, that the earlier silence and defensiveness helped make Shatila and Sabra happen. It is almost as if God, peeking at the sermons the rabbis had prepared for Rosh Hashanah, responded by hardening the hearts of certain Israeli officials—as well as hardening still harder the thick-sheathed hearts of Lebanese "Christian" Phalangists who had done much murdering already. It is almost as if God grimly hoped that a really horrendous event, *takke* on Rosh Hashanah itself, might jar those rabbis, and the whole Jewish people, into a prophetic response.

If so, the horror worked. The first "prophet" to respond to the Shatila and Sabra massacre (perhaps he deserves the quotation marks removed) was the anonymous Israeli soldier who responded to a Palestinian woman's shrieks of pain and grief by protesting to his commanding officer—not once, but again and again, in the face of being told "B'Seder. Its O.K." The next were the reporters—especially Zev Schiff of *Haaretz* and Hirsh Goodman of the *Jerusalem Post*, may their names be inscribed for a blessing—who saw clearly what was happening and reported it with honesty. (In one sense, to be a *navi*, an ancient prophet, was simply to see the naked truth, in all its levels, and to say it aloud—to be an extraordinarily good news reporter.)

Three or four hundred thousand Israelis marched in the streets, demanding not only that there be an independent inquiry but that Begin and Sharon resign. They argued that it is not necessary for one to be a deliberate criminal accomplice to mass murder, in order to be so abysmally ethically blind and stupid in permitting and encouraging it to happen that one is unfit for high office.

And—still far more weakly, but certainly at a greater strength than ever before in American Jewish life—American Jews publicly demanded an independent inquiry. Many of them also called for Begin's and Sharon's resignations, and some began listening with new seriousness to Israeli and American groups that were critical of official Israeli policy. On Yom Kippur many more rabbis did speak out, and clusters of their congregants who had never before raised questions began to debate.

So the prophetic voice spoke aloud. For the present "kings" of Israel the crucial question is whether they will listen to the present "prophets" of Israel. Will they respond and change—or will they ignore or even try to destroy the prophetic voices? Will the present kings of Israel act more like David or more like Ahab?

For the present "prophets" of Israel, there are several difficult questions. One is whether they can continue to voice their prophecy, indeed with a stronger, deeper bite, and still preserve their knowledge that kingship is also legitimate. Still remember that even illegitimate acts by a state do not destroy the legitimacy of that state itself as an expression of the people's self-determination. The new "prophetic" voices must keep reminding the world that wrongful acts by the government of Israel do not justify either anti-Semitism or calls to dismantle Israel—and yet not be infuriated or intimidated by rising anti-Semitism into abandoning their prophetic criticisms of Israeli policy.

Our "prophetic" voices also need to reexamine the sources of their message. Very few of them spoke explicitly of God or Torah. The Israeli Orthodox religious Zionists of *Oz v'Shalom* ("Strength and Peace") did, and so did some American rabbis who criticized the war or the massacre. But *Shalom Achshav* ("Peace Now"), B'nai B'rith, and AIPAC talked instead of "Jewish values," or even of "American-Israeli friendship." In a secularized society, this is not surprising. But is it enough?

"God" does not need to be lifted out of history and excluded from nature in order to be God. There are many moments in Torah, Talmud, and Kabbalah, not only in modern Jewish philosophers like Martin Buber or Mordecai Kaplan, when God appears in and through the voices and actions of human beings. So it might be argued that we can reasonably keep our attention on human values, human action, when we criticize our modern Kings. Yet I think it is important for *us* to be conscious that when we talk about the ultimate unity of menschlichkeit and seichel, decency and prudence, what-will-be with what-ought-to-be, we are hearing the God Whom the Prophets also heard. This consciousness accomplishes two things: it strengthens our sense of connection and continuity with the most ancient generations of the Jewish people. And it makes clear that our values are grounded not in any temporary situation or society but in our sense of ultimate reality. These goals will also be more achievable if we treat our own hard-won wisdom, our own tales and ethical commitments, as the newest layer of Torah. Not only do our ideas draw on the Torah of the last three thousand years, but they also become part of Torah that will go forward for the next three thousand years.

It therefore seems to me that for the sake of regathering the fallen, scattered sparks of Jewish peoplehood, the prophetic as well as the kingly forces must push themselves to understand how their thoughts and feelings stem from and connect with Torah.

So let me undertake this effort—for myself. It is clear that the underlying issue in the Lebanon War was the relationship of the Jewish people to the land of Israel, and to another people that lives in the same land and claims a profound relationship to it. How would I apply Torah to this question?

I read Torah to assert—

That God promised the Land of Israel to the people of Israel on permanent and irrevocable but intermittent "loan" (for "ownership" of that Land, like all land, belongs to God);

That Israel's actual possession of the Land has been (and may be) intermittent, because possession depends on how well Israel follows the commands of Torah to hallow the earth and human society;

That *every* intervening exile from the Land that is caused by Israel's failure, no matter how long the exile, will be followed by another chance;

That in our generation, the contemporary state of Israel is the form the Jewish people's continuing experiment in fulfilling Torah in the Land takes;

That Israel is commanded *also* to live among the nations, in order to learn from them and teach them; in order through dialogue-in-action to renew its own, and their, holiness and creativity.

These readings are not unusual in the Jewish community, though the last one among them is not universally accepted. But there is one more reading of Torah that far fewer people in the Jewish community would accept:

The Land is promised twice. In some sense God has also promised a relationship with the same land—maybe, but not necessarily, the same relationship—to another people: the children of Ishmael, in our generation represented by the Palestinian people.

God knows this is not traditional Jewish theology, yet I believe that in our era it has become truthful, Torah-faithful Judaism. And I believe it is crucial to our understanding of ourselves as *am segulah*, the vanguard people, for us to accept this troublesome belief.

Why would God promise the same land twice to two different peoples, even if the two promises are somewhat different?

And why do I say there are two promises?

First, the text of Torah (Gen. 16–17; 20–21). The story of the struggle between Abraham's two wives and their two sons—Hagar and Ishmael, Sarah and Isaac—is the paradigm of the struggle between Jews and Arabs. (According to the traditions of both peoples, the Jews are descendants, physically and spiritually, of Abraham, Sarah, and Isaac; the Arabs are, physically and, since the coming of Islam, spiritually as well, the descendants of Abraham, Hagar, and Ishmael.)

In that story, Sarah insists that for Isaac's good Ishmael and Hagar must leave the family. Abraham is troubled but God upholds Sarah's wishes. (We will come back to why the separation between the two brothers is necessary.) God promises to continue the covenant of Abraham through Isaac; but God also promises to make of Ishmael a great nation, and prophesies of Ishmael: He will be a wild jackass of a man (that is, a nomad); he will lift his fists against everyone and all will lift their fists against him; and finally—finally, finally! when? finally!—"he will dwell face to face with all his brothers."

Somehow, somewhen, Isaac and Ishmael must learn to live in each other's presence—after having been separated. Does this mean they will live in the same land? The verse, the prophecy, is not clear. Yet it is clear that in their own lifetimes the two are reconciled when Abraham dies (Gen. 25). They meet again at their father's grave in Hebron—the grave that in our own generation has become the scene of bitter contention, of raised fists and worse, between their descendants. And Isaac goes to live at the well that God had revealed for his brother, the "Well of the Living God Who Sees."

Why were the brothers separated? And how can they be reconciled?

To understand, we need to remember that Isaac was the younger son—and that over and over in the Book of Genesis there can be peace between brothers only when the younger, the weaker, has prevailed over the older, the more powerful. *Then* can come a reconciliation.

To understand, we also need to remember that Isaac's name (in Hebrew YiTzChaK) means "Laughing Boy." And we have to remember that when Sarah accuses Ishmael of "making sport with" or "mocking" Isaac (Gen. 21:9), the word she uses is "MiTza-CheyK"—from the same root of "laughing." *The same root.* The problem is not that the two brothers are so different; it is that they are so similar.

The difficulty is that Ishmael is a cloudy mirror to Isaac, and vice versa. The problem is that neither son can grow up to be "his own person" unless they can grow up separately. The danger is that their similarity will drive both of them crazy.

And that is what we see before us now, if we look at history as well as at the words of Torah. For the voice of God speaks not only in the letters on the scroll, but also in the thundering facts of history. So to say that God has promised the Land to both peoples is not only to quote a verse of Ishmael, but to say that when we examine history it is clear that both peoples *feel* and *act* committed to the Land.

Israelis and Palestinians are similar in that they love the same land. They are also similar in that they cannot—either of them—bear to recognize that the other *also* loves the land. That the other *also* has a claim to the land. That the other is more like them than different. Each of them seems to feel—"If the other *does,* I *don't.*" Neither seems able to grasp the possibility that the land has—somehow, "somewhy"—been promised twice.

And not only in relation to the land, but also in their experience of exile, there are some similarities. The Palestinians in their short exile have suffered a (milder) version of the torments that the Jews have suffered in their age-long exile. The Palestinians have even become the alternately upwardly mobile and downwardly victimized "Jews of the Middle East" (as many Arabs call them, with mixed respect, envy, and hatred—just as some Western Christians speak of the Jews).

Reconciliation? Living face-to-face? Let us come back to that after I explain how the history of modern Zionism fits into the picture I have sketched.

In the last century there have been many modern Zionisms. Some have been explicitly religious, others explicitly secularist and anti-religious. Some have been left-wing, others right-wing in their version of the new Jewish community they were building. Some were fraternal, others domineering in their outlook on the Palestinian Arabs.

All of them, even the ones that called themselves secular, drew on the religious-Jewish passion for the land of Israel. On the two millennia of Jewish prayers, three times a day, to return and there be permitted to build a holy society. On the knowledge that God's covenant with Israel had never been revoked and never would be— that the Diaspora was both an exile and an education, was both in order that the Jews could learn God's Teaching deeper and teach God's Teaching better. And the knowledge that someday the exile would end.

Is it possible for Jews to explain this passion to modern Christians, or Muslims—especially to leftists? Maybe. Try saying to them: Imagine—if you empathized with the Vietnamese during the American War against them—that the United States had "won." Had poisoned the land and decimated the people and driven out those who were left. The Vietnamese, as those Americans who met them recognized with wonder, loved their land with an awesome passion. How long would they have insisted on remembering it? How long would they have prayed, mourned, celebrated, walked, flown in efforts to return? How long before they would have stopped planning to return? *How long before others would have said they had no right to return?* Twenty years? One hundred? Five hundred? Two thousand?

And then say to them: The Roman Empire did that to the Jews. And the Jews remembered for two thousand years. And not only remembered. Planned. Acted.

It is true that others—Christians and Muslims especially, out of religious theories that they had supplanted the Jews—soon concluded that the Jews had lost any right to return. But that notion the Jews did not accept. Always, always, there were efforts to return.

To what end? So that the Jews should not remain forever *luft menschen,* "air people," floating above reality, full of hot air, "spiritual" without mattering to material life. For the Jewish vision has always been that the most soulful holiness did not matter unless it was applied to "matter"—to body. The command to share out all the wealth and let the land rest in the year of Jubilee—that command should not remain forever a lot of hot air blown across the lips of Torah scholars. Someday it must be *done,* and we need a land to do it with. Or if we fail, to fail because we had the chance and blew it.

And here we come to the heart of the Covenant, and why God promised the Land twice. God wanted, wants, the Jews to be a holy people, a kingdom all of priests——a "vanguard" people, you might say. A holy people that teaches by example all the peoples how to be holy peoples.

Such a people needs a land to be holy with. (That was why Martin Buber was a Zionist. Just as the Prophet Samuel did not want there to be an Israelite king, Buber did not, in the beginning, want there to be a Jewish *state*—but he did want a self-governing Jewish community in the Land of Israel. And when its history took the form of statehood, like the Prophet Samuel he acquiesced.) That need for a land is a "right," as well as a responsibility, an obligation. And by giving the Land of Israel to the vanguard People of Israel, God teaches that *every* people has a right, and an obligation, to a land on which it can live out its particular pattern of holiness. (A vanguard is special only because it is first in the line of march and takes the brunt of trouble. To be in the vanguard means that you expect the rest of the march will get there too.) The Jewish people in its quest for self-determination in a land of its own is a vanguard for all the peoples—all of whom must, and may, seek self-determination in lands of their own. Palestinians too.

But surely each people to its *own* land! Palestinians to some land other than the Land of Israel!

But the vanguard people has a special fate. A land for every people, a people for every land—yes. But the earth has no rigid "natural" boundaries between the lands and peoples. Every people must learn to share the earth with other peoples.

So the vanguard people must learn to share *its* land with another people. It may even be true—mysteriously true, mystically true, and geopolitically true as well—that *only* if the vanguard Jewish people learns to share its land with another people will the peoples of the earth learn to share the earth with each other in peace. And in our generation, it may even be true that if the Palestinians and Israelis cannot learn to live face to face with each other, the peoples of the earth may not live to work the earth at all. Perhaps it is no accident that many scenarios for World War Last begin with an Israeli-Palestinian collision.

Am I saying that God's promises to the children of Isaac and the children of Ishmael are the same? I do not know. If we use both history and the human heart as guides to God's will, along with Torah, it seems to me that the *kind* of relationship the Jews and the Palestinians have to "that land" may not be the same. Jerusalem is unique to the Jews; it is very special but not absolutely unique to Muslims. The point that many Israelis make is also true: Arabs have many sovereign states, the Jews but one—cannot Palestinian Arabs find some self-expression in the others? The facts are clear: *some,* but not enough. In other words, there may be differences between the promises. But that both peoples have a stake in the Land seems obvious now—except to both of them.

We do not need to be happy about the monumentally hard tasks that we—and the Palestinians—face. It is true that to love and be committed to a land that God has promised twice is no easy task. God's double promise was perhaps a harsh and bitter joke. And perhaps the laughter that was Isaac, the laughter that came from Ishmael—was laughter because they got the joke. Got the joke—and still could laugh, and therefore at last make peace. Can we learn that laughter?

Now suppose we come down to earth. What shall we *do?*

For the Jewish people, the theology I have sketched above comes out this way: We must (1) build a holy society among ourselves in the

Land of Israel; (2) accept that Palestinians must have a place, *should* have a place within the Land to build their own society under their own government (to me it seems clear that the West Bank and Gaza should be that place); and (3) celebrate the continuance of the Diaspora in a dialectical and complementary relationship with the state of Israel.

And what should our cousins Ishmael do? They, the Palestinians, should begin by getting over their present unwillingness to acknowledge the right of the Jewish state to live in peace. I do not mean by accepting merely that Israel is—"unfortunately"—there to stay, but accepting that it *should* be there; that the existence of Israel, far from negating the Palestinians' right to self-determination in the same land, confirms that right. And then they should try to build their own society, by their own lights of holiness. Not for us to say how, so long as they let Israel live in peace.

What does this mean about outside proposals for a settlement in which Palestinians and Jordanians together work out a peace settlement with Israel—proposals like the Reagan plan? It means, I think, that we Jews should welcome such efforts—but keep two caveats in mind. The first is that so long as Israel is kept safe—by a peace treaty and by physical arrangements like demilitarization and observation patrols on the Jordan River—it is not our business how the Palestinians on the West Bank and Gaza choose to govern themselves. The second is that Israel is more likely to gain from negotiating *directly* with some representative of the Palestinians than by negotiating only with the United States as a more or less honest broker. Even an honest broker gets a cut on the deal. The more crucial the United States turns out to be in arranging whatever deal gets arranged, the more power the United States will have in the resulting arrangement—and the less self-determination there will be for *both* Israel and the Palestinians.

Who the Palestinian representatives should be is not a cut-and-dried matter. It need not be the PLO, but it cannot be puppets of an Israeli government, either. Perhaps free elections on the West Bank/Gaza for a Constituent Assembly could get the process going.

What may be especially valuable about proposals like the Reagan plan is that they may signal that some outsider—the United States—is prepared to look both the Children of Israel and the Children of Ishmael in the face. To see us both clearly, bring us both to the Well of the Living God Who Sees. Perhaps that is what it will take for us to be able to see each other face-to-face, not as in a dark and cloudy mirror. I do not know that the seeing will be soon—or easy. The story was first lived, and written, about four thousand years ago. But perhaps the endtime of this story is at last upon us. As world disaster—or as reconciliation.

But whether or not what we and the Palestinians do with each other affects the rest of the world in some profound way—teaches all the peoples how to share the earth, or how to destroy it—it is almost certain that what we are able to do with the Palestinians will profoundly affect our own identity. If Ishmael had died of thirst in the desert, would God have prevented Isaac from dying under the knife? In our own generation, if we let the knife fall upon Ishmael, will we be able to survive our own spiritual thirst? Or will we too die, in a wilderness of our own making?

Our tasks of reconnecting the sparks of secularist activism and Torah, the sparks of Diaspora and the Land of Israel, the sparks of prophecy and kingship, are intertwined with our task of somehow healing the most ancient shattering of all—the shattered connection between Abraham's two children.

As we search out how to do this, we must renew and rework and repair the shattered outermost spheres of Jewish peoplehood: the sphere of our relationship, or lack of it, with God; and the sphere of our relationship, or lack of it, with all the other peoples.

9. Finding the Invisible God, Hearing the Silent Word

Once—for just one generation in its long history—the Jewish people lived in such a way that the sphere of "worldwide Jewish peoplehood" and the sphere of "face-to-face local community" were the same. That was when the whole people wandered together in the wilderness, moving from where it had been scattered in the villages of Egyptian slavery to where it would again be scattered—in villages of self-direction in the land of Canaan/Israel.

In the moment between these two eras of normal localism, the people—according to tradition—traveled as a single large-scale village. It was during this generation that all the concentric spheres of Jewishness, from individual to nation, came into being as spheres—for it was then that all of them acquired their Center. Indeed, to represent this new reality, the Ark of the Covenant, with the very Presence of God resting upon it, traveled at the center of the marching, wandering tribes.

It is the absence of this Center that is perhaps the most profound aspect of the modern shatteredness of Jewish peoplehood. For the worldwide Jewish people in the Modern Age is divided not only by its division into those who govern themselves in the land of Israel and those who live among and are governed by others in the Diaspora—but even more deeply, in its understanding of what it means to be Jewish. There are those who continue to see God at the center of the Jewish people, and those who—if they try to see God there—see nothing, and have concluded there is nothing there (only the Jewish people).

In short, the deepest division and the most basic shatteredness emerges from the division between those Jews who see themselves as "religious" and those who see themselves as "secular." This is of course par excellence the result of modernism. For us today, the question is whether there is any possibility of regathering these particular sparks; whether in the post-modern period it is possible to transcend this split.

In order to test the possibilities, let us return for a moment to that supernal moment during the generation of the Wilderness when the Center was most apparent and the concentric spheres came into being.

The entire people Israel is standing at Sinai. From all around them and from within themselves, they hear an overwhelming single word: *Anokhi,* "I!"

Each one of them feels this "I" as his own, her own.

The whole people feels it as a unity—together, all one "I."

Still in the same moment, the entire universe becomes Anokhi, "I."

This "I" is all there is; there is no "Thou," no "Other," no verb, no predicate. Only the subject of the sentence, only an "I."

Sinai itself has become a giant mirror. As the "I" thunders, each Israelite sees the people mirrored: one great organic flowing, caring body politic of time and tribe. They see more than the people mirrored: the wilderness, the shimmering heat waves rising from its surface, the network of shrubs and butterflies, the ordered ranks of stars and suns and moons, the whirling galaxies, the spirals of time and change and history, the towns and nations of the world, the woven tapestries of art and custom, the patterned laws of science: world upon world, infinity upon infinity. They see themselves, part of an unfathomable Whole, not facing it but integrated in it.

For an instant each of them is infinitesimal, a tiny rhythmic breathing conscious cell in some vast breathing conscious Ultra-human. For an instant, each of them is infinite, containing in one enormous self all the worlds of fact and meaning. These instants are themselves infinitely pliable: they last for just a flashing moment, they stretch out for eternity. No: they are not "they," *it* is a single instant that feels both like a flashing moment and like eternity, both infinitesimal and infinite. All time, all space whirls like a Moebius strip through a vast expanse curved in an unspeakable dimension—while it holds but one surface and one edge.

The helpless kinfolk tremble, topple, fall to the ground that seems to disappear beneath them even while they feel its textures with every inch of blazing, open skin. Their bodies quiver; every nerve is finely tuned, all awake, all responding with a more than sexual passion to the touches, tastes, the savors and the insights surrounding them—not only surrounding them, but inside too: inside their mouths, their bellies, every empty opening filled and every limb reaching out to fill an emptiness in the world.

So quickly that they cannot sense or describe the passage, they shift back and forth from microcosm to macrocosm—back and forth from the sense that they are All There Is—Anokhi, "I"—to the sense that Everything is all there is, that they are part of everything and therefore less than nothing, only a cell of that great Anokhi of the world come conscious.

At Sinai they do not stand face-to-face with God; they stand *inside* God's skull, behind the face; they look out through God's eyes and see themselves. Anokhi.

And reeling, stunned, all balance gone, they fall, roll, stumble away from the Mirror in the Mountain, they close their eyes and shriek to see that they can still see Everything, they close their ears and hear the Voice still ringing in their bones, they back away and try . . . to forget. To blot it out. To not be "I."

And gradually they are able to become a separate "thou." Gradually they are able to hear the "I" become "I am YHVH *your* God Who brought *you* out . . . " Gradually they are able to disentangle themselves, to distinguish between the voice in their throats and the voice in their ears. Gradually they are able to distinguish themselves from the ground beneath them, to distinguish the pain in their tightly clenched fists from the pleasure in their open mouths, the breath within them from the wind around them, what they are doing from what they should be doing.

Gradually they are able to move from *Naaseh*, "We *will do* because we all All There Is," to *Nishma*, "We *will hear* and obey—because the Other has spoken to us."

Gradually they are able to distinguish commandments: "*You* shall keep Shabbos." "*You* shalt not kill." The commandments become explicit in order to replace what is organic with what is organized; to replace harmonious wholeness with planned patterning. No one needs to command an artery to channel streams of blood; but now the organic unity is gone and commands are necessary. The original holy vessel has been shattered, and only commands can reunite it. So now the people need to hear commands.

Ruefully the people linger, trying to remember the Anokhi and trying to forget it at the same time, relieved that they have been able to escape and frightened that they will never be able to escape, and already wishing that they knew how to recreate the moment and still trembling, tingling, with the impossibility of what they have just done.

This is one midrash, one way of interpreting and understanding the story of Sinai. It arises partly from the biblical text that describes the experience of the Jewish people at Sinai, partly from strands of traditional interpretation, and partly from wrestling with that text in the light of direct, living experience of the Jewish people today.

To understand that experience and make use of it to reconnect some scattered sparks of Jewish being, it is necessary to step back from the intensity of Sinai, the intensity of our own experience. Just as the people needed to step back from the intensity of Sinai into a series of logics and commands, so we need to step back into a language of weighing., balancing, understanding. Why *this* particular midrash for *this* particular generation?

So let us take one step back . . .

In this understanding of Sinai, for the moment of Anokhi there was no distinction between "mysticism" and "secularism." The Consciousness that not only suffused and gave life to, but *became* the life of all the infinite worlds was "God"; there was not God on the one side and the secular, the world, on the other. There was no way to leap out of the world in order to have a "mystical" experience. And there was no way to turn away from God by turning toward the "secular" world. It was the full experiencing of the secular world itself that was, is, the mystical experience. And it was from this vision of utter wholeness that the Israelites fled—and modern Jews, modern human beings, still flee—into seeing "I" counterposed to "Thou," "God" counterposed to "the world."

Once this separation, this duality, had been established it became one of the great tasks of the Jewish people to hold both ends of the rope, so as neither to "ascend" into the utterly spiritual nor "descend" into the purely material.

In the period of modernism, it has been harder and harder for large parts of the Jewish people, as well as the other peoples, to keep perceiving the presence of God. The world, and human actions in the world, have become clearer, firmer, more fully understood; God has become much harder to hear, vaguer to see—and by our own generation, invisible, inaudible. Within the Jewish people, more and more individuals and groups gave up holding "both ends of the rope." More and more Jews have proclaimed themselves secularists. They have retreated from spiritual experience into the world of action, action in the world. And some Jews have retreated in the other direction, into abandoning the world in favor of living a holy life of prayer and Torah study. They are fewer; but for them as for the others, the old harmonious vessel had been shattered. "The world" and "spirit" had become scattered sparks of possible holiness, each degraded by its separation from the other.

So if postmodern Jews must reunite the sparks that have been separated under the impact of modernism, then one set of sparks that must be reunited are "secularism" and "religion," or perhaps more accurately those different sparks of the Jewish people who call themselves "secularists" and "religious."

The fact is that most of the Jewish people now has a secular view of the world, of itself, and of Torah. Millions of Jews no longer feel that Torah carries any authority for them, any attraction that would make wrestling with Torah worth the effort. Both the life-giving and deadly sides of modernism have brought this about. What room is there for God in a world where human beings know and can master every "miracle"? Can feed the hungry, heal the sick, touch the moon, use sun-energy to burn a city? What room is there for Torah as the Word of Revelation, in a world where scholars can trace and label each chapter, every verse, as belonging to one or another literary source in Egyptian or Babylonian intellectual life, in the Northern or Southern line of Semitic folk tradition?

Is there to be any possibility that the Jewish people as a whole will decide to reunite these sparks again, to walk again the religious path of understanding and acting in the world? If so, that path will have to take into account the fact that for two generations most of the Jewish people—the holy people, a nation of priests—have been secularists. This is not only a sociological fact, it is a theological fact. For "theology"—the explicit statement of an attitude toward God and God's Word—always comes ultimately from the people's understanding of the world, from their pain and fury, their hopes and joys. Let us look briefly at the past:

The "theology" of biblical Jews was built upon their fears and hopes about their relationship as a self-governing people to the land that nourished them. Their great questions centered on their ability as a people to live there safe from the attacks and conquests of other peoples, free from oppressive kings or murderous idolatries that might erupt within their own community, secure in the round of the natural year that gave them grain and fruit and herds of sheep and the next generation of their own children. Their answers to these questions focused on the sacrificial system that used the products of the land as the people's connection with God, and on the recognition of God's exclusive Kingship in commanding justice and rebuking tyranny.

The "theology" of the Rabbinic Era of Jewish life, from the Talmud on, was based on the people's pain and fury, hope and joy in living as a far-flung many-faceted culture under many different political and cultural systems. For that era, one of the great questions was how to understand the exile of God's people. Their answer was to take it as a sign of God's power and caring—rather than as a sign of God's impotence or carelessness. Another of the great questions was how the people could share a relationship to the same God when they no longer shared a single political community or relationship to the same land, and therefore no longer shared the sacrificial system that was built on the produce of the land. Still another was how to draw on the Torah for guidance in governing themselves internally, under economic and political conditions utterly different from those in which the Torah was written down; and another was how to understand the Torah as Revelation without freezing it, preventing it from being reinterpreted in civilization after civilization, century after century. The answer to these questions was the use of words: words of prayer and Torah-study, words given ultimate significance through the concept of the twofold Torah, Written and Oral.

In an analogous way, the "theology" of our own era must be based on the questions asked in pain and fury, hope and joy, that move our own generation. These questions may seem too simple. They are not—but they are simple and basic. In one sense they stem from very old disquietments—how do we keep in touch with God? Why does God not protect us from conquerors and tyrants, droughts and pestilence, exile and despair? But these basic, ultimate questions take new forms under the conditions of postmodern society:

If human beings are able to do what we used to believe only God could do—to destroy all life on the planet, to create new living forms, to understand the questions of nature that God threw out as challenges to Job—why do we need to imagine God? Are we not become as God(s)?

Do we inhibit and avoid our sense of our own responsibility for the future of the world if we ask God to make peace, pursue justice, secure prosperity, heal the sick?

Shall we blame God for the Holocaust—in which case, why should we any longer pray to a cruel and ugly God? Or shall we blame human beings for the Holocaust—in which case, why should we pray to an impotent or absent God?

Since we can see and describe the evolution of Jewish religious tradition through the techniques of secular history, reduce to sociology what the tradition itself called Torah—how can we any longer pretend that this tradition stems from God, from Revelation?

Since we can at least begin to see, describe, and control the processes by which human beings achieve feelings of alienation or of wholeness, why do we need to posit God as the Source of wholeness?

I believe these questions are aspects of a basic one: "Now that human beings have or can get mastery over all the real-life problems that face us, why do we invoke, debate about, a mysterious entity we label God?"

It is this question, the ultimate question of secularism, that is now posed because of the deepest religious feelings of the Jewish people. Sometimes the question focuses on the new fact of conscious human mastery over natural science; sometimes on the new fact of conscious human mastery over the social organization of human beings; sometimes on the new fact of conscious human mastery over the process of achieving knowledge and self-understanding; sometimes on the new fact of the beginnings of conscious human mastery over the human psyche. In any sphere where it is raised, the question seems to corrode our traditional experience and understanding of God: God as Creator of the natural world, God as Liberator who acts in history, God as Teacher through Torah, God as Spirit who inspires.

To be authentic to our lives, a theology that speaks for our generation must speak to this eclipse of God—must explain God's absence in terms of God's ultimate presence.

These questions and this problem speak to one side of the painful separation of the sparks in the Modern Age: the side in which secularism triumphs. These are the questions by which the religious become secularists. But there is another side of the separation, and another set of questions: questions by which the secularists became religious. In some ways these questions are very old; they are the questions of awe and wonder that always led to religious thought and feeling. The main thing that is new about them is that they *are* new; that they come *after* and *out of* the triumph of secularism, and indeed come from secularists. And there is one other way in which these questions are new: since they do come after the triumph of secularism, they demand new answers. Once the old images of God are dead, if we wish to make a new connection with God we will need new images—not resurrected old ones.

What are *these* questions, the questions of a baffled secularism? They are the questions that challenge the crucial secularist truth: the truth of human mastery. Mastery over the natural world, mastery over history, mastery over knowledge and ideas, mastery over our own spirits and selves.

These questions challenge that truth because they arise from its very truthfulness:

What does it mean for the human race to be masters of the world, if that very mastery makes itself a nullity? If, as it seems, the more total our control of the world the more likely we are to "total" the world? If acting like a master leads inevitably to nullity, then are there, after all, limits on our mastery? Limits of a kind we never had to understand before? Limits that come from a reality beyond us, a reality in which we are grounded rather than a reality that we create? In other words, if acting like masters of the world would destroy the world, are we really masters of the world at all?

What is the meaning of our discovery that every act of observation changes what is being observed? What is the meaning of Goedel's proof that no system of mathematics is self-contained, that no mathematical system can be defined and proved by using only the rules postulated in that system; that it is necessary to use a higher system to explain and justify the one we want to work with? Do these discoveries teach us that our deepest learning is an infinite loop, a Moebius strip of concept, fact, and conception? Once we look deep into the patterns of the world and see ourselves staring forth from the patterns, are we not forced to see a Pattern deeper, a Pattern that includes us and does not arise from us? For no infinite process can be explained in its own terms.

What does it mean that when we have discovered a profound pattern in the world, our response is awe? Awe is what we owe and give to mystery, not to the resolution of a mystery. Why do we feel and act as if such a discovery were not the simple satisfactory uncovering of a hidden fact, the solution of a practical problem—but rather the unveiling of a deeper Veil, the discovery of a mystery? Why—when we examine our own secular behavior with a secular eye—do we see ourselves trembling in awe?

To be authentic to our lives, any secular philosophy that speaks for our generation must speak to this self-transcending aspect of secularism—this tendency of secularism to force itself to look beyond itself.

So in our generation it is not only the disappearance of God that must be explained as an eclipse, an absence that can be understood only in terms of an ultimate presence. It is also the disappearing act of secular human mastery that must be so explained. We must imagine both a way of looking at God that explains God's invisibility and a way of explaining the secular fact that the secular triumph is self-annihilating.

The effort itself is awesome. No one comes to it without feeling tentative and shy. Yet the beginnings of such an effort already exist. On the "secular" side, the beginning exists chiefly in the work of— remarkably enough—a secularist historian of mysticism, Gershom Scholem, and the work of his historian-biographer, David Biale, which explains and extends Scholem. On the "religious" side, it exists in the efforts of a number of American rabbi-theologians who are loosely part of the movement for Jewish renewal.

What Scholem does is to treat Jewish history as an unfolding spiritual process, and the writing of Jewish history as itself an unfolding of the inward, hidden meaning of this spiritual process. If the history lived is a kind of Torah-with-Talmud, then to Scholem the history written—the historiography—is a kind of Kabbalah. Biale brings this implicit approach of Scholem's into explicit consciousness, and thus becomes a kind of midrashic explicator in this new "Kabbalah"—using the same method of "secular" historiography to both explain and enrich the method.

How is this stance different from that of classic secularist historians? It is different in that Scholem and Biale treat the history they are examining not with the cool and clinical detachment of the secular historian examining mere changes in the ideas of the people—but as something more profound, more in touch with reality, more *Torah*.

What is emerging among the newer theologians of the movement for Jewish renewal in America is a focusing on the aspect of God that is immanent, fully present within the world, rather than that aspect which is transcendent—wholly outside the world. This is by no means an utterly new way of experiencing God; there are passages in almost every generation of Jewish thought that view God this way, and indeed some of the metaphors and symbols the new theologians use are ancient ones. But it seems to me there is a new commonality, a new shared vision, in which the immanent aspect of God has a stronger place than Jews are used to.

The new theologians are using several different overlapping metaphors for the immanent God: the God of Elijah the Prophet, Who appeared as the "still small voice" within the prophet rather than as the thundering God of Sinai; the God of the Aquarian Age; the God of the Third Era of Jewish peoplehood; the Shekhinah, God's Presence in the world, most present in the midst of the circle of a congregation that sits in circles, rather than at the far end of a stretched-out congregation seated in rows; the God Who is present throughout the Song of Songs precisely because God is never named there.

Let us look a little more carefully at these people and what they have been saying:

Some of their approaches carry overtones of the work of Mordecai Kaplan, who almost two generations ago articulated what became known as Reconstructionist Judaism. Kaplan urged that God be understood as Process—as a human process, the Process that leads humankind toward goodness and holiness. Kaplan treated the symbols and practices of Jewish tradition as useful tools in walking the holy path. He came to his doctrine with no shiver of awe—at least none his readers and followers could feel. He wanted precisely to eliminate the supernatural and mystical. He was in tune with that generation, for he was trying to use the word "God" in such a fashion that American Jews who had no direct mystical experience and felt intellectually fulfilled by secular science and philosophy, Jews who were imbued with John Dewey's pragmatism and instrumentalism, could feel the word "God" had meaning.

Kaplan's work and thought continue. Among those closest to his views and most creative in applying them to daily life is Harold Schulweis, the congregational rabbi of a large Conservative synagogue in California. He has encouraged the congregants to form havurot and his board members to become para-rabbis able to deal with the life-crises of the members. Schulweis argues for a "Predicate theology" in which the Divine attributes of justice and loving kindness are seen as holy traits of human beings, who elevate Divinity by practicing them.

Yet for the very reasons that Kaplan was in tune with the generation of the thirties and forties, he was out of tune with the generation of the sixties and seventies. The movement for Jewish renewal that emerged in the late sixties and early seventies came with an experience of and a desire for ecstatic dance, intense song, intimate community, mystical communion. This was not just a question of a song-and-dance style: the style was authentically the shape of the movement's content. It is true that the movement itself was often more aware of its style than of its content, but the content was deeply felt: from the heart of our rational universities came the message that reason is not enough. It was this deeper message, as well as the one of style, that was different from the message Kaplan brought. For if Kaplan spoke at the peak of the modern, secular triumph, the next generation came to its voice when that very triumph had turned—literally—to ashes.

One of the most important teachers of a newer generation, bridging in unconventional ways the chasm between materialism and mysticism, is Zalman Schachter-Shalomi, a rabbi who was originally trained by the Lubavitcher Hassidim and is at the same time a professor of Jewish mysticism at Temple University; a serious student of the disciplines of Zen, Sufism, yoga, encounter psychology, and Christian mysticism; and the de facto rebbe of a "New Age Hassidic" group called B'nai Or (Children of Light). Schachter-Shalomi suggests that the great astrological ages of Aries, Pisces, and Aquarius—the Ram, the Fish, and the Water-bearer—be taken as real in both the cosmic and historical sense. Cosmically, in these three ages God's Self-revelation has been mostly expressed by God in successively different ways; historically, in these three ages God has been mostly understood by human beings in three successively different images. To begin with, God reached out as and was received as utterly external, transcendent, the Revealer; then, as infused into the world but still distinct, distinguishable; finally (but of course not really finally) as utterly indistinguishable, utterly the world rather than "in" it.

Schachter-Shalomi points out that in the earlier eras there were foretastes of the later ones, and in the later there have been continuations of what came earlier. For *all* these orientations describe truthfully aspects of a God Who cannot be cramped into only one image—and Who, in a fourth age, will once more be experienced as astoundingly different.

Among a quite different constituency of more settled, somewhat older Jews, a parallel and somewhat similar approach to Jewish history has been taught by Rabbi Irving Greenberg, the founder of the National Jewish Resource Center. Greenberg has been developing the notion of three great eras of Jewish peoplehood: the Biblical Age, the Talmudic-Rabbinic Age, and a Third Age that began with the Holocaust and the establishment of the state of Israel. In this Third Age, the Holocaust makes traditional Jewish thought far more problematic, and the state of Israel offers the possibility of a much more secular definition of the Jewish people as a civil society, developing in a conscious way its own spiritual life.

Still other rabbis have been moving in similar ways to break down the conceptual barriers between secularism and mysticism.

Arthur Green, a Conservatively trained rabbi, founder of the first havurah, and historian of Hassidism who teaches at the University of Pennsylvania, writes of God as a profound Unknown whose "known" and changing images are built up out of the great projections and reflections of the Jewish people's vision of the future, so that what we know of God mirrors a fully communal community. Lawrence Kushner, rabbi of a creative, havurah-style Reform congregation in Massachusetts, is the author of several books that are the first authentic fusions of an "American" and a "Kabbalistic" sensibility—or perhaps it would be more accurate to say the first wholly natural expressions of a Kabbalistic sensibility through the experiences of everyday American life. Kushner speaks of "the Torah of Elijah," who heard the Voice as a still, small voice within rather than an explosive energy from outside. Edward Feld, a Hillel rabbi at Princeton University, is grappling with the question of revelations of God taking different forms in different situations. God was revealed in the Holocaust, says Feld, not in earthquake events but in the tiny acts that in normal situations would have been ordinary acts of human love and kindness, but when done by people who were under extreme pressures to act inhumanly, become both signs of and carriers of God's own presence.

It is noteworthy that all of these writers for whom some version of the secular-religious dichotomy is the central issue are male. Yet their thought moves in the same direction as that of a smaller, younger group of Jewish women who are "doing theology" as part of their struggle to transform Jewish thought patterns and institutional structures that are mostly male.

And the group of men I have described may themselves have been influenced by the direct experience of the entrance of women into Jewish study and prayer as equals—carrying with them, explicitly or implicitly, their own spiritual experience. Mordecai Kaplan, for example, "invented" the bat mitzvah in order to meet the needs of his four daughters. Greenberg, though an Orthodox rabbi, has shared with his wife Blu Greenberg an intense struggle to examine the evolving spiritual roles of Jewish women and men. And so also with all the others.

The new women theologians emerged from a Jewish feminist movement that began by criticizing and opposing the traditional exclusion of women from leading prayers, becoming rabbis, and leading Jewish institutions. Then some of the Jewish feminists began to see the basic structures of Jewish religious thought and the Jewish way of experiencing God as male-dominated. Not only was God called "He," "Father," "King," but the very insistence on God as transcendent, distant, seemed to them erected on "male" life-experience—rather than growing out of the more "female" experience of closeness, inwardness, and flow.

Several of these women have begun to define alternative visions of God. Rabbi Lynn Gottlieb's mime and storytelling often focuses on the Shekhinah, that female aspect of God Who, according to the rabbinic tradition, went into exile alongside the Jewish people when the Temple was destroyed; went into exile as a Presence in the world. Gottlieb draws on many female symbols as metaphors for God's presence in the world: the womb, the lunar cycle, the inner space of the circle. Judith Plaskow is a feminist theologian who has worked both inside and outside Jewish tradition. She argues that drawing on female symbolism from Jewish tradition and using it alongside or even to replace male symbolism would not draw deeply enough on women's real spiritual experience. If women fully surfaced their spiritual lives, she suggests, "God" would emerge for many of them as a process of their own spiritual growth.

Other Jewish women—many of them in conversations rather than writing—have begun to raise similar questions, all leading in the direction of a much more "immanent" way of describing "God" or a much more "spiritual" way of describing "the world." Arising from issues that are somewhat different from those involved in the secular-religious dimension, these early stirrings of thought toward a feminist Judaism seem to be moving in the same direction as the fusion or hybrid of secularist and mystical thought that I have described. As the process of the women's critique of the ancient images of God and Torah develops, and as men continue to make connections with the process and open up the more buried portions of their selves to it, the critique itself will probably change and give birth to new ways of approaching a spiritual life.

Most of this thinking is in its early stages, still tentative and cautious. My own thoughts—also tentative—point in the same general direction, toward a theology focused on the immanent aspect or perception of God:

First of all, at the level of direct experience, I begin with the "vision" of Anokhi at the beginning of this chapter: the experience that the infinite universe as a "whole" is conscious, and that infinite conscious wholeness is God.

Second, drawing more on intellect and feeling, we see no God today because we are looking in the wrong place. We grew used to looking for God "out there," or at least (in the Talmudic Age) in exile "right next door" to us. But now God is "no longer" *out there;* God is not, in our era, most easily discerned as The Other. Instead God has fled *into* the world. For us to experience God at all, we have to perceive that moment of Anokhi. Looked at one way, that moment means everything is God. Looked at another way, it means that nothing is God; everything is secular.

The reason we experience having Divine powers is that we have them. The burst of human mastery in the last three centuries is real, and our first response is to discover that the Master of the Universe is gone. He *is* gone (and I use "He," with all its masculine overtones, deliberately). But we have something crucial yet to learn: that the disappearance of the Master does not eliminate the Mystery. The examinable, definable process of human action is *not all* there is: that process carries within it the Awesome, the Mysterious, and is connected with the Awesome and Mysterious outside it.

Do I mean that the human race is now God, or owns God, or shapes God? No. Even the whole infinite conscious universe may not "be" God, for there are probably levels of God beyond Anokhi, transcendences we are not able to explore. The human race is not God; but God *is* the human race, and more, and more, and still More.

It is not easy to attach labels or metaphors of intellect or feeling to this way of experiencing life, metaphors or labels that will convey its meaning to ourselves or others. If we were to seek a bodily reference point, we might contrast the experience of a *shrug* with the experience of a *shiver*. That is, we can greet the new face of human mastery either with a secular shrug—the Universe has lost its meaning if we are all there is—or with a mystic's shiver, a shudder, a tremble: the Universe has gained a deeper Mystery if the Powers of God have fled into the world and the human race. For in some ways such an experiencing of God is rooted in the mystic's sense that everything below replicates everything above.

Or if we seek to use not bodily but intellectual labels or metaphors for the life-approach that we are seeking, perhaps we can suggest how difficult the search is by giving it the name of some strange hybrid: "mystical secularism," or "the fusion of Kabbalah with Reconstructionism."

What metaphors and symbols could we develop in order to celebrate and strengthen our sense of God within us? What metaphors and symbols would help us to experience not only the awesomeness of the powers within us, but also the awesomeness of our need to limit those powers, our need to let them ebb as well as flow, to celebrate the rhythms and cycles that begin with birth and continue with maturation and fulfillment, but then move on to decline and death, leading toward a new birth? How could we learn rhythms not only in our "private" or communal lives, but also in the life of the planet and of the human race—where for the past four hundred years we have acted as though the curve of growth led ever upward, needing no pause, no hibernation, no encapsulating in a seed that could begin again?

For our generation, these questions might be addressed by bringing together the new feminist images that we have already explored, with much older mystical images: the Kabbalists' vision of the Shekhinah, the female aspect of God, Who knows not straight lines but cycles and spirals, Who knows the swelling and thinning of the moon, Who knows the meaning of exile. As we weave mysticism and feminism into one fabric, we might even celebrate the Shekhinah as the One who knows the cycles of the earth and social change come to because Her "menstrual cycle" is the Jubilee cycle of harvesting and fallowness, accumulation and sharing, the death and rebirth of the land and of society.

To experience God in this way might give the Jewish people a dialogue like this—a dialogue authentically arising from those silent questions burning in their throats:

"If we can create life, destroy life, understand the secrets of nature, why do we need to imagine God? Have we not ourselves become as God(s)?"

"Yes, we have. We have become utterly powerful, able ourselves to bring the Flood upon the earth. And *therefore* we need to be conscious of God as the rhythmic fountain of ebb and flow within us, the wellspring which knows how to ebb before drowning life in a flood of too much life-giving water."

"But if we ourselves are able to shape our own societies and are responsible to *make* peace and justice, do we need to look toward God to do this? Do we need to ask some other to send the Days of Peace and Justice?"

"Yes, we do; because the more fervently we praise the Other, the more we can love the otherness among ourselves. The more deeply we can experience the Other, the more deeply we can know that to build the Days of Peace and Justice is to experience fully, empathize with the otherness in other human beings. When I know that God in Exile dwells today not in the Western Wall but in the exiled body of my enemy, and in the exiled body of my own self's buried soul and body, then I can, must, make peace with, create justice with that Other."

"If I assert that human beings are *merely* human beings, far less than the transcendent God Who is to be loved far more than they, then I can oppress and kill them for the sake of my God—Whoever and Whatever my God is. And if I say that human beings are merely human beings and there is no God at all, then I can oppress and kill them if I have the whim and the power. Only because of a prudential calculus will I refrain."

"But if I say to them and to myself, '*You and I* are God together, *you and I* bear God within us; except for us there is at this moment no other God; I will not obey you as a God and I will not demand that you obey me as a God, for both of us together are God, in our otherness toward each other we are God the Other.' If I can say all this, then I am neither willing to kill nor willing to be killed; then I am filled with the love that leads toward peace and justice."

"But if *you and I* are at this moment God, then is whatever we agree to do between us godly? Without a transcendent God, always critical of whatever human society exists, who is to criticize the Holocaust—or even, *l'havdil*, the ordinary cutthroat tactics of the marketplace? Who is to reach toward the next rung?"

"We are, of course. The immanent God is not only "within us," but within the whole world. Once we are conscious that the whole world is Anokhi, "I," then we are also conscious that the world is unconscious of its unity. It is this unconsciousness that is the shatteredness that needs redemption. The consciousness that God *is* immanent, the world is One, is what stands critical, transcendent, as a judgment on our failures."

"Shall we blame God for the Holocaust? Then why should we pray to a cruel and ugly God? Or shall we blame human beings for the Holocaust? Then why should we pray to an impotent God?"

"We should blame the God who is in part *within us;* and we should pray in order to awaken our own Godly compassion and our own Godly power. By not merely speaking outward to God in each other (that too) but also speaking within ourselves, speaking across the great chasm between our "ordinary" selves and our selves conceived, felt, as part of God—we experience the chasm within ourselves, feel what could be our wholeness. We give ourselves and God the power and loving-kindness to prevent a holocaust."

"Since we can track by secular means the historical development of Torah, since we can see how it grew from human needs and embodied in its contradictory passages all the political and cultural disagreements within the Jewish people, why should we call it Revelation and the Word of God?"

"Because it is precisely the contradictions that are the Revelation. Because we know the Torah's holiness precisely from the knowledge that it is no seamless garment but a flawed and torn and *almost* perfect one that needs mending to be perfected. Because the deepest Revelation is the one that demands we join the revealing process."

This last part of the dialogue moves from the "visibility" of God to the "audibility" of God: from the Vision to the Voice. Traditionally, Torah was heard as the communication from a transcendent God to the People Israel. If we can now more easily sense God as immanent, within us rather than outside us, what do we make of Torah? Can the Jewish people, should the Jewish people, now take Torah seriously as the framework of thought and struggle in which and through which we continue being Jewish? To examine that question seriously requires that we focus our attention on what Torah means and has meant to the Jewish people.

In most of the first era of Jewish peoplehood, the Biblical Era, Torah seems to have been understood as its own texts suggest: as the written-down words of a direct eruption of powerful Teaching from the most profound source of truth in the world. From the Creation until Sinai, the story seems to be told directly by an omniscient historian reporting God's direct intervention in history. From Sinai on, the "Five Books of Moses" describe themselves and explain the process of experiencing Torah as the searing voice of God transmitted to and through Moses and the later prophets: a force of truthfulness so direct, so overwhelming that its voice shakes and tears them, convinces them what to say to the people—sayings that are remembered and then are written down.

This is not the whole story. There are aspects of the prophetic books that have a different sound—like the story of Elijah's "silent voice" within. And some of the pieces of "Literature" that were only later accepted as part of the Bible—the Song of Songs, Esther, Ruth, Proverbs, Ecclesiastes—describe their own origins as something other than a direct transcription of the Divine Voice. One Bible scholar, Richard Friedman, has pointed out that from the direct Creative Word of God in early Genesis into the transmission through Moses and then the Prophets into the Writings, down to Esther where God does not appear at all, there is a bumpy but continuing downward slope of direct intervention by God in the world—and a rising slope of human action. But the dominant note of the early period was that Torah, Teaching, is the direct message of an Other, God, Who uses human mediation only in the form of the Prophet—the mouthpiece or transmitter.

In the long Talmudic Era of Jewish peoplehood, Torah was understood differently. The Talmudic rabbis introduced or discovered the concept of the twofold Torah. The Teaching, they said, included of course the holy documents that recorded what had been said by God at Sinai and to the Prophets since. But it was the rabbis who debated over certain items of literature and when there was disagreement among them voted—voted!—on whether certain books were imbued with the Holy Spirit. They also spoke of a more esoteric Torah—one communicated by God to Moses but never written down during the Biblical Age. Instead, it was transmitted only by word of mouth from human to human as specific interpretations of the written text—and also, much more important, as a *process* for interpreting the text.

Through this process the "oral Torah" became discernible by scholars, who then could unveil levels or aspects of the Torah that had always been present but that remained invisible until they were needed. Thus the human share in making Torah clear was in principle expanded from that of the sheer "transmitter" or "mouthpiece" to that of examining a text, weighing, debating, explicating, sometimes agreeing, sometimes agreeing to disagree. Through this process, human beings of different times, places, and civilizations became able to discern the Teaching that would apply to their new and sometimes contradictory situations. Yet through the permutations, knots, and twists of practice ran the blue thread of the Revelation of Sinai—a Revelation of both "content" and the process by which that content could be understood.

During the last two centuries, this Rabbinic understanding of Torah has for most Jews been unraveling. The application of modern historical and sociological techniques has revealed that in the Five Books themselves there are different styles, different approaches, different literary and cultural origins, different institutional values. As for the debates of the rabbis, modern scholarship has shown that their own life-situations and their own positions on the economic and political issues of their day had a profound impact on the directions in which they chose to interpret Torah.

For most Jews, the result was that "Torah" came to seem purely the deposited wisdom of the Jewish people—basically no different from an anthology of "secular" literature. For many Jews, this particular collection became no more interesting than any other, and they ceased to study it with the passionate attention that had for centuries distinguished the Jewish people. For others, it became the fascinating record of the historical development of their own people, more interesting than Homer or Shakespeare because it was their own— just as one's own baby photographs or those of one's own grandfather are much more interesting than the practically identical photos of a neighbor's. For many, it became a grab bag which contained some profound truths about human nature and some quaint, ridiculous, infuriating, or disgusting views of and directives about life and the world.

On the basis of any of these views, it was reasonable to "pick and choose" aspects or sections of the whole corpus of the Teaching. As the integrated vessel of Jewish peoplehood separated into fragments, some chose to discard almost the whole of the Talmud; others chose to celebrate chiefly the Prophets; and still others chose to ignore them completely. The crucial fact was that once the long line of Teaching had been shown to have the contradictions and gaps characteristic of any human product, its status as God's Revelation vanished or diminished.

In the past generation, the first steps were made to absorb this secularization of the Torah and go beyond it. Franz Rosenzweig, colleague and comrade of Martin Buber in the brief German-Jewish intellectual flowering of the 1920s, took the question of the somewhat contradictory "documents" in Torah one step forward. Yes, he said, there are indeed the "J," "E," and "P" documents that the historians discern; but "R," as the scholars called the *Redaktor* or editor, is really *Rabbenu*—our Teacher: that is, the process of pulling together the different separate documents into the Torah text we know was the Teaching process that created Torah.

More recently, the poet and literary scholar Joel Rosenberg, a participant in the movement for Jewish renewal, took another crucial step. The nineteenth-century historians and sociologists had diminished the sense of Revelation in Torah by pointing to its internal contradictions. Rosenberg stood this approach on its head by celebrating the internal contradictions as the very stuff and meaning of Revelation. Suppose, he said, that Torah had been utterly seamless, utterly perfect. It would have been possible only to stand back and admire the Perfection. But because Torah had a fold here, a crack there, a rough place somewhere else—because it is indeed the joining of two great and partially contradictory approaches to the world—it invites and demands that we join in making it whole. By learning, applying, questioning, feeling, arguing, we participate in the Teaching. This, Rosenberg suggested, is the deepest expression of the Jewish experience of Revelation: that it forces us to join in Revelation. The Torah itself is a midrash on itself; so it teaches the midrashic process as the basic meaning of Torah, beneath and beyond the content.

The implication of this approach is that the "secular" fact of human conflict is what can make up the "spiritual" fact of Torah. Or, better, it is the "secular" effort to unify and transcend the conflict that is the deepest "spiritual" search. It is recognizing what is broken and trying, always trying, to mend it—and always failing, almost failing, almost succeeding, that makes Torah. It is precisely this process, the historical development of Torah, that *is* Torah.

Perhaps the irreducible minimum of Torah is the legend that, as the mystics say, the Root of the Universe opened Its Throat in the Aleph, the soundless vowel that begins the Anokhi, the"*I*," that starts the Ten Commandments. For perhaps this soundless vowel, this letter that is all process with no content, teaches that the Root of the World stands as a counter-part to us, wants to encounter us and argue with us.

Perhaps the irreducible minimum of Torah is the Torah's statement that at Sinai the people heard both—or either—"You shall *keep* the Sabbath" and "You shall *remember* the Sabbath," and that in some sense all of the people heard both words while all of them were hearing only one. So ever afterward they have struggled to choose between these words or to synthesize them—never quite succeeding in either.

Perhaps the irreducible minimum of Torah is the comment of the Talmud upon the contradictory opinions of the great teachers Shammai and Hillel: "These *and* these are the words of the living God."

Perhaps the irreducible minimum of Torah is the rabbi's answer to his quarreling *hassidim:* First "*You* are right!" and then "*You* are right!" and then above all when his wife challenges him with "They cannot both be right," his answer to her: "And you also are right!"

But is Torah *only* process, *only* historical development? Does anything and everything go? Abandoning Torah? Replacing Torah? No. The irreducible minimum of Torah is that the Jewish people be struggling with Torah—with all or any of the teachings of the past.

When the Jewish people three thousand five hundred years ago wrestled with the primeval festivals of birthing lamb and sprouting barley in the springtime, and learned to make of them a festival of giving birth to freedom—that struggle was, and gave us, Torah. When the Jewish people two thousand years ago wrestled with the festival of firstfruits and learned to make of it the season of the Giving of our Torah—that struggle was, and gave us, Torah. When the Jewish people one hundred years ago wrestled with the minor candle-lighting feast of Hanukkah and turned it into a celebration of the guerrilla resistance of the Maccabees, that struggle was, and gave us, Torah. And if one hundred years from now the Jewish people struggles again with Hanukkah and turns it into a celebration of light against the growing darkness, hope against despair, that struggle too will be—and give us—Torah.

In terms of Torah, the breakthrough of the Second Era of Jewish peoplehood—the era of the Talmud—was to give us the twofold Written/Oral Torah: was to give us the divinely revealed process by which human beings could unfold the words of the written Torah in order to give us the words of the oral Torah. The breakthrough of the Third Era of Jewish peoplehood must be to give us the sense that when we ourselves struggle with Torah, knowing that it is we human beings who are struggling, it is Torah that we are making—not merely "secular" literature. For as in this era we experience God within us, so in this era we experience Torah as the Teachings of the God Who speaks silently within us. The human role in the speaking of Torah has grown from era to era—from the role of transmitter in the Biblical period to the role of unveiler in the Talmudic Period to the role of speaker in our own.

If it is human beings who we say are speaking "Torah," is it just a trick of language to call it Torah that they speak? Am I simply disguising secularism with some seductive language about God and Torah? Or to put the question in a different way, what are the implications and practical results of hearing Torah in this fashion?

One implication of listening for the "small and silent Voice" within us is that we are still in some sense experiencing Torah as that Teaching that comes from Otherness. It is not Torah to plunge into doing the first, superficial notion of Torah that floats into our heads.

To make what we teach, learn, and do into Torah it is necessary to sound our selves, to sound our depths—each of us, and between us. The Other that we seek is both each other, the tremor of communion that quivers between us when we are together listening for Torah, and in each of us that deeper spark of God—which also shakes us, makes us tremble, when the spark sputters and sizzles to leap across the gap.

So to say that "the God within us is now teaching Torah" may point toward a technique, almost a technology, of arranging ourselves so as to make it more likely that what we speak is Torah. We could imagine that:

First we immerse ourselves in mikveh, plunge ourselves into the ritual pool or river that reminds us of the Ocean around us and within us;

Next we clothe ourselves in the four-cornered garment with its ritual fringes that reminds us we are constant wearers of the Torah;

Next we seat ourselves with our texts at the center of a circle in which we can clearly see the shivers on each other's faces, hear the tremors in each other's voices;

Then we draw on the written and oral traditions of Torah, on our "secular" knowledge of the world, and on our deepest feelings to create new Torah. We keep ourselves conscious of the political and social and institutional wishes, interests, and conflicts among us; we try not to suppress them or eliminate them but to be clear about them, to learn from them, to see what these very tugs and conflicts teach us about the pulls and tugs of God in history;

And finally we decide how to act, accepting disagreements in the spirit that both *these* actions and these *other* actions may be the expressions of the living God.

Is there anything new to this model, anything the rabbis of the Second Era did not do? I think there may be several things:

Our own emotional reactions to a text of Torah we should consider truthful midrash. That is, we can keep an eye on the emotions that a passage stirs up among the community that is reading and studying it, in order to understand the intent or meaning of the text.

For example: a reading of the Torah passage on the trial by ordeal of a wife suspected of adultery creates tension, suspicion, fury in the congregation that hears it. It especially creates tension between men and women. The passage that follows immediately in the text is about the vow of the Nazirite who becomes physically or emotionally lonely, a hermit, one isolated from the currents of society. The text goes out of its way to specify that either a man or a woman can become a Nazirite. As the congregation hears this passage, its tension and suspicion cool. It becomes—like the Nazirite—thoughtful, meditative, a little withdrawn. And then the Torah moves into a repetitive chant of the twelve identical gifts brought by twelve leaders of the twelve tribes to the dedication of God's Dwelling Space. The congregation begins to sway, feel soothed, feel even bored by the text. The text itself has both induced and dissolved the kind of furious jealousy and conflict it has been talking about in the initial passage. Now—suppose the women discover, realize, that all the twelve gift givers of the twelve tribes are men. The women discover this in the new context created by the new tone of the text. Will their reactions be another wave of their original fury? Or will it be something new—perhaps a fusion of anger with determination, a decision that the sanctuary is worthy enough for them to bring their own gifts—that the Torah has been waiting, inviting them to do this? That the gifts do not need to be identical and boring in order to be equal?

In this way we can consciously recognize our reactions as a guide to the meaning, the intention, of the Torah. We ourselves have become an element of Torah—not merely readers of the words upon the parchment, not even interpreters of the words upon the parchment, but bearers and channels, *embodiments* of the words.

With this new way of hearing Torah, we are able to—indeed, we must—involve a far broader spectrum of Jews with a far broader spectrum of experience and skills than could the Jews of the First or Second Eras. In the Biblical Era, in order to connect with God it was necessary either to be a priest or Levite by birth and thus permitted to join in the sacrifices, or to be a prophet, and thus able to hear directly and speak truthfully the naked Word of God. Both priesthood and prophethood were scarce commodities. Among the rabbis of the Talmudic Era, there were two requisite skills—and to be part of the Torah process, a Jew had to possess them both: sensitivity to the changing needs of human beings, and an extraordinary familiarity and facility with the specialized and subtle literatures of Torah.

To be a "Torah-speaker" in our new understanding would still, of course, require sensitivity to the changing needs of human beings. But in the circle alongside those who had profound knowledge of the Torah literatures could sit those with skill to express and discern human feelings in the face and body; those with skill in analyzing society and history; those with skill in healing the body and spirit; those with skill in understanding the processes of physics, chemistry, biology; those with an eye and ear for art and music . . . in short, the "secular" skills.

Is there any hope that people who now view themselves as "secular" and as "religious" can together begin to share a relationship with God and Torah of the kind I have described?

On the side of the religious, the necessary great leap of consciousness will be understanding that the growth of secularism needs to be seen neither as a horror to be opposed nor as a problem to be tolerated, but as a faithful response to God's absenting of the Divine Other from Otherhood; in short, that the emergence of secularism is a "religious" event.

On the side of the secularists, the necessary great leap of consciousness will be understanding that for secular reasons—notably the survival of the human race—it is vital to allow the mystic's shiver of awe to emerge from its hidden place; that, in short, the re-emergence of religion is a "secular" event.

10. Among the Nations

The outermost sphere in the pattern of Jewish life is the sphere in which the Jews speak and respond to other peoples. In this sphere, as in all the others, the present moment is a time of troubles. When "What is Jewish?" becomes a hotly debated question, "Who is a Jew?" and "What is the Jewish people?" soon follow.

And this time of troubles in the "outermost" sphere does not remain simply "outermost," simply a question of "foreign policy" that affects only the macropolitics of Jewish leaders dealing with the other peoples. It enters the life and consciousness of most Jews as an intimate question—posed by the possibility of intermarriage.

Why are we living through such an upheaval? Could we respond in any way that would both be authentically Jewish and be authentically responsive to our own postmodern lives and identities?

First, before we explore these questions as history and theory, a simple story:

In 1981, a Jewish friend of mine—a real friend; between us a caring, serious friendship—fell in love with a man who was not Jewish. My friend was not simply a casual, uncaring Jew; she was a passionate and brilliant artist whose art often came from and explicitly referred to themes of Jewish thought and tradition. Her interpretation of those themes, and her relationship to existing Jewish groups and institutions, was unconventional—but real. She wrestled—with God, and with the Jewish people.

And yet . . . and yet . . . and yet, she prepared to marry a man who was not Jewish. She came with her lover to tell me—in trembling, they later said. In trembling because of all their friends, I was the likeliest to be deeply troubled by their getting married.

And I was. *Really* troubled, because I had no simple answers. It was clear to me that my friend's lover was talented, loving, impassioned—himself a wrestler. It was clear they were intelligently in love, not out of blind romanticism but with clear and open eyes. It was clear that my friend was improved, heightened, by their love.

And it was clear that her lover was not Jewish, and that he had no authentic internal reason to become a Jew.

Above all, however, it was clear to me that all this clearness was making me unclear. Making me feel troubled, unable to simply say a *"Mazel Tov"* in pleasure or a curse in anger.

So for days I lived with my trouble. Wrestled, wondered, let myself feel troubled: happy, unhappy, happy. And then I asked myself:

"My *un*happiness about this marriage grows out of Torah and the Jewish past. Is there anything about my *happiness* with it that also grows out of Torah and the Jewish past—or does all my happiness arise from the liberal-American aspect of myself?"

And when I asked myself this question, there arose for me the image of the Rainbow—the Torah's many-colored symbol of the unity in variety of humankind and all creation. The rainbow: given by God as a sign of the covenant of continuing life, after the dread disaster of the biblical Flood. The Rainbow: our *particular* tradition's way of speaking about universalism. The Rainbow: in its very shape and colors a symbol that only out of many comes a unity; that only in unity do the many achieve coherence without abandoning their particularity.

This image of the Rainbow came without thought or planning. It came as a dream comes: my own unconscious drawing on Torah, the collective dreamwork of the Jewish people.

So then I turned to conscious thought: could this symbol become an appropriate symbol?

I hunted through the shops of Washington to find seven scarves of the seven rainbow colors. I knotted the seven scarves together and gave this "rainbow" to my friends. Use it in your wedding, I offered. Not the symbols of a Jewish wedding—the canopy, the wine, the broken glass. But this: the Jewish symbol for God's covenant with all of Noah's children.

They did. They had young cousins wrap this cloth of seven colors around them. And for me, this Rainbow healed the wound of my internal tug-of-war. Not without a scar: real wrestle leaves a limping walk. But healed. Able to say that in our present turmoil, Torah knows that we can see the Rainbow. That the time for the Rainbow has come, the time to see that our particular color, our particular covenant, both includes and is included by the universal covenant.

Includes and *is included*. As the DNA, which from the heart of every germ cell generates our bodies, lives also in each cell our bodies generate. As the merest speck of any hologram both is a part of the whole, and can be used to generate the whole.

In our generation, this must be the model of the relationship of the Jewish people with all the other peoples. We are ourselves—a special, a chosen, a vanguard, a choosing people. And we carry within us the crystal of the human race, perhaps of all creation—a universal wisdom that itself celebrates particularity in path of life.

Of course our struggle toward a new understanding of the Jewish people's role among the nations is not easy. There are precedents for our confusions, our pain. Whenever an old "era" of Jewish people-hood is ending and a new one is trying to begin, the boundaries of Jewish peoplehood are being redrawn.

We can still see the hints of this process as it took place in the formative stages of the Biblical Era, by looking at the passages of Genesis and Exodus that describe the relationship of the "Israelites" to the descendants of Ishmael, Esau, Lot, and all the other peoples. We read of closely related peoples and of distant ones. There are descendants of Noah—all human beings, who are not simply dismissed as barbarians and idolators but honored as co-covenanters with God in the "Rainbow Covenant" after the Flood. There are the closer cousins who are described as offshoots of Abraham's family—Ammon and Moab, Ishmael and Esau—with whom there are tensions, struggles, and reconciliations. Some of these cousins are described as having their own relationships with God. After several generations of "drawing the line," excluding and including, a peoplehood is achieved that defines itself as the descendants of Jacob, renamed Israel the Godwrestler.

In the wilderness after the Exodus from Egypt, the Torah tells us that the line was drawn again. The tradition tells us that a "mixed multitude" left Egypt—some who did and some who did not trace their tradition to Abraham and Sarah, Isaac and Rebekah, Jacob and Leah and Rachel. Among those who accepted the Torah and Moses' leadership were some who had not been of Israelite tradition; among those who rejected the Torah and Moses were some who had been Israelites.

Some historians believe that only part of the culture and community that became the People Israel had in its own ancestry the band of nomads that emerged from Egypt, experienced Sinai, and crossed the Jordan. Perhaps, they say, that band had a set of traditions connecting them with one or several of the Patriarchs and Matriarchs in Canaan. When they reentered Canaan, they would have met there a variety of peoples, some of whom had traditions that "dovetailed" with their own—and of these, some were hostile and others were ready to match not only traditions from the past but also life-styles for the future. Some, perhaps, identified more with Isaac, and some with Jacob; some, perhaps (especially those of the north of Canaan), with Joseph and his offspring Ephraim; others, toward the south, with Judah.

According to this view, the Torah as we know it, was a knitting together, the most artful creation of a patchwork quilt from several different, overlapping communities and traditions. What this knitting together did, inwardly, was define the content and process of Revelation—the binding force that held the people together in dealing with nature, history, politics, and their own individual spiritual lives. What this knitting together did, externally, was to define who was not part of the people—whose ethnic heritage, as of the moment of the consolidation of an Israelite politics and culture, was seen as part of a separate peoplehood, and whose life-path was too different to be considered Israelitish.

It is hard to tell at what point during the Biblical Era the notion of who was an Israelite, a Jew, crystallized. We do know that the issue opened up again in the formative period of the Talmudic Era—the period just before and after the Destruction of the Second Temple. There was an enormous wave of conversions to Judaism—

so enormous that some scholars believe that one-tenth of all the inhabitants of the Mediterranean basin were Jews. (Remember that the Mediterranean was the seat of the Roman Empire, by far the greatest power of its day. To compare, imagine that 10 percent of the citizens and subjects of the British Empire in 1900 had been Jewish, or 10 percent of those who lived under American sway in 1947—in North and South America, Europe, and Japan—had been Jewish.) Within the synagogues were myriads of "God-fearers" who accepted the basics of Jewish thought but not all of the commandments regarding food, tithing, and sacrifices. This pool of new Jews and semi-Jews was probably the arena in which Christianity based most of its early successes—and even the question whether Christianity could be seen as a sect within the Jewish people was open for at least a century.

In the moment of intense heat generated by the Hellenistic shattering of the Biblical Jewish vessel, the very shape and boundaries of Jewish peoplehood melted, flowed, and were reshaped. They recrystallized as the heat of the impact cooled, and as Talmudic Judaism took its shape so did the new version of Jewish peoplehood—each of them defining, and interwining with, the other.

Now we are in another such moment of intense heat, arising from the modernist shattering of the Talmudic Jewish vessel. The present number of conversions *to* Judaism is unparalleled, in any time or place since the crystallization of the Talmudic Era almost two thousand years ago. Marriages between people of Jewish and non-Jewish family origins—often after conversion of the non-Jewish partner, often not—are also at unprecedented levels. And so are fear and protest of these developments.

In the wake of all this, who will be a Jew one century hence?

• Imaginably, the Israeli Orthodox rabbinate and its Diaspora brethren will have won their battle to apply the halakha of the Talmudic Age; to apply it not only to immigrants to Israel but to Jews everywhere; and to use, no doubt, the enormous research capability of computer technology to ferret out breaks and violations of that halakha. In that case, the Jewish people will be a rather small band of descendants of provably Jewish mothers, plus a few people converted by Orthodox rabbis.

• Imaginably, the tugs and pulls, carrots and sticks of Diaspora life in postmodern society will have finished off the Jewish communities of America, the Soviet Union, and Europe—and Israel will have survived, on a secular rather than an Orthodox basis. In that case, the Jewish people will consist of most of the citizens of Israel and hardly anyone else—except perhaps communities that view themselves as practically "overseas Israelis." Jewishness will be shaped by participation in or commitment to the civil and secular Israeli society.

• Imaginably, the movement for Jewish renewal will succeed in redefining the practices of Jewish life so that an amalgam of different "kinds" of Jews, in the Diaspora as well as Israel, will be continuously and heatedly accepting each other as Jews. A number of people whose grandparents and parents were not Jewish will have joined one or another version of the Jewish community because they liked the people or the practice. There might be a good many more Jews than there are today; there might be about the same number, with a much more intensely and identifiably Jewish life-path than that of most Jews today

Questions of conversion and intermarriage are becoming hot among a wide variety of Jewish communities precisely because there is a transformation of Jewish life in process. And not only Jewish life: large numbers of people without Jewish family origins would not even be getting interested in becoming Jewish if the triumph of modernism had not shattered the assumptions of Western Christian society.

That is the important other side to be recognized by anyone who is interested in the effects of modernism upon Judaism: it is *all* the premodern worlds and vessels that have been shattered, not only Jewish peoplehood. Now that the self-canceling effect of modernism is manifest, it is not only the vessel of Jewish peoplehood in which the work of regathering sparks is under way. But just as the Jewish vessel will be different from its past analogues when it has been reshaped, so will the other vessels—national, ethnic, and religious. And the boundaries between them will also be different.

We can try to understand the old boundaries and imagine new ones. The rabbis taught the blessing, "Blessed are You, Lord our God, Ruler of time and space, Who chose us from all the peoples and gave us His Torah." The whole question of this "chosenness" has haunted the Jewish people. Chosen to lead? Chosen to be outcast? Chosen to be holy? Chosen to be different?

During the Rabbinic Age, the Jewish answer to this question went like this: "The Jews have received from God a special discipline, a life-practice intended to shape us into a holy people. This is both a special burden and a special joy. When we accept this burden and live out the discipline, we become a model community, a living model for the holiness that God demands of all human communities. In order to do this job well, we have to be separated in the practice of our discipline. If we come close to succeeding, we know that some people will be inflamed against us precisely because our approach toward holy life will stand as a rebuke and irritant to them. On the other hand, some people will be attracted to at least some partial version of the Torah if we live it well. But if we fail to live by this standard, God will punish us."

This way of hallowing the Jewish life-path worked well enough so long as the sociological facts reinforced the spiritual effort. So long as the Christian and Muslim worlds held the Jewish communities at arms' length, so long as Jews held little power and therefore little involvement in the moral and ethical complexities of using power, then the notion of the Jewish people as a "holy countercommunity" could be sustained. The Jews could embody in their "particular" peoplehood the great universalist ideals—the hallowing of personal life through calm, decency, love; the hallowing of social life through the search for justice, peace, and community.

But with the breakdown in the modern world of the social and political barriers between the Jewish and other communities, the blurring of distinctions between Jewish and other paths of life, and the Jews' own discovery that many Quaker, Navaho, Buddhist, and other communities also walk a holy path of life, the notion of the Jews as a "chosen people" has become embarrassing to many Jews and infuriating to many others. So the breakdown of the flesh-and-blood barriers between the Jews and other peoples coincided with the breakdown of the conceptual and intellectual patterns that had explained the Jews as a separate people.

Most of the efforts that have been made to deal with this breakdown can be seen as simplemindedly universalist or simplemindedly particularist. On the simplemindedly universalist side, Isaac Deutscher elevated to a goal and a vision one of the symptoms of breakdown: the "non-Jewish Jew." As Deutscher pointed out, those Jews who were most ardently committed to the universalist values that were embedded in Jewish thought have now found themselves, under the conditions of modernization, able to act out those ideals outside the Jewish community—in the general society. Once this was possible, they found themselves tugged to do it: "Why struggle for universal values in a narrow arena if we can struggle for them in a universal arena?" So they tranferred their energies from the Jewish community to the outside world in order to act out Jewish values. Deutscher, watching this process in himself and others, sees these non-Jewish Jews as the true heroes of Jewish practice—precisely because they abandon it. To accept this approach, however, would mean to weaken and soon to shatter the very womb from which the non-Jewish Jew sprang: to shatter the whole Jewish cultural-religious context from which the universalist vision arose.

The direction that Reform Judaism originally took (and has since abandoned) was a milder version of "non-Jewish Jewishness." It tried to simplify the whole intricate idiosyncratic weave of Judaism into "the struggle for universal social justice." Much of daily Jewish practice and ritual in such matters as food, the Sabbath, prayer, sexual life, and study of the tradition were viewed as outdated precisely because they were peculiar and idiosyncratic. Instead, universally held definitions and standards were adopted as the measures for obedience to the Torah's commands to "pursue justice." This attempt at universalization through the abandonment of peculiarity sidestepped one major question: Was anything in the unique life-patterns uniquely useful as a model, a pattern, a pointer for those seeking universal peace and justice?

Even the Labor-Zionist, Socialist-Zionist, and Socialist-Bundist formulas for dealing with this whole question had some ironic similarities to the "non-Jewish Jew." For while they reaffirmed Jewish peoplehood in a very powerful way, even while they asserted that political self-determination for the Jewish people could be made a model for all the world's peoples as an examplar of justice and freedom, they urged that the internal political content of that self-determining Jewish people would be defined by modern non-Jewish thought: socialist and social-democratic thought, generated since the eighteenth century by the European labor and socialist movements. These ideas and approaches had often been developed by "non-Jewish Jews." The effort among Zionists to take these ideas from the level of the individual Jew to that of the Jewish state, and the effort among Bundists to carry them to the level of a culturally autonomous socialist Jewish community in Eastern Europe, were in an ironic way a collectivization of Deutscher's dream. They sought the "non-Jewish Jewish state," or the "non-Jewish Jewish working class."

On the other hand, from some segments of Jewish life there came the opposite response: a focus inward, toward the protection of Jewish particularity and peculiarity and away from the assertion of a universal vision or the making of universalist connections. Revisionist Zionism, for example, asserted the importance of a Jewish nation-state for the sake of the Jewish people, purely; some parts of the religious community, filled with fear of and contempt for "the goyim" viewed the Jewish mission as utterly self-contained and self-reinforcing. These currents of Jewish life and thought responded to the new interlacing of Jews and non-Jews in modern societies by seeking to use political boundaries or rigid versions of religion to restore their separation from non-Jewish communities—except to treat them as actual or potential enemies.

There were three interrelated problems with this approach: First, since much of Jewish thought and practice did in fact express universalist themes, it required a self-impoverishment of Jewish culture.

Second, since these universal themes speak to the profound hopes of many or all human beings, this approach required the expulsion (*de facto* or *de jure*) from Jewish life of those who responded to these themes. And finally, if the freedom that Jews sought was intended for Jews only, why should non-Jews help them struggle for it? The rejection of the universal visions left the "Jewish particularists" no non-Jewish allies in the struggle for the freedom of Jews to express themselves in their own way.

The larger question of the role of the Jews among the other peoples stands before our own generation. Is there any more satisfactory answer than these rather simplistic versions of universalism and of particularism?

I believe that the direction we must move toward is one in which the whole web of Jewish thought and practice is seen again as a model for the wider human community—but seen in a new way. In premodern society, Jews saw the seamless Jewish vessel *in its inwardness* as such a model. But the model was separated, ghettoized, and we could scarcely imagine using the model as an active force to reach out in order to help transform the world. In modern society, Jews thought we had a choice: inward or outward. Forget the world, or strip ourselves of our Jewishness in order to improve the world.

In the postmodern world, the Jewish task becomes to know that we are chosen not *mi kol ha-amim, "from* all the peoples," but *im* kol ha-amim, *"along with* all the peoples." Our task is to see that our being chosen both *includes* and *parallels* the choosing of the other peoples—that our chosenness both carries in itself the microcosm of universal wholeness, and also makes us an element, a part, of the macrocosm in its universal wholeness. Our task is to see *within* our own particular path the Rainbow of universal truth, and to hear the call for us to carry this many-colored Rainbow to the many-colored peoples. Our task is to be not merely a passive model but an active force. Our task is not to strip ourselves of our Jewishness, but weave new Jewish cloth from those strands of universal modern thought that will blend with the strands of our own ancient wisdom, and then to go actively to the other peoples to encourage them to weave their own new clothing—so as to warm us all.

Enough rhetoric. What will it mean to do this, in a particular case, on a particular issue? Let us address an issue that raises at the most profound level the relationship between the Jewish people and the rest of humankind. The danger of a universal holocaust, a thermonuclear catastrophe that could destroy all life on earth. What is the Jewish responsibility, and what is the Jewish teaching on this question? What is Torah?

We might begin by thinking that since the Torah is so ancient and the H-bomb so new, the one can have nothing to say to the other. Yet suppose we ask the Torah, with an open mind and heart and spirit, "Where can I find a teaching about the H-bomb?" And pause. To let the stillness, the "white fire" of the spaces on the parchment of the Torah as well as the "black fire" of the letters on the parchment, flame up at us. To see what comes.

For me, what arose was the story of the Flood and the Rainbow. For this story is the only one we have in which it is all earth that stands in danger. It is almost as if the story has been preserved as a treasure all these generations until there would arise a generation when the danger to all of earth was real.

That generation is our own. What can we learn?

First, we learn that the human race is responsible to save not only itself but all the species. Noah is commanded to take them all into the Ark. Today we know there is only one Ark that is large enough and various enough to contain all the species: the Ark of Planet Earth. And today we know that we human beings are all responsible to float her. Indeed, the story teaches us that decent human beings are obliged to act—not only experts. Noah was no expert on rain, or ships, or animals. He was a reasonably righteous person. That was all; that was enough.

Second, we learn that the Torah does not call this a "war." When all life is in danger, we should stop talking of the danger as if it were a war. The human race is used to wars. Wars are lost or won; wars are just or unjust. If we destroy all humankind, no one will win, no one will lose; justice and injustice will be gone. In wars, the side with more weapons will probably win; in thermonuclear collision, beyond a certain threshold the number of "weapons"—better to call each bomb a portable Auschwitz—will not matter. Every time we talk about thermonuclear "war" we are tricking ourselves.

Let us use instead the imagery that comes from ancient midrash on the story of the Flood: the midrash that, as embodied in a Black spiritual, tell us: "God gave Noah the Rainbow Sign: no more water; the fire next time." We might better speak of the Flood of Fire—or translate that into "holocaust," the *all-burning*. In any case, let us learn from the Torah not to make the Flood of Fire more likely by thinking and speaking of it as if it were a war.

Third, we should notice that the story of the Flood has an extraordinary sense of time. The story goes out of its way, over and over, to name the dates on which the rain begins and ends, the waters recede and the earth reappears, the ground becomes dry and the Rainbow appears. These dates have never been used in Jewish practice. They never had to be. Now they are available to us when we need them—need a date to commit ourselves to keep the world alive, as we need a date (at Pesach) to experience our liberation and a date (at Shavuot) to experience receiving Torah. The day of the Rainbow Sign was 27 *Iyyar*. We can, should, make it the day of experiencing the Rainbow. In Jewish communities across North America during 1982 and 1983, Jews did in fact observe the Rainbow Sign with teach-ins and services focused on the prevention of nuclear holocaust.

The Flood story has still more to teach us about time. It teaches that the life cycles of time are crucial to preventing the death of life.

When the Flood begins, the normal cycles halt. The Torah says that just before the rain began to fall, there were seven days of waiting. The rabbis teach that during those seven days the sun rose in the West and set in the East. In other words, the seven days of Creation were being run backward—and so the sun reversed itself. During the time on the Ark—exactly one solar year, a lunar year plus eleven days—the rabbis say that all the animals and humans on the Ark refrained from sex—refrained from initiating the life cycle. When Noah wanted to test out the dry land, according to midrash of the modern havurot, he tried to restart the great cycles of night and day, death and life. First he sent out a raven—black as the night, named *arva*, like *erev*, the "evening," and then he sent out the dove—white as the morning, named *yonah*, like *yom*, the "day." The raven, bird of carrion, cleared the earth of the dead carcasses that were the end product of the last life cycle before the Flood. The dove brought back for food the olive branch, the first new life that had sprung up after the great disaster.

Noah's pleading for renewal of the cycles won God's approval and response. In the Rainbow Covenant, God gives the promise of renewing and preserving life by mentioning precisely the cycles of seedtime and harvest, cold and heat, summer and winter, day and night.

What are we to learn from this? In our times, "productivity" has destroyed the sense of holy time, holy cycles. The human race has become so drunk on its new abilities to produce goods that it has forgotten to rest, contemplate, meditate, reevaluate, celebrate. And this hyperproductive mode, in which time is only a commodity, a raw material of production, has brought us to the brink of hyper-destruction. In a world that thinks Shabbos is a waste of time, the H-bomb is inevitable. The story of the Flood and Rainbow remind us that we must renew the cycles, renew our celebration of them— in order to live.

Finally, there is the teaching of the Rainbow itself. That it comes on Mount Ararat is both surprising and important. The Flood was universal. Yet the Torah specifies a real place—Mount Ararat—for its ending. Why there? Because from Ararat, the mountain peak that looms in Turkey high above the Middle East, the Fertile Crescent is a unity. As the earth looks like a unity from space, so the "whole known world" looked from Ararat. That was where the human race looked like a single family. Indeed, the Rainbow itself was like a projection into the heavens of the great Middle Eastern Crescent of human settlements—and the varied colors of the Rainbow remind us that we can only preserve human unity if we accept human diversity. For the Rainbow is not merely an undifferentiated white light.

Yet the Rainbow is also not merely a myriad of colors. In the Rainbow colors take a shape. Those who have observed the awesome explosion of an H-bomb have reported how beautiful, how terrifying, are the myriad flashing colors that appear within the mush-room cloud. All the colors of the rainbow. For the H-bomb *is* the Rainbow—shattered.

Perhaps one deeper lesson of the Rainbow story is its lesson to the Jews about the relationship between our particularism and our universalism. We, the Jewish people, are especially commanded to bring our special contribution to the universal effort to prevent a nuclear holocaust and save the earth. We must bring our special color to enrich the Rainbow. Perhaps we should be the ones to say that an effort to save the earth must bear high not only the warnings of disaster, but also an ensign of hope, an ensign of new possibility. The Rainbow was a symbol of hope, God's reminder that not only human beings but even God must have a symbol of hope if life is to be renewed. And the content of that symbol is renewing the cycles of life.

Finally, perhaps the deepest lesson of all for the postmodern world is again our special Jewish contribution: the lesson of doing midrash on the ancient stories. For all of the human race faces the problem of where to turn for Teaching, if we can now see that the ideas and practices of modernism are useful, dangerous, and insufficient. If modernism is useful, it is not good simply to turn back to the premodern religious traditions. If modernism is dangerous, it is not good simply to reject the ancient traditions. The midrashic process returns and renews: It does neither, and both.

Would that method be useful to other communities with long traditions that have been damaged by the last five centuries of modernism?

The midrashic method has worked for millennia and continues to work because Jews—including Jews who have learned a great deal from the truths in modernism—have come to the ancient texts with passion to hear in them new teachings for their own generations; because we neither bow down to the texts nor turn away, but wrestle: we, as who we are; the text, as what and who it is. Both we and the text change in that process. Communities of "the faithful"—that is, those who stay truly in the wrestle—find new meaning when we bring our lives to the tradition.

Would Christians, Muslims, Buddhists find new meaning in their own ancient texts if communities of the faithful wrestled with them in this way? Already the emergence of Christian *communidades de base* (local communities) doing this in Brazil, and developing a theory and practice of decent social transformation, hints at the possibilities. So do the efforts of small groups of Iranian Muslims and American Sufis, Iroquois Indians, and Vietnamese Buddhist priests. Everywhere there are hints that the "premodern" traditions and world views we call "religions" are taking on new meaning and importance at the social and political level in the "postmodern" world.

The Jewish people went through a great midrashic transformation once—when the Temple was destroyed, the people scattered, and the Talmud created. The shattered vessel and the scattered sparks of our Biblical peoplehood we were able to regather into a new vessel, a new holy pattern. The transformation was traumatic, but it worked—and on the other side of the event, the Jewish people was once again able to see and recognize itself: to know that despite all changes, the same people had lived through one continuous flow of history. The experience of having successfully transcended that trauma is not the least of the lessons we could be bringing to the other peoples.

The sparks that we have begun to reconnect—loving with learning, money with mitzvah, politics with spirituality, the home-grounded with the far-dispersed, the kingly with the prophetic, the religious with the secular, the foreigner with the in-group, God with the world—all these are the sparks that the other peoples also need to gather in.

It is no accident, this similarity. There is a level—hard to reach and harder to remain at—where we are really one. I think back to the Sinai moment of *Anokhi*, the Infinite "I." I have experienced this moment—lived it, touched it, tasted it, felt it. What this moment teaches is that even the truth of Torah is a paler expression of the One Truth, the truth that the world is a Unity. (As the rabbis said, "Sleep is a hint of death; dreams, a hint of prophecy; Shabbos, a hint of the Messianic Age; the sun, a hint of the heavenly light; *and the Torah, a hint of the ultimate wisdom.*")

That vessel of unity has been shattered by forgetfulness—a deliberate forgetting, an amnesia chosen out of panic at the intensity, the impossibility, of the experience of Oneness. Out of panic the Israelites at Sinai scrambled to withdraw themselves from the Unity and to receive a specific Torah of their own. They needed a Torah that would address their own life-situation and bring it closer toward the Unity they had just fled. So their Torah taught them how to bring their own food, their own sexual and family lives, their own political structures closer toward the Unity that they were trying to forget and to remember at the same time.

So in almost the same moment they—we—moved in a three-step dance. First we moved toward Sinai, seeking the experience of Unity, seeking to merge ourselves into the Holy Vessel of the Unity. Then we shattered the Holy Vessel by pulling ourselves out of it. And, finally, we returned to begin gathering the sparks of holiness, to bring them closer to each other and to the great reunification.

I imagine that all the peoples that have experienced a covenant, or a moment of enlightenment, have also had a flash of insight into their own participation, their own part-ness, in the Ultimate Unity. And they have all backed off into a partial vision. Therefore our various Teachings overlap in part, contradict each other in part, reinforce each other in part.

Sinai is the story of how we went through this process for ourselves. But our Torah also tells the story of how all the peoples sought, felt, fled from, and began to rebuild the Unity. This story is told in the rhythm of the Flood and the Tower. The story of the Flood begins with the confounding of all boundaries: humans, animals, plants are all mixing themselves together sexually and genetically. They seek fluidity and flow. The Flood itself is simply the continuation and consequence of this confounding: flow and fluidity overflowing. The water obliterates all boundaries, mixes everything together. It is destructive. But out of it comes a truth: there is but one family of those who dwell on earth: all human beings are of one family, and they have lived for a year aboard one single boat with all the plants and animals of earth. And together we receive the Rainbow Covenant, the covenant that bridges even earth and heaven. "We are one family!"—says the covenant. "It is true that we have no boundaries between us."

And then the human race pursues the opposite truth. Where before we had tried to obliterate all distinctions, now we try to erect a great distinction: the Tower of Babel. Remembering how the Flood had obliterated every landmark, we raised up a landmark that could never be wiped out. And this too led naturally to its own fulfillment: distinctions were erected between us. Truly, every land was marked with a difference; for in every land sprang up a separate language, a tower of strength to its inhabitants and a watchtower to warn off all other peoples.

We feel the sadness of these distinctions, but we know the sadness holds a kind of joy. For the Jewish Torah teaches us that out of the babble of new peoples came the line that led to Abraham and to the Jewish people. And all of us, of every people, know the joy we take in our own language, how it teaches us a vision of the world, and how we shape it to bring nearer the wholeness of the world. To every people the covenant comes again, in light refracted by the prism of its own language. We each receive a curve of color from the Rainbow.

Afterword: Gathering Sparks

In the Rainbow, God gave the earth the glory of the seven curving colors.

In the ancient Temple in Jerusalem, the Jewish people gave to God the Menorah of seven burning lights.

Our rainbow. Our seven fires, burning not to bring destruction but to enlighten the world, burning to let us see that all of us are the children of Adam, the children of Eve, the children of Noah, bearers of the Image of God.

God's Rainbow comes only for a moment, lifts and awes us, vanishes. Our Menorah we can keep lit forever. Or we can let it darken.

Our seven lamps are kindled by the seven rainbow colors.

Our seven lamps rekindle the seven rainbow colors.

As above, so below; as below, so above.

But we know the Menorah can be shattered—*has* been shattered. This book began with an image of the high Menorah shattered, struck in its very height by fiery lightning, struck to ashes, and with an image of the sparks and embers regathering to make a new Menorah, traced in light.

We have lived through the moment of such a shattering—and now we are living through the time when we are finding sparks and embers in the ashes, sparks to make a new Menorah traced in light.

The task of regathering is hard. But we should take comfort from the knowledge that we have done this task before.

The story of that other time is still before us, written in letters of stone and rays of light. It is an eerie story, not only about the Menorah as a symbol of Jewish peoplehood but also about a physical Menorah of seven burning lamps.

The physical Menorah, the golden seven-branched Menorah that stood in the Holy Temple in Jerusalem, was shattered. The Imperial

Legions carried it in triumph to be degraded in the streets of Rome. And with its physical capture, came the political, economic, cultural, and religious shattering of what had till then been the Jewish people.

Even today, on the Arch of Titus in the Imperial City, Jews can see in sculpted stone the shape of the seven-branched Menorah from the Temple, brought as booty to be melted down for the Imperial treasury.

Jews can see it in the Arch of Titus. For against all logic and prediction, the Jewish people—shattered by Imperial Rome—regathered. Indeed, God and history have written a sardonic footnote to the Arch of Titus. Inside the walls of the Old City of Jerusalem, a block from Jaffa Gate, there is an ancient block of stone. It is ignored by almost everyone who bustles past. But a visitor who peers closely can see carved on it the letters "LEG X." It is a relic of the Roman Tenth Legion—the legion that conquered and destroyed Jerusalem.

Today, in a vibrant city full of Jewish culture, politics, and commerce, that block of Roman stone serves as the base for a homely, ordinary street lamp. Giving light: a strange renewal of the old Menorah. And a strange reversal of the Arch of Titus: for where the Arch turned the light from the Menorah into stone, this street lamp turns the stone back into light. Light to live by.

We know what Titus did not know: that the shattered vessel of the ancient House of Israel could be regathered. That the sparks and glowing embers in the burned-out wreckage could be reshaped—not into the Temple as it was, but into a new pattern of the Jewish people. A new, nonphysical Menorah, for the task of the Jewish people is not merely to survive but to keep turning stone back into light.

In our own lifetime, the new kind of Menorah that the Jews created from the burned-out wreckage of the Temple has itself been burned and shattered. So we too have the task of regathering the sparks, shaping a new Menorah. What can we learn from the Jews who did this work before? The Jews of that day drew on Hellenism, on the universal knowledge of their day—on the light of the universal Rainbow—to help them rekindle the lamps of their own Menorah. And the Menorah that they kindled gave back new light, century after century, to the universal Rainbow.

And so today. We see behind us the flames of Auschwitz and Hiroshima; we see before us the flames of a worldwide holocaust. So we know that to regather the sparks of our own covenant, we shall have to help regather the sparks of all the covenants. The original Kabbalistic legend of the shattered vessel and the gathering of the sparks arose out of the past life-experience of the Jewish people, and it spoke to the future path-making of the Jewish people; but it spoke not of the Jewish people alone but of the whole created universe. As we move to regather our own sparks in every sphere—from the single Jewish person to the worldwide Jewish people—we will find ourselves more able to gather in the universal sparks.

If we do not, the sparks will remain apart, each burning toward a fire that may consume us all.

I am troubled to see this last harsh sentence standing at the end of a hopeful book on Jewish and human renewal. Yet the sentence belongs there. That certain books may have to end on a note of pain the Jews have always accepted, but when such books are read aloud the line of hope before them is reread:

As we move to regather our own sparks, we will find ourselves more able to gather in the universal sparks. Return us to You, O Breath of Life, and we shall return; renew our days as of old.

To All the Rabbis, and All Their Disciples

This book was written in two spaces: in Washington, D.C., toward the end of my twenty-three years there, and in Philadelphia, in the first six months of my sojourn. It owes much to people in both places.

First, I must say again, over and over, what I have said before: to all my comrades, all my teachers, in twelve years of Fabrangen, there is no way to say all that needs to be said of love and learning. There is this: I love you, and I learn from you.

As I find myself still learning and growing through playful, truthful midrash, I remember with gratitude that in 1969 it was Harold White who introduced me to the wonders of rabbinic midrash.

And to the newest of my teachers: my colleagues and students at the Reconstructionist Rabbinical College and Swarthmore College, my *haverim* and *haverot* in B'nai Or, the Feminist Theology Group and the Minyanim of Germantown, and the Philadelphia chapter of New Jewish Agenda: my joy in studying, davvening, and living with and among you.

Many of the ideas in this book appeared first in *Menorah*, the journal of Jewish renewal I edit and write for. With the help of God and many writers, artists, and subscribers, there will appear in *Menorah* many more passages of midrash, observation, autobiography, and analysis. Whoever find themselves passionately committed to Jewish renewal—and also find this book a useful thought-path for it—might experiment with subscribing to *Menorah* and writing or drawing for it.

For helping these thoughts become a book I have many people to thank—and only myself to blame. Jacob Agus, Rebecca Alpert, Alan

Berg, Ronald Brauner, Ivan Caine, Jeffrey Dekro, Arnold Eisen, Edward Feld, Nancy Fuchs, Arthur Green, Irving Greenberg, Susannah Heschel, Diane Levenberg, Hillel Levine, Joel Rosenberg, Arthur Samuelson, Zalman Schachter-Shalomi, Harold Schulweis, Drorah Setel, Steve Shaw, Ira Silverman, Carol Simon, David Teutsch, Max Ticktin, Sheila Weinberg, Jonathan Woocher, and Barbara Zukin read part or all of the manuscript and gave me their suggestions and criticisms. I often have and often have not followed their advice—which is why they are to be thanked for the pitfalls I avoided and I am to be blamed for the pitfalls I fell into.

I—and I believe all serious Jews—owe special thanks to Ira Silverman, president of the Reconstructionist Rabbinical College, not only for his work on behalf of the reconstruction and renewal of the Jewish people, but also for his proof that *menschlichkeit* and *seichel*, creativity and solidity, spiritual openness and the ability to raise money, are not mutually exclusive qualities.

My children David and Shoshana—children no longer—remain my best teachers in what they say and how they act. May they, and all their generation, live out the full span of their lives; may I, and all my generation, act to make it so.

Today my father is seventy-five years old. For him, Henry Waskow, and for my mother, Hannah Waskow, my first teachers, I have not only love but admiration; not only thanks but comradeship.

For Israel and all who wrestle with God, for the rabbis and all our teachers, for their disciples and the disciples of their disciples, for all who study the Teaching, may there be abundant peace, long life, compassionate caring, and a decent livelihood—from the Source of all in heaven and earth.

Blessed be the Breath that breathes all life, all space, all time; the Breath that shapes the sparks of fire into light—and not destruction.

AVRAHAM YITZCHAK YISHMAEL
ben Chanoch v'Chana
18 Shvat 5743/February 1, 1983

About the Author

ARTHUR WASKOW is on the faculty of the Reconstructionist Rabbinical College in Philadelphia and has also taught in the religion departments of Swarthmore College and Temple University. He edits *Menorah*, a journal of Jewish renewal, and is the director of RAINBOW SIGN, a Jewish project for the prevention of nuclear holocaust.

He was born in Baltimore in 1933 and took a bachelor's degree from the Johns Hopkins University and a doctorate in United States history from the University of Wisconsin. He worked as a legislative assistant for a United States Congressman and wrote four books on nuclear strategy, deterrence, and disarmament. He was one of the founding fellows of the Institute for Policy Studies, and through the 1960s was active in writing, speaking, politics, and direct action against the Vietnam War.

Waskow's involvement with serious Jewish work and thought began in 1969 with the writing of *The Freedom Seder;* deepened through the 1970s in Fabrangen, a havurah or participatory congregation in Washington, D.C.; and became his chief life-focus with the publication of *Godwrestling* (Schocken, 1978), *Menorah* (which he founded in 1979), and *Seasons of Our Joy* (Bantam, 1982). He helped found the National Havurah Coordinating Committee and New Jewish Agenda.

He is now writing *Rainbow Sign: The Shape of Hope,* a book on the seeds of hope for a decent and livable society that are now sprouting among several religious traditions.

If you have comments or questions on Jewish renewal or would like information about writing for or subscribing to the journal *Menorah,* you may write to Arthur Waskow at the Reconstructionist Rabbinical College, Church Road and Greenwood Avenue, Wyncote, Pennsylvania 19095.